Hélène Adeline Guerber

The Story of the English

Hélène Adeline Guerber

The Story of the English

ISBN/EAN: 9783741186714

Manufactured in Europe, USA, Canada, Australia, Japa

Cover: Foto ©ninafisch / pixelio.de

Manufactured and distributed by brebook publishing software (www.brebook.com)

Hélène Adeline Guerber

The Story of the English

ECLECTIC SCHOOL READINGS

THE
STORY OF THE ENGLISH

BY

H. A. GUERBER

NEW YORK ∴ CINCINNATI ∴ CHICAGO
AMERICAN BOOK COMPANY

COPYRIGHT, 1898, BY
AMERICAN BOOK COMPANY.

All rights reserved.

STORY OF THE ENGLISH.

W. P. I

PREFACE.

Down to the colonial period, if not to the Revolutionary War, English history concerns American children just as much as it does their brothers and sisters who speak the same language on the other side of the broad Atlantic. It is therefore very important that our boys and girls should as soon as possible become familiar with its salient events.

To interest them in their own race, introduce them to their mother country, and make the past as vivid as possible, characters, customs, and places have in this book been depicted principally through anecdotes, many of which have become classical, although not all are admitted into works intended for more mature minds.

The gradual evolution of English law, the growth of liberty, and the various changes in religion are as unintelligible as uninteresting to the average child; so they have been touched upon very briefly, and in the most simple way.

The principal object has been to make pupils so familiar with the prominent characters of English history that these shall henceforth seem like old acquaintances, and, in addition, to use every device to make history so attractive to youthful minds as to rouse their enthusiasm and stimulate them to further study.

Although all the main facts have been given, least space has been allotted to modern times. That is not only because many of the events which have occurred within the past two centuries are more difficult of comprehension, but because any intelligent child is sure to have them brought to his or her notice in other books. For that reason, also, the wars in America are merely mentioned, and pupils are referred to United States histories for detailed accounts of them.

To enrich young minds and to emphasize the need of patient endeavour, courage, faithfulness, gentleness, truthfulness, and all other desirable qualities, all that is good has been heartily commended, and all that is base or dishonourable has been made to appear in an unfavourable light. Nevertheless, it has also been the writer's aim to cultivate a spirit of fairness and charity towards all men.

Much reading and research stand back of this little book, and the author is indebted to historians, biographers, novelists, poets, and artists for the material of which it is composed. It is with the hope that the road to literature and history will seem easier and more attractive, after the way has been made somewhat smoother by these little paving stones, that this book is placed before the public.

The pronunciation of difficult proper names has been indicated in the text, in order to make easier the reading of the book, and to prevent the formation of incorrect habits of pronunciation. The symbols used for this purpose are self-explanatory in most cases; the diacritical marks are explained on p. 343. Besides this, the pronunciation of all proper names is more fully indicated by diacritical marks in the index.

CONTENTS.

		PAGE
I.	Early Times	11
II.	The Druids	13
III.	The Britons	17
IV.	Cæsar in Britain	21
V.	Queen Boadicea	24
VI.	The Great Walls	26
VII.	The Great Irish Saint	29
VIII.	The Anglo-Saxons	31
IX.	Brave King Arthur	34
X.	The Laws of the Saxons	36
XI.	The Story of St. Augustine	38
XII.	Three Great Men	41
XIII.	The Danish Pirates	42
XIV.	King Alfred and the Cakes	46
XV.	Alfred conquers the Danes	49
XVI.	A King's Narrow Escape	53
XVII.	The King and the Outlaw	55
XVIII.	The Monasteries	57
XIX.	An Unlucky Couple	58
XX.	St. Dunstan	61
XXI.	King Canute and the Waves	63
XXII.	A Saxon Nobleman	67
XXIII.	Lady Godiva's Ride	70

		PAGE
XXIV.	The Battle of Hastings	73
XXV.	The Conquest	76
XXVI.	Lords and Vassals	79
XXVII.	Death of William	82
XXVIII.	The Brothers' Quarrels	84
XXIX.	Arms and Armour	88
XXX.	The "White Ship"	91
XXXI.	Matilda's Narrow Escapes	93
XXXII.	The Story of Fair Rosamond	96
XXXIII.	Thomas à Becket	99
XXXIV.	The Murder of Thomas à Becket	101
XXXV.	Richard's Adventures	105
XXXVI.	Richard and the Saracens	107
XXXVII.	The Faithful Minstrel	110
XXXVIII.	Death of Richard	113
XXXIX.	The Murder of Arthur	117
XL.	The Great Charter	119
XLI.	The Weak Rule of Henry III.	124
XLII.	A Race	126
XLIII.	Persecution of the Jews	128
XLIV.	The Conquest of Wales	131
XLV.	A Quarrel with France	134
XLVI.	The Coronation Stone	137
XLVII.	The Insolent Favourite	140
XLVIII.	Bruce and the Spider	143
XLIX.	Death of Edward II.	147
L.	The Murderers punished	150
LI.	The Battle of Crécy	152
LII.	The Siege of Calais	156
LIII.	The Age of Chivalry	159
LIV.	The Battle of Poitiers	162
LV.	The Peasants' Revolt	166
LVI.	Richard's Presence of Mind	168

		PAGE
LVII.	A Tiny Queen	171
LVIII.	Henry's Troubles	174
LIX.	Madcap Harry	176
LX.	A Glorious Reign	179
LXI.	The Maid of Orleans	183
LXII.	The Beginning of the War of the Roses	187
LXIII.	The Queen and the Brigand	189
LXIV.	The Triumph of the Yorks	193
LXV.	The Princes in the Tower	196
LXVI.	Richard's Punishment	200
LXVII.	Two Pretenders	202
LXVIII.	A Grasping King	205
LXIX.	The Field of the Cloth of Gold	207
LXX.	The New Opinions	211
LXXI.	Death of Wolsey	214
LXXII.	Henry's Wives	217
LXXIII.	The King and the Painter	220
LXXIV.	A Boy King	222
LXXV.	The Story of Lady Jane Grey	226
LXXVI.	The Death of Cranmer	230
LXXVII.	A Clever Queen	233
LXXVIII.	Elizabeth's Lovers	235
LXXIX.	Mary, Queen of Scots	238
LXXX.	Captivity of Mary Stuart	241
LXXXI.	Wreck of the Spanish Armada	244
LXXXII.	The Elizabethan Age	246
LXXXIII.	Death of Elizabeth	250
LXXXIV.	A Scotch King	252
LXXXV.	The Gunpowder Plot	254
LXXXVI.	Sir Walter Raleigh	257
LXXXVII.	King and Parliament	260
LXXXVIII.	Cavaliers and Roundheads	263
LXXXIX.	"Remember"	266

		PAGE
XC.	The Royal Oak	269
XCI.	The Commonwealth	271
XCII.	The Restoration	275
XCIII.	Plague and Fire	278
XCIV.	The Merry Monarch	280
XCV.	James driven out of England	283
XCVI.	A Terrible Massacre	286
XCVII.	William's Wars	288
XCVIII.	The Duke of Marlborough	291
XCIX.	The Taking of Gibraltar	294
C.	The South Sea Bubble	296
CI.	Bonny Prince Charlie	299
CII.	The Black Hole of Calcutta	303
CIII.	Loss of the Thirteen Colonies	305
CIV.	The Battle of the Nile	309
CV.	Nelson's Last Signal	312
CVI.	The Battle of Waterloo	314
CVII.	The First Gentleman in Europe	319
CVIII.	The Childhood of Queen Victoria	320
CIX.	The Queen's Marriage	323
CX.	Some Wars in Victoria's Reign	327
CXI.	The Jubilee	334

GENEALOGICAL TABLE 340
THE SOVEREIGNS OF ENGLAND . . . 342
INDEX 343

MAPS.

GREAT BRITAIN AND IRELAND . . *opposite* 11
FRANCE 114
INDIA 302
WORLD, SHOWING BRITISH POSSESSIONS . 332, 333

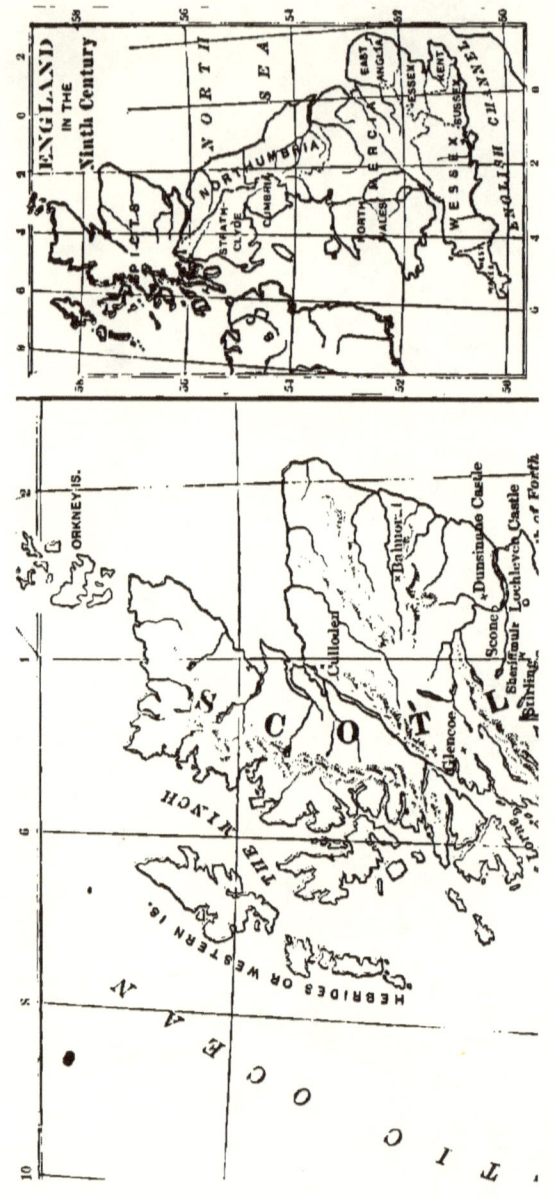

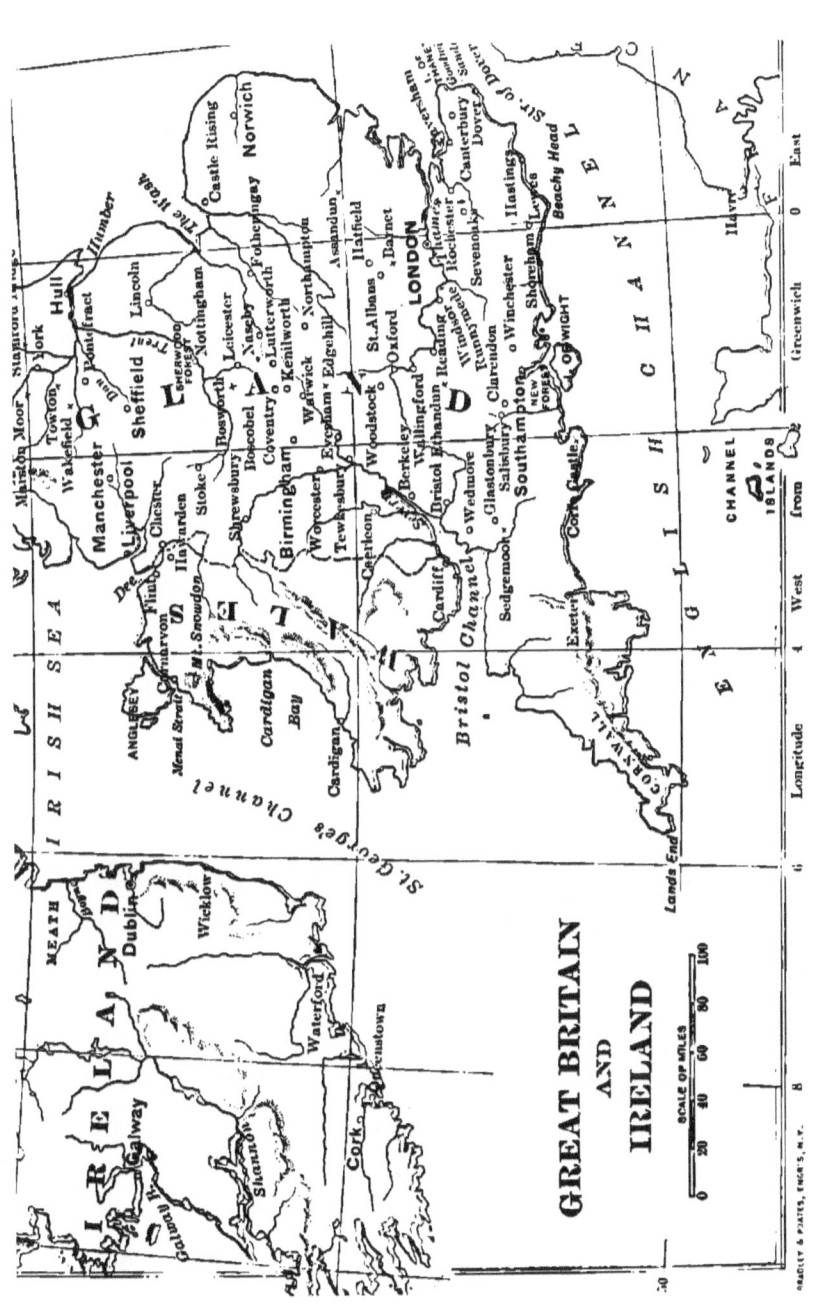

THE STORY OF THE ENGLISH.

I. EARLY TIMES.

IF you look at a map of Europe, you will notice two large islands and many small ones at a short distance west of the mainland. It is the story of the people who have lived upon these islands that you are now going to hear. As you can see, the islands are so small that no matter how far inland you travel, you are never more than one hundred miles away from the water which hems them in on all sides. On the north and west there is the Atlantic Ocean, on the south the English Channel, and on the east the North Sea.

These islands are now called the United Kingdom of Great Brit'ain and Ireland, and they form one of the foremost countries of the world. Great Britain includes England, Scotland, and Wales, besides the many little islands near by; and as the language, laws, and customs of Great Britain are mostly English, you will find that you will hear more about England than about the other parts of the realm.

Nobody knows just when the history of England really

begins, because it commenced long before people learned how to read or write, or keep any kind of record of passing events. Many, many years before Christ, these islands were inhabited by a rude race, who hunted and fished, lived in caves, dressed in the skins of the beasts they had slain, and often made war against one another. We know this because, from time to time, farmers have dug up stone arrowheads and spears, knives and axes made of flint, and have found the bones of these ancient men and women. Among the ashes of their fires there have also been found the bones of the animals whose flesh they ate, or the shells of oysters and clams.

As these early inhabitants used stone weapons, their time is generally known as the Stone Age. In the course of time the people grew more civilized, discovered metals, and learned how to make better weapons. Some of these weapons have also been dug up: they belong to the second period, which is called the Bronze Age. Such stone and bronze weapons are carefully kept in museums, where you can see them to-day, although the people who once used them have been dead for thousands of years.

The British Isles are far out in the ocean, and since the ships which ancient people used were as clumsy as their knives and spears, the early inhabitants of this country could not leave their homes to visit the mainland. They did not need to do so, for these islands are very fertile, owing principally to the mist which rises from the sea, and which keeps the grass in England green nearly all the year round.

On bright, clear days, when there is no mist at all, people standing on the coast of France, at the spot where the English Channel is narrowest, can just see the tall white chalk cliffs on the southern coast of England. These cliffs are so dazzlingly white that the people who lived in France used to call England the White Land. This name was translated into Latin by the Romans, who called the country Al'bi-on, a name which you will still sometimes find in poetry, but rarely in prose.

The white cliffs of Great Britain roused the curiosity of the early inhabitants of France, the Gaels (gālz), to such a point that some of them at last went out to sea in their little boats, which were fashioned of roughly woven willow, and covered with skins so as to be water-tight.

In such rude craft the Gaels, after a time, either paddled or drifted to England; and when they found what a beautiful country it was, and saw that game was plentiful, they settled down there. These Gaels, however, were only one tribe of a very large nation which is known as the Celtic race. They talked a language of their own, of which there are many traces in the Gaelic, a tongue which is still spoken in some parts of Ireland and Scotland, but which is very unlike our English.

II. THE DRUIDS.

THE Gaels were a very rude people, but they were a little more civilized than the first inhabitants of Britain. They went out on their hunting or fighting expeditions under the leadership of one of their number, who, on account of his strength or skill, was chosen to be their chief.

They had also learned how to build mud huts, which they placed close together and surrounded with a wall of tree-trunks and mud. This wall protected their dwellings from the attacks of the wild beasts which ranged through the forests then covering the greater part of the island.

The Gaelic villages multiplied until they soon dotted the southern coast of England. Then, little by little, the Gaels improved, and learned to make a kind of cloth, which they used for clothing instead of the skins of wild beasts, and to fashion clumsy earthenware pots, in which they cooked their food.

But, just as the Gaels had driven away the first inhabitants, of whom we know so little, they were, in turn, driven away themselves. Another tribe of the same race, called the Celts, now came from the mainland; and as they were more civilized than the Gaels, and had better weapons, they forced the Gaels to retreat before them into the interior of the country.

The newcomers knew how to plough, and sow, and reap, as well as to hunt and fight. They brought with them their priests, who were called Dru'ids, and began to practise in England what is known as the Dru-id'ic religion, or Dru'id-ism.

These priests were the wisest men of the Celtic nation, and they knew something of agriculture, arithmetic, astronomy, medicine, etc. They were very careful, however, to teach what they knew only to a few of the most intelligent men of the tribe, who thus became Druids too, and were greatly respected by their less learned companions.

At first the Druids used to teach their disciples by repeating over and over again the things they knew; and as it is easier to remember poetry than anything else, most of their knowledge was put into a sort of rhyme. The Druids wore long white linen garments and strange golden ornaments. They selected one of their number to be their chief, and obeyed him in all things. The chief is said to have worn a little golden box, which contained a serpent's egg. But you must not imagine that this was an ordinary snake's egg. Oh, no! The Druids said it was a magic egg, and that if the box were put into the water it would swim against the current.

Now the Celts and Gaels were so ignorant that they believed all this, and listened attentively to everything the Druids told them. But although the Druids did make them believe some very silly things, they also taught them some very useful knowledge. For instance, these priests told them that there was one great and powerful God, who had made them and enabled them to live. They said that this God was so great that no temple could hold him, and hence they always worshipped him out of doors.

Sometimes the Druids held their services under a huge oak tree, in the depths of the great forest. Then would tell the people that the oak was an emblem of the great God whom they worshipped, while the mistletoe, a little plant which grew on its bark, was like man, who was so weak and small that he could not live for a moment without the help of God.

The Druids had very solemn services at times; and once a year they used to march out into the forest, accompanied by holy women who were supposed to have the gift of prophecy. These women wore long white linen robes, had crowns of vervain on their heads, and carried golden sickles, with which the Druids cut down the mistletoe while chanting a sort of hymn. The herb thus gathered was used for medicine, and the Celts believed that it would cure almost every disease.

In different parts of England, you can still see huge stone altars or tables, which are called dolmens. The rocks which form these altars are so large that it is not easy to understand how the Druids built them; but it is evident that these wise men knew something about machinery, and secretly made use of this knowledge to put them up. The ignorant people, however, believed that the

Stonehenge.

stones had moved into their places at a mere touch of the Druids' magic wands.

Although the Druids generally offered up a horse or some other animal, they sometimes laid human sacrifices on these great stone slabs, in which little grooves were cut to receive the blood. As they fancied that such a sacrifice was agreeable to God, the victim sometimes offered to die of his own free will. In times of war, prisoners were sacrificed; but when they were very numerous, the Druids made a huge wicker cage in the shape of a man, crammed it full of captives, and then set it afire, while they intoned their chants.

Besides the stone altars, the Druids are also supposed to have built one of the strangest monuments in the world, that known as Stone'henge, on the Salisbury (sawlz'ber-y) Plain in England. There, around a huge stone altar, you can see two circles of upright stones, which were once connected by flat slabs laid on top of them. Learned men now think that this was one of the Druidic temples, and hence left open to the sky; but it was built so long before real history began, that the people, unable to account for its origin, declared it had risen by magic, in the course of a single night, from stones spirited over the sea from Ireland.

Stonehenge (restored).

III. THE BRITONS.

THE Gaels and Celts were followed by a third tribe of their own race, called the Brit'ons, from whom the country took the name of Britain. They, too, came from the mainland, and, being more civilized than the Celts, drove them away from the coast into the interior. The

Celts, in their turn, drove the Gaels still farther away, and forced them to go and live in the mountains of Scotland and Wales, where it was cold and foggy, but where there was plenty of game.

The Britons, however, had just the same religion as the Celts, and so they brought over more Druids, of their own tribe, who finally settled in the island of An'gle-sey. Here they founded a school, where they would keep a pupil at his studies for twenty years, making him learn by heart all they knew. Besides the Druids, there were teachers, or prophets, and a class of men called bards, who went about from place to place, singing the great deeds of heroes, which they or the Druids had woven into songs.

The Britons were braver and stronger than the Celts, and had better weapons. Their main pleasure was to terrify their enemies. To do this, they used to utter fearful cries, and brandish their spears. Each spear was provided with a noisy rattle, which made a great din when shaken or flung. It was fastened to the warrior's wrist by a long strap; and after a Briton had flung his spear at an enemy he would jerk it back by this strap.

As the Britons wore big moustaches, and painted their bodies blue, you can readily imagine how strange they looked, and how they must have frightened their enemies. They were fierce and quarrelsome, and rode small horses, which they had trained to fight too. These shaggy little ponies used to dash into the very midst of the fray, and stand still while their riders dismounted; but as soon as they felt their masters on their backs once more, they would rush off, knocking the enemies over and trampling them under foot. After the Britons had settled in England, they learned to make rude war chariots, to which they harnessed these intelligent little horses, which they guided by signs. To make more havoc, the Britons fastened scythes to their chariot wheels, and, driving rapidly into the very midst of the enemy, mowed their foes down like ripe grain.

Now, although the Gaels, Celts, and Britons were so rude at this time, there were other nations in Europe who had progressed faster, and had already reached a high degree of civilization. Towards the south, along the shores of the Mediterranean Sea, there were many prosperous cities. Most of these had been founded by the Phœ-nï'-cians, who, as they owned but a little strip of land on the coast of Asia, turned to the sea and became great navigators. Already, one thousand years before Christ, the Phœnicians had coasted all around the Mediterranean Sea, and we are told that they even ventured out into the Atlantic Ocean, through the Strait of Gi-bral'tar. They soon began to carry goods from one place to another, and thus became great traders.

Men in those days were always fighting, so they wanted armour and weapons; and as copper is not quite hard enough for this purpose, they needed something to mix with it so as to harden it. The Phœnicians knew that tin was just what was needed; and as they could not find enough of this metal near home to supply the demand, they sailed off in search of tin mines elsewhere. They soon found some in Spain, and got tin from the natives in exchange for cloth and trinkets; then, when they reached home, they sold this tin at such profit that they soon became very rich. But since the tin mines in Spain could not furnish as much metal as the Phœnicians wanted, they soon sailed all around Spain, and along the coast of France, in search of more. Here some merchants told them that they could find all the tin they wanted in Britain; so the Phœnicians, if old stories be true, crossed the Channel and landed in England. There the Phœnicians found mines so rich that they are still worked to-day, nearly three thousand years after they were first discovered.

As the Phœnicians made large profits by their tin trade, they were very careful not to tell any one where the mines were situated; and whenever any one inquired where they got their metal, they would always answer, "From the Cas-si-ter′i-des," or Tin Islands.

Many years later, the Romans, who were great fighters, and needed a great deal of tin for the manufacture of their weapons, were very anxious to find these islands; so they fitted out a vessel and sent it away with orders to watch and follow a Phœnician ship, and not to give up the pursuit until the Tin Islands had been reached.

The Roman captain was a bold and clever man, so he managed to sail after the Phœnicians for a long while unseen; but finally the Phœnician captain discovered that he was followed, and that the long-guarded secret was likely to become known to his foes. Rather than let them find it out, he resolved to sacrifice his boat and crew.

So he changed his course a little, and lured the Roman vessel on into shallow waters, until it came on a sunken reef and was dashed to pieces. The Phœnician vessel could not escape the same fate, but the captain and his crew managed to cling to the spars until they were washed ashore or rescued. The men on the Roman vessel, however, all perished; and it was not till two hundred years later, and in a different way, that the Romans found out where the Tin Islands were situated.

IV. CÆSAR IN BRITAIN.

IN exchange for the tin from the mines of Wales and Corn'wall, the Phœnicians brought the Britons many useful things, and taught them how to make better weapons. But as few people besides the Phœnicians ever came to Britain, the inhabitants progressed very slowly, and were still savages when Jul'ius Cæ'sar, the most famous of Roman generals, conquered Gaul, the country which is now called France.

Hearing from some merchants that the Britons had sent help to the Gauls, Cæsar made up his mind to cross the Channel and punish them. Vessels were prepared to carry the Roman legions (or regiments) across the water; and one night, when a favourable wind was blowing, Cæsar and his men embarked. Early the next morning they drew near the tall white cliffs at Do'ver; and, seeing no good landing place there, Cæsar bade his men sail eastward along the coast until they came to a shelving beach.

Warned by the merchants that Cæsar was coming over to conquer them, the fierce Britons had assembled there. They watched the coming of the Romans, who gazed with surprise at them; for their bodies were painted blue, and they uttered blood-curdling cries as they brandished their spears and shook their war rattles.

Although surprised, the Roman soldiers under Cæsar were too hardened warriors to be frightened; and as soon as the water was shallow enough, the standard bearer sprang out and waded ashore, closely followed by his companions. Then the Britons and the Romans had a fierce battle; but in spite of their great bravery, the Britons were defeated and forced to make a treaty with Cæsar. As some of the tribes in Gaul had taken advantage of his absence to revolt, Cæsar did not remain in Britain to continue his conquests, but hastily recrossed the Channel. When he had put down this rebellion, he found that the Britons did not keep their promises, so he crossed the Channel once more, with a larger army, to force the Britons to obey him. They resisted fiercely, but vainly, under the able leadership of a brave chief named Cas-si-vel-lau'nus.

These two expeditions into Britain were made in the years 55 and 54 B.C., and it was thus that the Romans became masters of the country where the tin mines were situated. Cæsar himself wrote an account of both campaigns in his "Commentaries," a Latin work which is still read in our schools. In that book the country is called Bri-tan'ni-a—a name still used in poetry to-day.

The Britons, thus brought into contact with the Romans for a short time, made some progress; but, instead of keeping the treaty they had made, they proved for a while very rebellious subjects. During the next one hundred years the Romans were too busy elsewhere to pay much attention to them; so it was not till the time of the emperor Clau'di-us that legions were again sent out to their island.

This time the Britons were led by Ca-rac'ta-cus, who fought for nine years before he was conquered. The Roman general then took this Briton chief to Rome, where the captive was forced to march in chains in the victor's triumph. As the barbarian slowly passed along the streets of the Eternal City, amid the deafening shouts

G. F. Watts, Artist.
Caractacus led in Triumph through Rome.

of the people, he gazed in awe at the beautiful buildings, and bitterly cried: " Alas! how is it possible that a people possessed of such magnificence at home could envy me my humble cottage in Britain?"

This remark was repeated to the emperor Claudius, and, although he was not noted for his kind-heartedness, he was so touched by the Briton chief's bravery and homesickness that he set him free, as well as the other captives of his race.

V. QUEEN BOADICEA.

IN defeating Caractacus, the Romans had become masters of the southern part of the island only. Many Britons were not subdued, and, helped by the Celts and Gaels, they often revolted. The Roman generals stationed in Britain put down one revolt after another; but finally Sue-to'ni-us, one of them, declared that he was sure the Druids advised the Britons to fight. He therefore made up his mind to go and attack the priests in their island of Anglesey, and set out with his legions.

As Suetonius drew near the Druid stronghold, he saw that the priests had been warned of his coming, for they rushed forward to meet him, uttering strange cries and curses. They were armed, and fought fiercely, while the women, too, attacked the enemy with lighted torches, uttering shrill screams, and wildly tossing their long hair.

In spite of the brave defence of the Druids, Suetonius landed on the island, killed the priests and bards, overthrew the altars and temples, and cut down the sacred oak trees beneath whose shade they had been wont to gather. But while he was doing this, some other Roman soldiers cruelly illtreated Bo-ad-i-ce'a, the queen of one of the Briton tribes, and insulted her two daughters.

Escaping from their hands with her unhappy daughters, Boadicea drove in her chariot all through the land, calling the people together, and telling them how shamefully the Romans had treated her and her poor children. As she spoke, the men's eyes gleamed with anger; and at her appeal, they all took up their arms and swore to avenge her. Led by this woman, the Britons went forth to fight the Romans, took their principal city, killed the seventy thousand strangers who dwelt there, and set fire to the beautiful buildings which the Romans had put up. But their triumph did not last long, for they soon met Suetonius coming back from Anglesey. He attacked them, and although the Britons fought more fiercely than ever before, they were soon completely beaten.

We are told that eighty thousand Britons died on that field of battle, and that Boadicea killed herself and her children, rather than fall into the enemy's hands and be taken to Rome to figure in the victor's triumph.

This victory left the Romans masters of the greater part of the island. All the Britons who were not willing to obey them fled to the mountains, to join the Picts and Scots, who were also Celtic tribes. Here the Romans did not dare venture, for fear they should lose their way and fall into an ambush. From time to time, parties of warriors would make sudden raids down into the country, killing, burning, and robbing wherever they went. Then, before the Roman soldiers could overtake them, they would carry their spoil back to the mountains, to hide until it was time for a new expedition.

To prevent these inroads into the country, which was rapidly becoming fertile and civilized, the Romans built large fortified camps at Ex'e-ter, Chester, and York, which last they made their capital. In these camps, or cities, they built beautiful houses, temples, and public baths, such as they had in Rome. There are still some traces of these fine buildings, and the well-made Roman roads, which connected the different camps, are still good to-day.

Little by little, the Britons learned many of the Roman arts; and in the first century of our era, some of them heard Christian soldiers tell the story of Christ, and became Christians. For many years Roman soldiers did all the fighting in Britain, while the young Britons who joined the army were sent to fight in other lands, under Roman generals.

VI. THE GREAT WALLS.

TO protect the northern part of Britain from the raids of the Picts and Scots, the Romans built three walls all across the island at its narrowest point. These walls, which are more than seventy miles long, are known by the names of the emperors by whose order they were built, and are hence called the walls of Ha′dri-an, of An-to-ni′-nus, and of Se-ve′rus.

As the Romans were noted for their solid masonry, their walls stood firm for many long years, and even now, nearly seventeen centuries after the last wall was finished, there are some parts of it still standing. Along the walls, at certain intervals, were towers where the Roman soldiers stood on guard night and day, so that the Picts and Scots could not force their way into the cultivated lands.

Nearly five hundred years after the Romans first set foot in Britain, and when the country was quite used to their rule, Rome was threatened by a terrible invasion of barbarians. The legions were all needed to protect the frontier nearer home, so an order was sent to Britain recalling all the troops.

The Britons were in despair, for those who were now left on the island did not know how to fight, and all the people were afraid of the Scots and Picts. But the Roman legions could not stay; so they gave the Britons

William Bell Scott, Artist.
Building a Roman Wall.

weapons, taught them how to fight, and bade them keep watch on the walls and drive back their enemies whenever they came down from Cal-e-do'ni-a, as Scotland was then called.

As soon as the Romans had left the country, the Picts and Scots marched southward. When they came near the great walls, they were surprised to see men on guard there, and hesitated for a little while; but they soon took courage, and, rushing forward, they climbed over the walls and drove away the Britons, who dared not resist.

There was nothing now to stop these marauders, who overran the whole country, destroying all that they could not carry away, and killing the inhabitants, or leading them off to sell them as slaves. Encouraged by success, the Picts and Scots came into Britain again and again. Each time they went a little farther south, and the inhabitants fled at their approach. The Britons could not protect themselves against the inroads of these barbarians, who were not much more civilized than the Britons had been at the time of Cæsar's invasion; so they wrote a pitiful letter to the Roman general in Gaul, begging him to come over and help them. This letter was entitled " The Groans of the Britons," and ran thus: " The barbarians drive us into the sea; the sea throws us back upon the swords of the barbarians: and we have only the hard choice of perishing by the sword or by the waves."

This letter reached the Roman general safely, but he could not help the Britons, because he had to defend Gaul against At'ti-la, the " Scourge of God," the terrible king of the Huns, who was sweeping all over Europe with his hordes of barbarians. As Rome itself was threatened, the Romans could not spare any troops to help the Britons, who, as you will soon see, were thus driven to seek help elsewhere.

VII. THE GREAT IRISH SAINT.

SHORTLY after the Roman legions had left Britain, and during one of their first raids over the wall of Severus, the Picts carried off into captivity a boy named Patrick, who was then about sixteen years of age. He was the son of a deacon, and was busy ploughing when the marauders fell upon him.

The Picts, after taking young Patrick back to their mountain homes, conveyed him over the Irish Sea to Ireland, where they sold him into slavery. For six years Patrick was obliged to watch his master's sheep on the hillside, and during that time he often prayed that he might escape.

Finally his prayers were answered, and after hiding for some time among the reeds by the shore, Patrick boarded one of the vessels which came to trade along the coast. From there he probably went to France, then to a monastery near the Mediterranean, and then to Rome.

He studied hard to become a priest; and when he was ordained, he went back to Britain, where his kinsmen were glad to see him. While there, Patrick was troubled by dreams and visions. It seemed to him as if the people in Ireland, or Hi-ber'ni-a, as it was called in the days of the Romans, were stretching out their hands to him, and begging him to come over to them.

At times he fancied that he heard the Irish saying, "We pray thee, holy youth, to come and henceforth walk among us." The result was that Patrick, either by the pope's orders, or of his own free will, finally made his way back to the country whence he had escaped as a slave.

With a few followers, he landed on the Irish coast. Thence he made his way on foot to Meath, where a pagan Irish king was holding a great festival. It was the custom, at that time, that no fire should be lighted until the king had given the signal by kindling his. But Patrick, not knowing this, and stopping to keep Easter on the hill of Slane, made a bright fire there.

When its light was seen, the Irish king sent a messenger to Patrick, bidding him come and explain how he dared to light his fire before the king. An old writer tells us that Patrick immediately set out with the messenger, but that, as he went along, many prodigies took place. First, darkness fell upon the earth; then the ground shook beneath their feet; and when some of the Irish magicians would fain have stopped Patrick, they were seized by invisible hands and tossed up in the air.

When Patrick appeared before the angry king, he began to preach to him; and such was this missionary's eloquence that he converted not only the ruler, but the whole clan. Journeying about from place to place, Patrick is said to have converted all Ireland, to have baptized more than twenty thousand converts with his own hand, and to have founded more than three hundred churches.

As Patrick lived so long ago, and as no record was kept of his life, many things are told about him which most people do not now believe to be true. Stories are told of his driving all the snakes out of Ireland into the sea, and of his working many other miracles.

The only thing we are sure of is that he converted the

Irish and founded churches and monasteries in the island. In the monasteries he established schools, which were visited by students from all parts of the world. These men became missionaries, preached in Scotland, England, France, Germany, Switzerland, and Italy, and were so enthusiastic and so earnest that they did a great deal of good.

Thus the schools founded by Patrick, the first Bishop of Ireland, were the foremost in Europe for about three centuries. The man who founded them is now called Saint Patrick, and he is considered the patron saint of the island where he was, in turn, slave, priest, and saint. His birthday, celebrated on the 17th of March, is one of the greatest festivals in Ireland.

VIII. THE ANGLO-SAXONS.

YOU have seen how the poor Britons had vainly appealed to the Roman general in Gaul to come and deliver them from the Picts and Scots, who were ravaging the whole country and driving them into the sea. When the Britons found out that the Romans could not help them, they began to look around them for other aid.

In the days of the Romans, light willow barks, covered with skins, had sometimes visited the shores of the island. These boats carried hardy warriors, who came from the shores of the Baltic Sea. They belonged to the Teu-ton'ic, or German, race—a race never subdued by the Romans, who were then masters of nearly all the known world.

These men were so brave that Vor'ti-gern, the British

chief, begged some of them to come over to Britain and help him drive back the Picts and Scots. One of the Teutonic tribes, the Jutes, consented; and about the year 449 a whole fleet of little ships came dancing over the sea, which the Teutons called the " Swan Road," because when winter drew near they often watched the birds flying or swimming southward over the waters.

The leaders of the Jutes, it is said, were two brothers, Hen'gist and Hor'sa, the descendants of Wo'den, who was the principal god of the Teutonic nations. The Jutes were used to fighting, and helped the Britons drive back the Picts and Scots. The marauders were forced to retreat to the other side of the walls, which were repaired and provided with defenders.

In reward for their services, Vortigern gave the Jutes the island of Than'et; and while some of them settled down there contentedly, others went back to their native country to tell what they had seen. But, as Britain was much more fertile than the land where they dwelt, they soon came back, with their families, to settle in it.

The Jutes were followed, before long, by another Teutonic tribe, the Sax'ons. As there was not room enough for them all in the island of Thanet, the Saxons settled on the mainland, where they were joined by other Saxons; and their numbers multiplied so fast that they soon covered much territory.

The Britons were forced to retreat before the newcomers; and as they were afraid of the Picts and Scots, and dared not go north, they withdrew to the west, where they took possession of Cornwall and Wales. Now that it was too late, Vortigern saw what a mistake he had made in inviting the Jutes to come over and help him. He could not quarrel with them, however, because he had married Ro-we'na, Hengist's beautiful young daughter. It seems that he had fallen in love with this maiden at first sight, when she came to offer him a drink, as was the custom in her country whenever a stranger came into the house.

The Jutes and Saxons spread farther and farther over the southern part of Britain, until they took entire possession of Vortigern's kingdom, driving him far into the west, where he died of grief. After the Jutes and Saxons came a third Teutonic tribe, the An'gles, who, in their turn, settled in the eastern part of Britain.

They killed all the natives who would not peaceably make way for them, sparing only the women and children, whom they made their slaves. But the Angles were not nearly so civilized as the Britons, who had learned much from their Roman conquerors, and they destroyed many of the Roman buildings, which they were too ignorant to admire.

When they first came over to Britain, the Anglo-Saxons — as the Angles and Saxons are often called for short — knew nothing at all about Christianity, and brought with them their own language, laws, and religion. This old Anglo-Saxon religion soon gave way before Christianity, as you will see; but the names of the heathen gods of the Anglo-Saxons are still found in our names of the days of the week. Thus, Sunday was the day of the sun god; Monday, of the moon deity; Tuesday was named after Tiu, god of war; Wednesday, after Woden, their principal divinity, and the ancestor of their kings; Thursday took its name from Thor, god of thunder; Friday, from Frea, goddess of beauty; and Saturday, from Sat'urn, a Roman divinity.

But, although there are now very few traces left of the old Teutonic religion, the Anglo-Saxon laws and language form the basis of the present English laws and language, so they are of great interest to the one hundred and fifty million English-speaking people of this century.

IX. BRAVE KING ARTHUR.

THE Angles, in the course of time, formed three kingdoms in Britain, which bore the names of An'gli-a, Mer'cia, and Nor-thum'bri-a. But, in speaking of the territory they occupied, they so often said that it was the Angles' land, that little by little the name was contracted into "England," and after the tenth century the whole country was known by this name.

The Saxons also formed three kingdoms, called Es'sex, Wes'sex, and Sus'sex, or the lands of the East, West, and South Saxons; and the Jutes took possession of that part of England which goes by the name of Kent. You see, the Britons had very little space left, and for some time they could not resist their powerful foes. But not very long after Vortigern's death, they were ruled by Arthur, a British chief whose name has become very famous, because many poets have written about him and about his great deeds.

It is so long since Arthur lived that we really know little about him; but we are told that he fought against the Saxons and defeated them in twelve great battles. Brave as Arthur was in war, he was no less gentle and courteous in peace, and the Britons were so proud of him that they were never tired of singing his praises.

After a time they began to fancy that he was more than a man; and when he finally fell in battle, and was buried in Glastonbury (glahs'en-ber-y), they would not believe that he was dead. They said that Arthur could not die, and that when he fell, sorely wounded, the fairies carried him away to their island home at Av'a-lon, to make him well.

They had such faith in Arthur that they thought he would come back, some day, to reign over all Britain and make his people happy. The bards, who loved to sing about Arthur, fostered this belief; and we are told that some of the descendants of the old Britons, the Welsh, as they are now called, still believe that Arthur will come back to his loving people.

After Arthur's death, the Britons were driven still farther away from their former homes, and some of them, crossing the sea, went to settle in France, in a province called Brit'tan-y. Here, and in Wales, the old Briton language is still spoken by many of the common people, and wonderful stories about King Arthur are still told by the fireside.

Many years later, when a new race had settled in England, stories of Arthur were told in every castle. As the warriors then wore armour, held tournaments, and went about to deliver the oppressed, they imagined that Arthur and his followers used to do the same. So they made up long tales about the adventures of Arthur's principal companions, who, they said, assembled in his palace at Caer-leon (car-le′on), and held feasts there, sitting at a round table. Because they did this, they were called the Knights of the Round Table, and poets have long loved to write about them. One of the last great poets who has retold their story is Tennyson, whose "Idylls of the King" you will read with great delight.

X. THE LAWS OF THE SAXONS.

THE Anglo-Saxons, having terrified the Picts, Scots, and Britons, so that they no longer dared come into the main part of the island, settled down quietly in the kingdoms they had founded. As there were generally seven of these kingdoms, they are known as the Hep′-tarch-y, or the Seven Kingdoms.

You must not imagine, however, that the Anglo-Saxons entirely gave up fighting, for they often quarrelled and waged war against one another. But whenever any great danger threatened them, the Seven Kingdoms united under the command of the bravest of their kings, who was given the title of *bret′wal-da*, or head of the army. Besides the king, there were the earls, noblemen who were the governors and judges of certain provinces; the thanes, who served the king; the churls, who were the farmers; and, the lowest and largest class of all, the slaves, or serfs.

The people believed that the Anglo-Saxon kings all belonged to the race of Woden, but the crown did not always pass from a father to his eldest son, as it does now.

Whenever a king died, the principal men of the tribe assembled in a council which was called the Wit'e-na-ge-mot, or assembly of wise men. Here they talked the matter over and elected a new king, who could reign only by consent of the people. The Witenagemot also met two or three times a year, to decide what had best be done, and what new laws should be made, or to judge any case which could not be settled by the earls.

Most of the Anglo-Saxon punishments were by fines, a larger sum being asked for the murder of an earl than for that of a churl, and the killing of a horse or a cow being rated higher than that of a slave. Each earl had a sort of court over which he presided, and when a man was accused of a crime, he could prove his innocence either by getting ten men of his own class to swear he had not done wrong, or by submitting to an ordeal.

Now, as you probably do not know what an ordeal was, I must explain to you that it was a test of some kind. For instance, there was the ordeal by water, in which the accused was forced to plunge his hand into boiling water. If, at the end of a certain number of days, his burns were healed, he was said to be guiltless; but if they were not well, he was condemned as guilty. Sometimes the accused had to pick up a bar of iron heated red-hot, or had to walk blindfolded over nine heated ploughshares, or to plunge his hand or foot into boiling oil or pitch. Of course, we know that it was impossible by this plan to find out whether a man was innocent or guilty; but the Anglo-Saxons fancied that God would plainly show them who was right and who was wrong.

In these trials by ordeal, if the accused was a friend of

the executioner, or if he had given him a present, the iron, water, or oil was not heated so hot as when the accused was an enemy, or even a stranger. So while some of the old Anglo-Saxon laws have proved worthy of being preserved, no one can regret that the trial by ordeal has been long ago given up.

XI. THE STORY OF ST. AUGUSTINE.

THE Anglo-Saxons had been masters of England for many years, when Eth'el-bert, the third bretwalda, married a French princess, Bertha, who was a Christian.

In the wars between the various Anglo-Saxon kingdoms, many captives were taken, and these were often sold as slaves. Besides this, many poor men were compelled by their hunger to sell themselves and their wives and children into slavery.

We are told that some English boys were brought to Rome by the slave merchants, and exposed there for sale on the market place. A monk named Greg'o-ry, who was passing by, stopped to look at them. Struck by the blue eyes, golden hair, and fair complexion of these children, he asked the merchant who they were. The man answered that they were Angles and heathens.

"Oh," cried the monk, "they would be indeed not *Angli* (Angles), but *angeli* (angels), if they were only Christians!"

This monk was so pleased, either by his own pun or by the good looks of the young slaves, that he wanted to go to Britain without delay; but his friends would not let him.

He did not forget the Angles, however; and when he became pope, soon after, he sent Au'gus-tine and forty other monks to preach the gospel to the Angles, or English.

Augustine travelled through Gaul, where he got some men who could act as interpreters, and then landed on the island of Thanet, on the coast of England. From here, he sent a message to Ethelbert, begging for an interview, and asking permission to preach to the people. As Bertha was a Christian, she coaxed her husband to receive Augustine; but the pagan king was so afraid the monk would try to influence him by magic, that he would not receive him indoors, and sat under an oak, fancying that so holy a tree would protect him from all evil spells.

Augustine now advanced with his forty monks, and showed Ethelbert a picture of Christ. Then he preached to the king to such good purpose that he consented to be baptized. Of course all his court followed his example, and we are told that on Pentecost day ten thousand Anglo-Saxons were converted, and that the Christian religion soon took the place of the worship of Woden all through England.

Churches were built in different parts of the country, the greatest being the Cathedral of Can'ter-bur-y, of which Augustine was the first bishop. There is nothing left of this old building, but the famous Cathedral of Canterbury (p. 40) stands on the very spot that it once occupied. Churches were also built, at this time, in London, on the sites of West'min-ster Abbey and St. Paul's Cathedral; and when we enter these buildings, we like to think that Christians have worshipped on these spots nearly thirteen hundred years.

In a very short time, the monks Gregory had sent visited all the different parts of England, and founded churches and monasteries, where many students came to learn all that the monks could teach them. Most of the

Canterbury Cathedral.

monks' books were written in Latin, so all the students learned to read and write in that language, rather than in their own. As it had not seemed best to the priests that prayers should be translated into English, the church services were also held in Latin, a language which the common people did not understand.

XII. THREE GREAT MEN.

YOU have heard how Augustine came over to England to convert the Anglo-Saxons. After his death he was made a saint, and he is the missionary of England, just as St. Patrick is the missionary of Ireland. There were many good men in the monasteries which were founded in England, and a few of them are still famous.

There was, for instance, a monk named Gil'das, who wrote a Latin history, in which he tells us a great deal about olden times in England. Copies of this book have been preserved, and it has been translated into English.

In the nunneries of the seventh century, the nuns and their servants used to spend the long winter evenings around the fire, telling tales and singing songs. In one nunnery there was a poor servant named Cædmon (ked'-mon), who was greatly embarrassed when his turn came. He had nothing to say, and felt so ashamed that he went out into the stable and wept. While he was there one evening, he heard a voice which bade him sing. First he answered that he could not; but when the command was repeated, he inquired, "What shall I sing?" "Sing the beginning of created things," answered the voice. So Cædmon, who had often heard the nuns tell about the creation, began to sing, and, to his surprise, he found that he was reciting a wonderful poem.

We are told that Hilda, the abbess of the nunnery, encouraged Cædmon to compose more verse, and that his poem, the first in English, gave Milton, one of our greatest geniuses, the idea of writing "Paradise Lost."

The first English prose was written, nearly one hundred years after Cædmon's poem, by the Venerable Bede. He translated one of the Gospels into English. He was very old, and when his great work was nearly finished, feeling that he was about to die, he bade his disciple hurry and write down the end of the translation.

"There is still one chapter wanting, Master," said the scribe; "it is hard for thee to think and to speak."

"It must be done," said Bede. "Write quickly!"

The work went on, but the master grew weaker and weaker; and when night was coming on, the scribe said:

"There is yet one sentence to write, dear Master."

Once more the master roused himself to dictate the last words, and a few moments later the scribe exclaimed: "It is finished!" "Thou sayest truth," replied the weary old man; "it is finished; all is finished!" And, sinking back upon his pillow, he died, leaving us the first English translation of one of the books of the Bible.

XIII. THE DANISH PIRATES.

ABOUT four hundred years after the Anglo-Saxons first came to settle in Britain, other men from the north began to appear on their coasts. These, too, made part of the great Teutonic race, and came from the shores of the Baltic Sea; but they were far less civilized than the Anglo-Saxons, and still worshipped heathen gods.

Their main object was to plunder, and, landing from their skiffs, they would attack the peaceful Anglo-Saxon

Herbert A. Bone, Artist.

"How the Danes came up the Channel a Thousand Years ago."

villages, and destroy all the property which they did not carry away. They came when least expected, and sometimes sailed off with their plunder before the terrified inhabitants could arm to resist them. These pirates were called, from their nationality, Danes or Northmen; and, from the bays where their ships sought shelter, vik'ings or bay-men.

The Northmen not only ravaged the coasts of England, Scotland, and Ireland from the seventh to the tenth century, but they also visited the coasts of the Continent. Such was the terror they inspired in England that a sentence was added to the Litany, and the people daily prayed, "From the fury of the Northmen, good Lord, deliver us."

Some of the chiefs of the Northmen were so brave and daring that their names have come down to us in history. One of the best-known among them is Rag'nar Lod'brog, a Danish king who invaded England in the days when Æl'la was head of the Anglo-Saxon Heptarchy.

When Ragnar's fleet appeared, with the big vessels called "dragons" and the little ones "snails," the people fled; but Ælla promptly assembled a large army to repulse the enemy. The two forces met in a bloody battle, in which Ragnar was defeated and fell into the hands of his enemies.

To punish the captive king for all the harm he had done to the English, Ælla thrust him into a pit filled with venomous serpents, which crawled all over him and bit him to death. But even while the serpents were torturing him, Ragnar remained calm and showed no fear.

As his hands were tied, and he could not use them to play on his harp, which had been flung into the pit after him, we are told that the dauntless old Northman began to play upon it with his toes. Then, to show the English how little he cared for their tortures, he began a song, in which he boasted how bravely he had fought, how many foes he had slain, and how he scorned his conquerors.

Singing thus, he died; but his death did not put an end to the Northmen's raids, for Ragnar's sons came over to England to avenge him. They captured King Ælla in battle, sacrificed him on one of the heathen altar-stones, and took possession of a large part of the country.

For many years after the death of Ælla, the Saxons and the Danes were always at war; and as more and more of these Northmen came over the sea, they took up more and more room. The part of the land occupied by the Danes was called the Dane'lagh, and the Saxon kings, weary of fighting, sometimes bribed them to keep peace. But, as the Danes delighted in warfare, the truce never lasted long, and bloodshed and destruction were soon renewed.

In these wars the Danes not only burned the wooden houses of the Saxons, but they also ruined the stone churches, which had been built at great cost by workmen brought from the Continent. These churches were decorated with beautiful paintings, and some of them even had stained-glass windows, which were then very rare.

The Danes destroyed these beautiful buildings because they hated the Christian religion, and because they wanted to secure the gold and silver vessels used for mass, and the large sums of money often kept in the churches. This money was collected by the priests, who always accepted all the gifts the people brought them, and claimed, besides, one penny from each household. As the money was sent to the pope to help build the beautiful church of St. Peter's in Rome, the tax has been called "Peter's pence."

King Eth'el-wulf, who first gave the priests permission to collect Peter's pence in his realm, was so pious a king that he made several journeys to Rome to visit the pope. Once he took with him his youngest son, Alfred, a prince who lived to be one of the most remarkable kings the world has ever seen.

XIV. KING ALFRED AND THE CAKES.

LIKE all the Saxon youths of his time, Alfred soon learned how to handle the arms of a soldier, but he knew nothing of what even the smallest children now learn in school. One day, when he was twelve years old, he and his brothers noticed that the queen was reading a book of Saxon poetry. You must not imagine that this book was a printed work, like those we have now. It was carefully written on parchment, or sheepskin, which was then used instead of paper, and the initial letters were painted in bright colours and surrounded by fancy designs.

Written books are called manuscripts, and as soon as the young princes caught sight of this illuminated, or painted, manuscript, they crowded around their mother to see and admire it. The queen, who was much more learned than many women of her time, told them it contained delightful stories, and promised that she would make a present of it to the first who could read it to her.

You may not think that this was a very great reward, as you can get a gaily painted book for a few pennies; but books in those days were so costly that they were worth more than a large farm.

Alfred was so anxious to win the prize, and especially to know what the book could tell him, that he lost no time in seeking a teacher and in beginning to learn to read. In those days, when there were no primers or readers, often no division between the words, and very little punctuation, it was much harder to learn how to read than it is now.

But Alfred was the kind of boy that would not give up; and although no one forced him to go to school, he kept at his self-appointed task, and tried so hard that he soon learned how to read. Then he went to his mother with the manuscript, and not only read, but also recited, the greater part of the poems it contained; and she was so delighted that she gladly gave him his hard-earned prize.

Having learned a little, Alfred was now eager to know more; and, hearing that nearly all manuscripts were written in Greek or Latin, he learned both languages, although he had no grammars, or dictionaries, or easy books such as you have now.

King Ethelwulf wanted Alfred to be king in his place when he died; but the Witenagemot decided that the three elder princes should reign first. These rulers were obliged to war against the Danes, who would not stay in the Danelagh; and we are told that Alfred laid aside his books and helped them fight eight battles in one year.

In spite of all this, the Danes spread farther and farther; and when Alfred became King of England, at the age of twenty-two, he found he had very little land left. Besides that, the Danes had destroyed so much property that all the Saxons were very poor. Even the king had hardly enough to eat; but Alfred was as generous as he was poor, and when one of his subjects once came to beg at his door, he bade his wife give the man half of the last loaf of bread in the house.

The Danes grew so bold that the king was forced, at one time, to assume a disguise and take refuge in the hut of a poor herdsman. Although these poor people had no idea that the wanderer was the king, they asked him to come into their little house, and gave him a seat near the fire. All the Saxons were noted for being good to strangers,

Sir David Wilkie, Artist.
King Alfred in the Herdsman's Cottage.

and they would have considered it very wrong not to treat them as well as they could.

One day Alfred was sitting near the fire, either mending his bow and thinking how he could drive the Danes out of the realm, or reading a book which he had hidden in the bosom of his dress. The herdsman's wife, who was baking flat cakes of bread on the hearthstone, bade her guest watch and turn them while she was busy elsewhere.

Alfred, thinking of more important matters, forgot all about the cakes, and let them burn. When the woman came back, she was angry with the king, and scolded him roundly, saying that, although he was too lazy to turn the cakes, he was ready enough to eat them.

Instead of punishing the woman for speaking so to him, Alfred said he was sorry to have let the cakes burn, and promised to do better another time. You see, although he was a king, he was not afraid to acknowledge that he had done wrong; and we are told that the next time the woman bade him watch her cakes, he did it very well.

XV. ALFRED CONQUERS THE DANES.

SHORTLY after this accident with the cakes, Alfred went to join his followers in a fortified camp in the centre of a swamp. Here he made a bold plan to conquer the Danes. Before he could carry it out, however, he had to know just how many Danes he should have to fight, where their camp was situated, how it was guarded, and where the general's tent stood.

To find out these things, Alfred disguised himself as a bard, took his harp, and walked boldly into the Danish camp. The soldiers were glad to see a bard, and, gathering around him, called for song after song.

Alfred now sang and told them all the stories he knew; and as he sang and played on his harp, he glanced around him and noticed the number of men. The soldiers were so pleased with Alfred's songs and jests that they led him to their general, Guth'rum, who, after hearing him sing and play, gave him some gold and praised his skill.

Alfred tarried in the Danish camp a few days, and made such good use of his eyes and ears that he found out enough to enable him to win a great victory over the Danes at Eth-an-dun'. He then signed the treaty of Wed'more with them, and gave them their choice, either to become Christians and keep the peace, or to leave England.

Most of the Danes preferred to stay, but a few of them joined a pirate chief named Has'tings, and a few years later they came back with him, to try to recover their lost ground. But Alfred again managed to defeat them, and made them promise to stay in the Danelagh, the part of the country which he said they might occupy. After this, the Danes lived on the northeast side of Wat'ling Street,—one of the old Roman roads which ran from Dover to Chester, passing through London,—while the Anglo-Saxons occupied the land on the other side of it.

To frighten away the pirate Danes, and keep the Picts and Scots in order, Alfred built ships, and once a year he sailed all around the islands, to see that all was well. This is considered the beginning of the English navy, and by the time you have finished reading this book, you will see that England owes much of her prosperity to her fleet, and that she is justly known as the "Queen of the Sea."

The beginning of King Alfred's reign was mostly taken up in fighting; but when he had made peace with the Danes, he began to think how he could best help his people. To make the best use of his time, Alfred divided his days into three equal parts: one for sleeping, eating, and amusement; one for business; and one for study.

As there were no clocks in King Alfred's day, and as the sundials marked time only when the sun shone, Alfred had candles made of such size and thickness that they would burn a certain length of time. These candles were notched to divide the day into equal periods. But the king soon noticed that the candles burned unevenly, owing to draughts. When you hear that glass was used only in a few churches, and that the palace windows were closed only by rude wooden shutters, you can readily understand that there were many draughts, and that when the wind blew the candles flickered, went out, or burned too fast. To prevent this, King Alfred had boxes made of thin pieces of horn, in which to place the candles; so he may fairly be considered the inventor of the first lantern.

The time which Alfred spent in study was devoted in part to framing wise laws for his people; and we are told that he executed justice so carefully that no one dared steal in all his realm. It is even said that golden bracelets hung on a tree in a lonely spot for more than a year, and, although there was no one near to guard them, no thief ventured to lay a finger upon them.

King Alfred not only made good laws for his people, but he established the first real schools in England. As there were no books in Anglo-Saxon, Alfred patiently translated many of the Greek and Latin works into his own language. He encouraged teachers to come and settle in his kingdom, and bought many manuscripts. We are told that he once gave a whole estate for a work on geography—a work which was considered wonderful then, although it gave far less information on the subject than the poorest and cheapest book printed in our day.

In Alfred's time, people studied languages more than anything else. There was, indeed, little else to study. Science and history were sadly neglected. In arithmetic, only Roman numbers were used, so even learned men found it hard to work out simple sums, and said that the study was beyond human understanding! But when Ar'a-bic numbers were introduced, in the twelfth century, arithmetic became much easier—so much easier that to-day children in the primary department can do sums that would have been almost impossible to the simple wise men of the ninth century.

You must not think, however, that the Saxons worked all the time. They liked to play, and when they could not run, or jump, or practise archery (shooting with a bow and arrow) outdoors, they sat by the fire, told stories, and sometimes played chess or backgammon.

King Alfred is remembered not only as a good general, a wise ruler, and a learned man; he is famous also for his patience, his perseverance, and most of all for his noble and truthful character. This is so well known that he is generally called Alfred the Great, or Alfred the Truth-teller. Although he always worked very hard, he was not strong, and after suffering for years from a terrible disease which none of the doctors of his time could cure, he died in the year 901. Just before he breathed his last, King Alfred said: "This I can now truly say: that so long as I have lived, I have striven to live worthily, and after my death to leave my memory to my descendants in good works."

It is because Alfred lived worthily that he has always been honoured as England's greatest king; and all the

English-speaking race has reason to respect the man who, among many other benefits, translated all the gospels into the Anglo-Saxon language for his people's use.

XVI. A KING'S NARROW ESCAPE.

KING ALFRED was buried in Win'ches-ter, and his son Edward, called the Elder to distinguish him from other kings of the same name who came after him, reigned in his place. The new king was busy, during the greater part of his reign of twenty-five years, in fighting the Danes, who wanted to invade his territory.

Edward the Elder was followed by his son Ath'el-stan the Glorious, who also had to struggle with the invaders. The Danes then had a very clever young leader named An'laf. He fancied that if he could get into the Anglo-Saxon camp, as Alfred had once made his way into the camp of the Danes, he would be able to find out just where Athelstan slept, and could come again with his army to murder the king in his sleep.

Disguised as a bard, so the story runs, Anlaf went into the English camp, where he was not recognized, and where he played so well that Athelstan gave him a piece of money. Now the young Dane hated Athelstan, and was so proud that he took the money only so that the king should not suspect who he really was. But as soon as he got out of the camp, he forgot all caution, and, digging a hole in the ground, buried the coin his enemy had given him.

One of the Anglo-Saxon soldiers, who had once served Anlaf, saw him bury the money, and recognized him. After watching him out of sight, this soldier told Athelstan all he had seen. But when the king angrily inquired why he had not spoken sooner, so that the Danish leader could have been captured, he answered: "I once served Anlaf as faithfully as I am now serving you. If I betrayed him, you could not trust me not to betray you. But now you know your danger, and I advise you to change the place of your tent, lest he should come and attack you when you do not expect him."

King Athelstan followed the soldier's advice, and it was well that he did so; for that very night Anlaf broke into the camp, and, rushing straight to what he took for the king's tent, he killed a bishop who happened to be sleeping there.

The Saxons fought all that night and the next day, so this encounter is often called the Long Battle, as well as the battle of Bru'nan-burgh. As Athelstan won the victory, the Danes left him thenceforth in peace.

Like Alfred, Athelstan was anxious that his people should learn as much as possible, so he had the whole of the Scriptures translated for them into Anglo-Saxon. He also encouraged commerce, and said that every merchant who made three journeys to the Mediterranean should receive the title of thane, or nobleman. It was no easy matter to travel in the tenth century, but the hope of winning this title induced many merchants to make these long and dangerous trips; and every time they came home they brought new things and new ideas to benefit the Anglo-Saxon people.

XVII. THE KING AND THE OUTLAW.

ATHELSTAN left no children, so he was succeeded by his young brother Edmund, who is surnamed the Magnificent. This prince was only eighteen when he came to the throne, but he was very brave. He conquered the province of Cum'bri-a, and gave it to Malcolm I., King of Scotland.

Edmund also defeated the Danes, who had risen up against him, and he might have done much more for his people had he not come to a very sudden death in rather a strange way. It seems that he had given strict orders that all robbers should be driven out of the country. A noted outlaw, notwithstanding this command, once entered the king's hall and boldly sat down at his table. Angry at this impudence, Edmund sternly ordered the man to go out. The robber insolently refused to obey, and when the king's cupbearer tried to turn him out by force, he began to resist. Then, before any one else could interfere, Edmund sprang up from his seat and tried to fling the intruder out of the house.

In the scuffle that ensued, the thief stabbed the king. The latter fell, and the people attacked the robber, who, leaning against the wall, fought with the courage of despair, until he was overpowered and killed.

Edmund was only twenty-four when he died, and as his children were babies, the Witenagemot chose his brother Ed'red for their next king. This prince soon had his hands full; for when the Danes heard that Edmund was dead, they again rose up against the Saxons. After defeating them, Edred decided that they should no longer be ruled by one of their own princes, but by an English governor who would keep them in order.

Edred was so young when he began to reign, that he generally followed the advice of a very clever priest called Dun'stan. While Dunstan was only a man like his fellow-men, he was unusually clever and able; so the common people fancied that he was gifted with powers more than human, and told strange stories about him.

They said that when he was only a boy Dunstan had already shown that he was not an ordinary child, and in proof of it they whispered that he walked in his sleep! Of course, we know that when a person is unable to sleep soundly and quietly, it is only a sign that he is not quite well; but the people in Dunstan's time fancied it was something very strange. When Dunstan saw that they admired all he said and did, he took advantage of that fact to get all he wanted, and, as he was very ambitious, he soon became the most important man in the kingdom.

Once, when his services were not needed at court, he took up his abode in a cell so small and low that he could neither lie down nor stand up in it. Here he prayed and fasted, and worked at a forge, and people came from far and near to admire him and exclaim in wonder at his great goodness. They often talked with him, and believed all he said, although we are told he once said that the devil came to visit him, and that he seized the fiend by the nose with his red-hot pincers!

XVIII. THE MONASTERIES.

KING EDRED, being as simple and credulous as the people, like them imagined that Dunstan was a saint, and obeyed him in everything. Dunstan, being a priest, wanted to have only priests who shared his opinions in England, so he began to found new monasteries in different parts of the country.

These monasteries were large houses, where many men lived together under the orders of one of their number, the abbot, or prior, whom they elected to be their master. The monks, as the dwellers in monasteries were termed, were good men who thought they could best serve God by promising never to marry, always to obey their superior, and, among many other things, to lead simple and holy lives.

Near each monastery, or forming part of it, there was a church or chapel, where the monks assembled several times a day, and even in the night, to say their prayers and sing hymns. They all ate their meals together in a large hall, called the refectory; and while they ate, one of their number read aloud to them from some holy book.

Each monk had his own sleeping room, a narrow little place called a cell, where there were sometimes a hard bed, a stool, and a crucifix; but very often the monks slept on the floor, with a stone or a log of wood for a pillow. Their only covering was a rough woollen dress which they wore summer and winter, and which was often fastened around the waist by a rope.

Each monk was expected to do something for the good

of the rest. Some of them studied, preached, and copied manuscripts in the monastery library, or *scri-ba'ri-um*, while others cooked, sewed, wove cloth, tilled the ground around the monastery, or watched the cows and sheep. They were good, earnest, and charitable men, so everybody loved and respected them, and the poor and ignorant often came to them for help and advice. As many people gave them land and money, the monasteries soon became very rich.

Besides the monasteries, or religious houses for men, there were similar places for women. These were called convents, or nunneries, and the women who dwelt in them, the nuns, were under the orders of an abbess, or prioress.

The nuns, besides looking after their own housekeeping, took care of the poor and sick, and taught young girls. Their main occupation, however, was needlework, in which they soon excelled. Besides sewing for themselves and for the needy, these holy women made fine lace and delicate embroidery, which they either gave to the church or sold to the wealthy.

XIX. AN UNLUCKY COUPLE.

DUNSTAN was the real ruler of England during the reign of Edred. When that king died, and Ed'wy, the sixteen-year-old son of Edmund, succeeded him, the priest was still at the head of affairs. But Dunstan had been master so long now that he often forgot to show the king due respect.

Edwy had married El-gi'va, a beautiful, gentle, and lovable girl. But as she was his cousin, and as they had forgotten to ask the pope's permission to marry, Dunstan made up his mind to separate the young couple. Now we are told that on the night of Edwy's coronation the young king slipped out of the noisy banquet hall, and went to join his bride and her mother in their quiet apartment. Dunstan was very angry when he perceived this, for he did not wish the king to see Elgiva any more, and he considered it very rude of the king to leave his guests.

The priest's temper so completely overcame his good judgment, that he rushed into the queen's rooms and dragged Edwy back into the banquet hall. Not content with this, Dunstan soon went further, and tried to separate Edwy and his wife. First he bade the king send her away; but, as Edwy did not obey, some stories tell us that Dunstan had the young queen's face branded with a red-hot iron, in hopes that the king would cease to love her when she was no longer pretty.

Young as he was, Edwy was too much of a man to desert the poor little queen; and, knowing that Dunstan had used some of the public money, the king promptly took advantage of this fact to banish him. But although Dunstan was gone, he had given his orders to a friend of his, who seized the young queen and had her carried off to Ireland a prisoner. Then, hoping to make more trouble for Edwy, this same wicked man stirred up the monks and the king's brothers to rebellion, awing the people by performing wonders which he called miracles, but which were probably clever tricks, such as are now done to amuse people.

Poor Edwy did not know what to do, and when he heard

that his beloved Elgiva, after escaping from Ireland to rejoin him, had been overtaken by her enemies and cruelly murdered, he became so ill that we are told he died of a broken heart, after reigning only three years.

As soon as Edwy died, one of his young brothers was placed on the throne, and Dunstan, coming back to England, again took the power into his own hands. The new king, Edgar, never dared disobey Dunstan in anything; and when he died, many years later, the monks who wrote his history, by Dunstan's order, declared that he was the best monarch that ever lived.

During his reign, Edgar not only fought the Danes, but frequently sailed around the islands with a fleet of three hundred and sixty ships, to overawe the people and prevent them from daring to disobey his laws. Eight princes are said to have recognized Edgar as their master, and on one occasion to have rowed his barge across the river Dee to do him honour.

Although Edgar was none too good himself, he made severe laws for his people, and insisted upon their keeping the Sabbath day very strictly. We are told that Edgar accepted from the Welsh king the tribute of three hundred wolfskins, instead of a money payment. The result was, it seems, that the Welshmen hunted the wolves in their mountains so persistently that soon not one of these wild beasts was left to frighten the people in England and Wales, and devour their sheep or their children.

One of the chroniclers tells a very romantic story. King Edgar, he says, wished to marry; and when he heard that El-fri'da, a Saxon princess, was noted for her beauty, he sent one of his courtiers to see if she was really handsome.

The courtier no sooner beheld this maiden than he fell in love with her himself, so, without telling her that the king wished to sue for her hand, he wooed and won her.

Upon returning to court, this man told the king that Elfrida's charms were not very great, and at first Edgar believed him. But after a while he began to suspect that his courtier had deceived him, and suddenly announced that he was going to visit the bride.

The courtier bade his wife wear her old clothes and make herself as unattractive as possible; but Elfrida, who was proud of her beauty, disobeyed him. She seemed so beautiful that the king wanted her for his wife, and with her aid he murdered the courtier who had deceived them both. Then Edgar married Elfrida, who, as you see, was not at all a good woman, although she was so handsome.

XX. ST. DUNSTAN.

WHEN Edgar died, the Witenagemot chose Edward, his eldest son, to succeed him. This choice greatly displeased Edward's stepmother, Elfrida, who wanted her own son to reign. One day soon after his coronation, the young king, who had been out hunting, stopped at Corfe Castle to greet his little brother, whom he dearly loved. As he was about to ride away, Elfrida came out on the doorstep to give him a cup of wine. Edward gladly accepted it; but while he was drinking, Elfrida made a sign to one of her servants, who suddenly drew his dagger and thrust it into the king's back.

Although mortally wounded, Edward drove his spurs into his steed, which galloped wildly away. The king soon grew too faint to sit upon his horse, and as he fell from the saddle, his foot caught in the stirrup, and he was dragged over the rough roads by the frightened animal. When his followers found him, Edward was dead, and by Dunstan's orders he was buried in the chapel of Westminster, which had just been finished.

On account of his death, this monarch is known in history as Edward the Martyr. He was succeeded by his little brother Eth'el-red, the child who was standing beside Elfrida when the murder was committed.

When Ethelred came to the throne, at the age of ten, Elfrida deprived Dunstan of much of the power which he had exercised during so many years and under four previous kings. The priest was so angry at being set aside that he withdrew to his seat at Canterbury, where, we are told, he died of chagrin. The monks, whom he had befriended all his life, were naturally very grateful to him, and either because he was better than some stories would make us believe, or because they did not know all the wrong he had done, they always regarded him as a very good man, and at their request he was placed among the saints of the Roman Catholic Church.

Elfrida had, as we have seen, not only made her son King of England, but reigned in his name. She was not a happy woman, however, for she was haunted by the recollection of the crimes she had committed. She therefore left the court to withdraw into a nunnery, where she spent the rest of her life in penance and prayer.

You have seen how some Danes had settled in England. A little before Dunstan's time, some other Northmen went with their leader Rol'lo to France. This Rollo was so tall and heavy that none of the Northmen's little horses could carry him, and as he was thus forced to walk, he was known among his people as Rolf Gang'er, or Rollo the Walker. He forced the French king to give him a province in northern France, which, as it became the home of the Northmen, or Normans, has ever since been known as Nor'man-dy. In exchange for the land, and the title of Duke, Rollo promised to consider the French king his overlord, and to do homage to him.

To do homage, a nobleman knelt before his monarch, placed both hands between the royal palms, and in that position took his oath of fealty, or faithfulness. Then, the oath taken, he stooped and kissed the king's foot.

When Rollo was told what he was to do, he angrily refused to comply. But after the French courtiers had argued with him some time, he called one of his men, and bade him go through the ceremony for him. The huge Northman obeyed with ill grace, and took the necessary oath. But when he was told to kiss the king's foot, instead of stooping down to do so, he violently jerked it up to his lips, thus making the king lose his balance and fall over backward.

XXI. KING CANUTE AND THE WAVES.

KING ETHELRED was a weak, ignorant, and timid monarch, and as he was never able to determine wisely what was best to do, he was surnamed the Unready.

Three times during his reign the Danes invaded his territory, and three times he paid them large sums to go away. This money was raised by a yearly tax, called the Dane'geld, or Danes' money, and the Danish king, Sweyn (swān), promised to keep the peace as long as it was paid.

Ethelred promised to treat all Danes kindly and to pay the Danegeld regularly, but he soon regretted his promise, and made a plot to have all the Danes in the kingdom murdered on St. Brice's day, in the year 1002. This massacre was carried out, and as King Sweyn's sister perished with the rest, he soon came over to England to avenge her death.

After some resistance on the part of the Anglo-Saxons, Sweyn became master of the country, and Ethelred the Unready fled to France with his wife Emma, who was a daughter of the Duke of Normandy. But the Danish king died the very next year, and, although an attempt was made to place his son Ca-nute' upon the throne, the Witenagemot sent for Ethelred, who again became king.

The Saxon monarch had learned nothing by his former misfortune, so before long the Danes came back, and war was waged between Canute and Ethelred's son Edmund Ironsides. After some time, the two forces met at Assan'dun in battle, and when the fight was over it was agreed that the land should be divided between the Saxon and Danish kings, and that the one who lived longest should be sole ruler. Ethelred having died during the struggle, Edmund Ironsides and Canute became kings. But the former did not live very long, and after his death Canute reigned alone.

Canute had been very stern and cruel at first, so as to

make the people afraid to disobey him; but when he became sole King of England he tried to please his subjects. Many of the Danes were sent home, the English were made his officers, good laws were established, and peace and order reigned throughout the land.

As Canute was not married, he took Emma, Ethelred's widow, for his wife, became a Christian, and went on a pilgrimage to Rome, to receive the pope's forgiveness for his sins. About ten years after becoming sole King of England, Canute conquered Norway, and because he thus ruled two kingdoms, he was regarded as a very powerful king.

Besides being brave, Canute was wise and just, so he had plenty of admirers; and his courtiers, hoping to please him, often remarked that he was sole lord of land and sea. This flattery was distasteful to Canute, so he made up his mind to give his courtiers a lesson.

One day, at low tide, he bade his servants place his throne far down upon the beach; and accompanied by his courtiers, in their richest robes, he went down there and took his seat. Grouped around him, and still paying their stupid compliments, the courtiers kept a watchful eye upon the waves, for they did not wish to get their clothes wet.

When the tide turned they ventured to suggest to the king that he have his throne set farther up on the beach. Canute carelessly said that he did not want to move, and that as they vowed he was lord of land and sea, he would bid the waves stand still. But although he stretched out his sceptre and ordered the water not to come near him, the waves rose higher and higher, till the spray drenched the courtiers' fine clothes and forced them and the king to beat a hasty retreat.

Canute on the Seashore.

When they were beyond the reach of the tide, Canute gravely told his courtiers that God alone was master of the sea, and made them feel so ashamed of their senseless talk that they never ventured to flatter him again.

XXII. A SAXON NOBLEMAN.

DURING the war between the English and the Danes, in the reign of Ethelred or of Edmund Ironsides, a Danish nobleman, separated from his companions, lost his way. As he was afraid of falling into the hands of the English, he began to look about him for a guide.

He soon discovered a poor little hut, and, boldly entering, asked the Saxon peasant who dwelt there to help him. Now you know the Saxons were noted for their kindness to their guests; so, although the peasant knew this man was an enemy, he gave him food and drink and promised that his son should guide him safely back to the Danish camp. But the peasant asked in return that the Dane should keep the youth in his service; for if the lad came back, and the Saxons discovered that he had helped an enemy, they would surely kill him.

The Dane, led back to his companions by the Saxon youth God'win, took him into his household, and found him very useful. Godwin was clever and ambitious, and worked so hard and so faithfully that he finally became one of the principal officers of Canute. We are told, further, that he even married one of the king's relatives.

Canute died after a reign of eighteen years, leaving his

kingdom to three of his sons, who were to be kings of Norway, Denmark, and England. The last-named throne he intended for his youngest boy, Emma's son, Har-di-ca-nute'. But another of Canute's sons, Harold, who was surnamed the Harefoot because he could run so fast, took possession of the greater part of England.

Godwin at first took the part of Hardicanute, and made war against Harold. But after a while he changed sides, and some historians tell us that one of his daughters finally married Harold.

Hardicanute, instead of fighting, lingered in Denmark, allowing his mother Emma to rule in his stead over the small part of England which Harold had not won. The sons of Ethelred, hearing there was war in England, now hoped to recover their father's kingdom; but they did not succeed. One of them, Alfred, was made prisoner and cruelly put to death. Although Godwin was accused of this crime, it could not be proved, so he was acquitted.

The English soon grew tired of being neglected by Hardicanute, and said they would rather belong to Harold, who thus became sole king. But when Harold died, Hardicanute came to England to rule over the whole country in his turn. Godwin, who had once deserted him in favor of Harold, now tried to win his forgiveness by making him a present of a beautiful galley, whose oars, rigging, and hull were gilded all over, so as to make it look like a golden ship. Hardicanute graciously accepted Godwin's present, but never fully trusted the man again. His reign was very short, for after ruling two years he died as he stood drinking at a wedding feast.

The English were now tired of Danish kings, so the

Witenagemot chose Edward, Ethelred's son, to rule over them next. Edward gladly accepted the crown, and the people welcomed him by a great festival. Some say that it was held every year, in memory of his coronation; but others claim that Hock'day, as the festival is called, celebrates the massacre of the Danes on St. Brice's day.

The people were still more joyful when Edward put a stop to the Danegeld, a tax which they had been forced to pay for many a year. Their new king was gentle and very pious, and spent so much of his time in penance and prayer that he was considered a very holy man and called the Confessor. He was very fond of the Normans, among whom he had been brought up, and would gladly have made them his sole advisers, but he did not dare to do so as long as Godwin lived. This Saxon nobleman was still the most important man at court, and he tried to gain more power by making the king marry his daughter Edith. Edward, however, never cared for her, and when Godwin lost his power, some time after, the poor queen was shut up in a nunnery, and all her property was taken from her.

As people fancied that the mere touch of so holy a man as Edward could cure them, many sick were brought to him; and for several centuries after this, it was the custom for the King of England to lay his hands upon people who were afflicted by a certain disease called the "king's evil," because he was supposed to have inherited Edward the Confessor's power to heal it.

Edward built many churches and monasteries during his reign, and would have liked to go to Je-ru'sa-lem to visit the Holy Sepulchre. He was not able to do so, however, for his Norman friends and Godwin were always quarrelling. Tired of these disputes, Edward once turned angrily upon Godwin, then restored to favour, and accused him of having taken part in the murder of Prince Alfred.

Godwin, who was then sitting at table, denied the crime, adding that he hoped the food he was then eating would choke him if he were not telling the truth. One story says that he choked to death on the next mouthful. According to another version, the king, in anger, bade him leave the country, and while he was doing so the Norman nobles pursued and murdered him in the place now known as Goodwin Sands. Still another story, and this is the most probable, says that while sitting at the king's table Godwin was stricken dead by an attack of apoplexy.

A few years later, after having given his people good laws, Edward the Confessor died, and was buried in Westminster Abbey, in the chapel which bears his name. With his death begins a new epoch in English history, when the Normans came in their turn to take possession of the land which had belonged to the Gaels, Celts, Britons, Romans, Anglo-Saxons, and Danes.

XXIII. LADY GODIVA'S RIDE.

BEFORE we go on to the conquest of England by the Normans, you will like to hear the stories of two events which have become very famous because two great English poets, Tennyson and Shakespeare, have used them as the subjects of a beautiful poem and a fine tragedy.

In the middle of the eleventh century, many of the English towns and villages were under the rule of harsh Saxon noblemen. One of these noblemen was Le-of'ric, Earl of Mercia and Lord of Cov'en-try. He was so anxious to get richer that he once imposed a heavy tax upon the inhabitants of Coventry.

When the people heard of this, they were in despair, for it was impossible to pay it and have enough money

E. Blair Leighton, Artist.

Lady Godiva.

left to buy food. As they knew it was useless to appeal to the hard-hearted earl, they went to his wife, the beautiful Lady Go-di'va, and implored her to help them, or they and their children would starve.

Lady Godiva was as good as she was beautiful, and although she was afraid of her cruel husband, she went to him, begged him not to tax the people, and promised to do anything he wished, if he would only spare them.

"Very well, then," cried the brutal earl; "ride through the town at noonday, naked, and the people shall not be taxed."

When Lady Godiva heard this, she shrank with horror; for she knew her husband would tax the people unless she rode naked through the town. But although she was as modest as beautiful, and would rather have died than do an unwomanly thing, she made up her mind to go through this frightful ordeal rather than see the people starve.

By her orders, a herald rode through the town, telling the people what the earl had said, and bidding them all stay in their houses, with closed doors and windows, and not glance out until it was twelve o'clock, and Lady Godiva had passed by. These orders were obeyed, and when the trembling Godiva stole out of her room, clad only in her long hair, which rippled down to her knees, no one was to be seen. She mounted her horse, rode all through the town, and back; and because she had done this, her husband did not tax the people, who were grateful to her as long as she lived.

We are told that there was only one man in the city who was mean enough to try to peep at Lady Godiva as she rode by. This man, who was a tailor, and who has ever since been known as Peeping Tom of Coventry, was severely punished, however; for before he had caught a glimpse of Godiva, he was stricken blind.

The second story is not so pleasant. During the reign

of Edward the Confessor, Dun′can was King of Scotland. Among his followers there was a nobleman named Macbeth′. He was a very ambitious man, and, advised by his wife, he murdered the Scotch king one night when the monarch was sleeping in his house. Duncan dead, and his sons having fled to England, Macbeth became king in his turn, and reigned over Scotland seventeen years.

But he never enjoyed the crown, and he and his wife were haunted by remorse night and day. An old prophecy had made Macbeth believe he would rule for ever, for it said he would be king until "Bir′nam woods came to Dun-si-nane′." But one day when Macbeth was in Dunsinane Castle, one of his servants cried out that the forest was coming. Macbeth rushed to the window in time to see that a large army had come to attack him, and that each soldier carried a leafy bough which he had cut in passing through Birnam woods. The prophecy had come true, for Birnam woods had come to Dunsinane, and though Macbeth fought bravely, he was slain by Duncan's sons.

The poet Shakespeare has written a grand tragedy about this story of Macbeth. The play is one of the greatest treasures of English literature, and when you are older you will read it over and over again with ever new delight.

XXIV. THE BATTLE OF HASTINGS.

WHEN Edward the Confessor died, in 1066, leaving no children, there were several claimants to the English throne. One of them was Harold, the son of Godwin, who was chosen by the Witenagemot to be the next king. It seems, moreover, that Edward the Confessor had picked out the same Harold to succeed him.

The Duke of Normandy, also a relative of Edward, claimed that the throne should belong to him. He said that Edward had once promised to name him his successor, and added that when Harold was shipwrecked in Normandy he solemnly swore to help the duke get possession of the English crown.

According to some histories, William, Duke of Normandy, had forced the shipwrecked Harold to make that promise. The Saxon prince, thinking an oath under such circumstances could not be binding, laid his hand upon a small relic which William placed on the table. But as soon as the words were spoken, the duke removed the cloth which covered the table, and showed Harold a pile of the holiest relics that could be found.

Of course, in these days a promise is a promise, but in the time of Harold it was considered more binding if made upon several relics than if upon one. If Harold really promised to give William the throne, he should have done so, but you will find in some histories that Harold made no such promise, and hence did not break his word when he accepted the crown.

However that may be, Harold was no sooner named king than he found himself compelled to fight against the Danes, who invaded his kingdom on one side, and the Normans, who were coming on the other.

Harold, who is known as the "Last of the Saxons," because he was the last Saxon king, promptly collected his army, and, marching rapidly northward, met and defeated the Danes at Stam'ford Bridge. But scarcely had he won this victory, when a herald came in great haste to announce that the Normans were crossing the Channel in many ships. Without giving his men a moment to rest, Harold marched them from Stamford Bridge to the shore at Hastings, where he arrived three days later, only to find that the Normans had already landed.

We are told that as William was leaving his boat he stumbled and fell. People were very superstitious in those days, so some of his followers began to mutter something about evil omens and bad luck. But William, who was very quick-witted, laughed aloud, and, seizing some sand in his hands, he cried that he now held England fast. This gave his men new courage, and when they met Harold's army at Sen'lac, a few miles away, they fought with great energy.

For a long while the battle raged furiously, and it seemed doubtful how it would end. Then, suddenly, a cry arose that William had been killed, and his men paused in dismay. But before they could turn and flee, he put spurs to his horse, and, snatching his helmet from his head so that all might see his face, rode through the ranks, crying, " I am still alive, and, with the help of God, I shall yet conquer."

The Norman soldiers, encouraged by these words, again attacked the weary Saxons, who fought bravely, in spite of the terrible rain of Norman arrows, until they saw their king fall dead. When the battle was over, and William remained victor, Harold's lady-love came to look for his body. She found it under a heap of slain, on the very spot where he had fought gallantly to the last. A Norman arrow was sticking through his eye into his brain, and his hand still grasped his sword.

Some historians say that Harold's body was buried in an abbey near London. Others declare that William ordered that he should be buried on the shore, saying, "He guarded the coast while he was alive; let him continue to guard it after death." Upon his grave, wherever it was, his lady is said to have put this epitaph: "Here lies Harold the Unfortunate."

XXV. THE CONQUEST.

THE great battle of Senlac, or Hastings, was won. Harold, "Last of the Saxons," was dead; and William, now called the Conqueror, was ruler of England. Although he had no real claim to the crown, William took it by force, and England became his by conquest.

This battle of Hastings, fought in 1066, is one of the great battles of the world, because it decided the fate of England, which was now to be ruled, not by a Saxon king chosen by the wise men of the kingdom, but by a monarch who spoke Norman French, brought new laws and customs, and meant to be absolute king.

William's wife, Queen Matilda, was so proud of his victory at Hastings that she and her women worked a wonderful piece of tapestry, sixty-eight yards long, on which the landing of William and the principal features of the battle are all represented. This wonderful piece of needlework still exists, and is known as the Bayeux (bah-yuh') tapestry.

The battle at Hastings was the only great battle which William had to fight, for the Saxons, who had been masters of England for about six hundred years, dared no longer

Coronation of William the Conqueror.

resist him. As William advanced, the towns opened their gates to him, and he marched right on to London, where he was crowned in Westminster Abbey, on Christmas day. There were great rejoicings at his coronation, but the occasion was marred by a terrible fire, which broke out during the service and did much damage to the city.

William, having become King of England, gradually took possession of the land, which he distributed among the Normans who had come with him into England. Thus Saxon land passed into the hands of the Normans, and many of the noblest families in England now proudly claim that they "came over with the Conqueror." At court, in church, and in all the noblemen's houses, Norman French was the language spoken; but Anglo-Saxon remained the speech of the humbler people, who, for the greater part, became the servants of the Normans.

The new masters of England not only brought over a new language and new customs, but they also began to build houses in a new style. They did not think that the low, rambling, wooden houses which the Saxons and Danes had occupied were fit for noblemen; so they sent over to Normandy for workmen to teach their new servants how to build Norman castles.

As you may never have seen such a castle, I will try to make you understand how it looked. In the centre there was a huge round or square tower, built of stone, with enormously thick walls, and with only slits for windows. This tower was called the dungeon, or keep, and was generally occupied by the lord and his family. They spent most of their time in the principal apartment, called the hall.

Around the keep there was an open space, paved with

stone. This was inclosed by one or more very thick walls, in which were built rooms for the servants, stables, granaries, armouries, etc. The outer wall of the castle was particularly strong, and was surmounted by a parapet and towers, where men at arms were always on guard.

Directly under this wall there was often a deep and wide ditch, filled with water; this was called the moat. When a person wished to get into the castle, a drawbridge was lowered over the moat, and the portcullis, or iron gateway which closed the entrance to the castle, was drawn up to let him pass into the inner court.

Cæsar's Tower, Warwick Castle.

XXVI. LORDS AND VASSALS.

WILLIAM THE CONQUEROR repulsed the Danes, who tried once more to gain a footing in England, and subdued the few Saxon lords who still opposed him. Then he built a few castles to keep order in the principal cities of his new realm. The most noted of these castles is the great Tower of London (p. 80), which you will often find mentioned in this book.

Although the conquest of England was made after only one great battle, it took twenty years before it was quite completed and the last attempts at rebellion were put down. Every time a Saxon lord disobeyed, or was killed

Tower of London.

in battle, his lands were given to some Norman nobleman, who, in return, swore to be faithful to William.

It was thus that with the Normans the feudal system came into England. Now, as you probably do not know what the feudal system was, I am going to try to make it clear to you. When a king gave lands to one of his followers, he did so on condition that the new owner should remain his vassal, or servant, and should supply him with a certain amount of money and men in time of war.

The lord or baron—for by some such title these noblemen were generally called—had full power over his territory, and could even make war upon his neighbours. He usually gave part of his estates to his followers, who in their turn promised to obey him. This kind of ownership of land—ownership depending on personal service—was called a *feud*, and hence this whole system was called feudalism. By it each lord was the vassal of a king, and the master of other vassals of lower rank.

To make sure that order should be maintained in his new realm, William held each lord responsible for the good behaviour of his vassals. It was also decreed that a bell should be rung every evening, as a signal that all the fires and lights should be put out. This bell was called the curfew bell; and as the people had no more light, they were obliged to go to bed early.

Instead of trying criminals by the old Saxon methods, by ordeal or by jury, the Norman barons introduced the fashion of making the accuser and the accused fight together, declaring that the innocent would always prevail. Of course this was not true, for the wrongdoer was often the stronger of the two; but for many years these fights, called judgments of God, or judicial duels, were often resorted to in England.

To make sure that he should know exactly how his land was divided, who owned each field and house, and how much tax each landowner could afford to pay, William had commissioners visit all parts of the realm. These men wrote down what they learned, keeping the record in a very old and celebrated book, which is called the Domesday or Doomsday Book. It is written on vellum, a very fine kind of parchment, and is carefully kept as a great curiosity in the British Museum.

You must not imagine that the Conqueror gave away all the land. On the contrary, he was careful to keep a large share of it for himself, and, as he was very fond of hunting, he had no less than sixty-eight forests full of game. As this did not seem enough, he laid waste a huge tract of more than one hundred and forty square miles, where thirty-six churches and many pretty villages had once stood. This land was made into a huge hunting ground, called the New Forest, and no one was allowed to hunt in it without the permission of the king.

William made several visits to Normandy, and on his return from one of these excursions, finding that the Archbishop of Canterbury had not been faithful to him, he put a learned man named Lan'franc there in his stead. This man helped the king to govern, and to settle the affairs of the English Church.

XXVII. DEATH OF WILLIAM.

KING WILLIAM was not a happy man, in spite of all his conquests. His three sons gave him much trouble, and once, when the two younger lads playfully threw some water upon their elder brother as he was passing under their window, a terrible quarrel broke out.

Robert, the elder, declared that his brothers had insulted him, and wanted to kill them both in his rage. When his father reproved him, Robert said he would not stay in England, and asked to be allowed to return to Normandy and govern this province, which his father had once promised him. William refused to grant this request, so Robert fled to Normandy, where, joining some discontented noblemen, he declared war against his father.

Forced to bear arms against his son, William crossed the Channel with an army, and after several years' warfare father and son met face to face in battle. As William's visor (the steel grating which protected a warrior's face) was down, Robert did not recognize his father until he had knocked him off his horse and was about to kill him.

Full of remorse, Robert begged William's pardon, helped him to rise, and offered him his own horse. But William was too angry just then to forgive him, and, vaulting upon the steed, he rode testily away. It was only some time after, and owing to the queen's entreaties, that father and son became friends once more. Shortly after this, good Queen Matilda, a descendant of Alfred the Great, died, and was sorely missed.

The rest of William's life was spent in warfare, and his last campaign was in France, where he went to subdue a revolt of the Normans, whom the French had induced to rebel. The Conqueror was old, stout, and in poor health; but when he heard that the King of France was making fun of him because he was fat, he vowed revenge.

He therefore attacked Mantes (moNt; map, p. 114), a small town, where, after killing most of the inhabitants, he had the houses set afire. As he was riding through the place on the next day, his horse stepped on some hot ashes, and, rearing and plunging wildly, flung the king heavily against the pommel of his saddle.

The blow was so violent that William was mortally injured. His men carried him off to a neighbouring village, where he gave his last orders. He said that his son Robert should have Normandy; his namesake, William, England; and his youngest son, Henry, a large sum of money.

The three young princes were so anxious to take possession of their inheritance that they all rushed away without waiting until their father had breathed his last. The king's servants followed their example and fled also, carrying off everything they could lay hands upon. Even the sheets of the bed upon which William lay were snatched away from him, and the thief escaped, leaving the king's body on the ground, where it had rolled.

Some monks found the dead monarch lying on the floor, all alone, and charitably prepared to bury him. But when they had dug a grave for him in a church William had founded, a man stepped forward and said that the ground was his. The king, he declared, had never paid him for it, so his body should not be buried there.

The priests bought the soil; but the grave proved too small to hold so large a corpse, and the priests had to force it into the hole, while the few spectators fled in horror. The king, who had won a large part of France and all England by his sword, was thus buried like a criminal; and as he had shown no mercy to any one, no tears were shed over his grave.

XXVIII. THE BROTHERS' QUARRELS.

WILLIAM II., or Rufus, so called on account of his red hair, hastened over to England and took possession of the treasure and of the principal royal castles. Then he was crowned king in Westminster Abbey, by Lanfranc, the good Archbishop of Canterbury.

As long as Lanfranc lived, William Rufus did not dare show how cruel, selfish, and grasping he really was. But when Lanfranc died, people began to see the king in his true colours. To get money was the new ruler's principal aim ; so he forced the people to pay heavy taxes, and made the churches and monasteries give him large sums.

The Anglo-Norman barons (those followers of William who had settled in England, married English wives, and had thus become Englishmen) did not want William Rufus to be their king. But William made such fine promises to the Saxons that they helped him against the barons, and thus enabled him to keep possession of the throne.

This was not the only war which William Rufus had to fight, for we are told that he and Robert attacked their brother Henry. They wanted to force him to give up some land which he had purchased from Robert. Of course this was very unjust and unbrotherly behaviour; but the war went on until at last Henry was besieged in the fortress on Mont St. Michel (moN saN mee-shel').

This castle stands on a huge rock near the French coast, and while it is connected with the mainland by a causeway at low tide, it is entirely surrounded by water the remainder of the time. On the narrow strip of beach at the foot of the castle, William was once thrown from his horse in the midst of the fight. He would have been killed had he not cried out, " Hold! I am the King of England." A soldier who was about to kill him helped him to rise, and in reward William Rufus took the man into his service.

The brothers now learned that Henry and his men had nothing to drink. Although Robert was not much better than William, he immediately sent Henry water for his men and wine for his own use. This generosity made William angry, but Robert hotly answered: "What! shall I suffer my brother to die of thirst? Where shall we find another when he is gone?"

Henry now had plenty to drink, but he could not hold out much longer; and after surrendering he left the country, with only a few followers.

In those days it was considered an act of great piety to journey on foot to Jerusalem, to visit the tomb of our Lord. When the Romans ceased to be masters in the East, the Sar'a-cens took possession of the Holy Land. They freely allowed pilgrims to come and go; but when the Turks took Jerusalem, in 1065, matters changed.

The pilgrims, who were often called palmers, because they brought home palms as relics, were now very harshly treated. One of them, a monk named Peter the Hermit, was so indignant at the cruelty of the Turks that, as soon as he came back to Europe, he won the pope's permission to preach a holy war against them.

He visited different parts of Europe, preaching so eloquently that most of his hearers vowed they would go and fight the Turks. Every one who promised to do this wore a cross on his shoulder; and because *crux* is the Latin word for cross, these men were called crusaders, and their wars, crusades.

Peter the Hermit was so earnest that many noblemen joined the first crusade; among others, Robert of Normandy, who promised to set out with an army. Now you know it is far from Normandy to Jerusalem, so before Robert could undertake this journey, he had to raise money to pay his travelling expenses.

When William II. heard this, he offered to lend his brother quite a large sum, on condition that Robert should promise to give up Normandy if he could not pay back the money at the end of five years. Robert consented, and set out; but as soon as he was gone William vowed that he knew his brother would never pay back the borrowed money, and that Normandy was already his. He therefore started out to take possession of his new lands, and was in such a hurry to get there that he haughtily cried, when the pilot objected that the sea was rough: "Sail on instantly; kings are never drowned!"

Because William thus took possession of his brother's lands, he was forced to make several wars. He was also called upon to resist the Norwegians, who made a last but unsuccessful attempt to get possession of England. William was still busy scheming how he could get more land and money, when his life came to a sudden end, after he had reigned thirteen years.

It seems that while he was waiting for a favorable wind to carry him over to Normandy, he went out to hunt in the New Forest. He gave Sir Walter Tyr'rel, one of his followers, two new arrows, and rode out with him and many others. In the course of the hunt, the king and Tyrrel, pursuing a deer, were separated from the rest of the party. According to some accounts, Tyrrel drew his bow to kill a stag, and his arrow, glancing aside after touching an oak tree, struck the king and killed him instantly. Tyrrel, dreading an accusation of wilful murder, rode to the sea, embarked on the first vessel he found, and joined the crusade, hoping thus to win forgiveness for his involuntary sin. Other accounts say that Tyrrel had nothing to do with the king's death, but a few declare that he was a real murderer.

The body was found by a charcoal burner, who carried it to Winchester in his cart. There William II. was buried with very little ado, for no one really regretted him.

XXIX. ARMS AND ARMOUR.

THE news of the sudden death of William Rufus no sooner reached his brother Henry, than he rode off in haste to Winchester, to take possession of the royal treasure. The keeper at first refused to let him have it, saying it belonged to Robert; but when Henry drew his sword, the poor man was forced to yield.

Henry I., the third Norman king of England, is surnamed Beauclerc (bo-klark'), or the Scholar, because he was more learned than most men of his day. He had spent much of his time in study, and was proud of his knowledge, for he had once heard his father say, "Illiterate kings are little better than crowned asses." But although Henry knew many things, he never thought it worth while to be really good.

To win friends he treated the Saxons very kindly, restored the laws of Edward the Confessor, married Matilda, one of the last descendants of their old royal race, recalled An'selm, Archbishop of Canterbury, whom William Rufus had banished, and gave offices to many priests. But, while he made friends of the Saxons, many of the Norman barons refused to acknowledge him as their feudal lord, and joined Robert when he came home from Pal'estine. As Robert declared war, Henry collected his troops; but when the two armies came face to face, a peace was made. It was then settled that Henry should keep England, but should pay Robert a yearly sum of money.

Henry had no intention whatever of keeping his promises, and, hearing that his brother was not on good terms with the Normans, he determined to gain possession of their province also. He therefore crossed the Channel with a large army, and met and defeated his brother at Tinchebrai (taNsh-bra'), in 1106. Robert was not only defeated, but carried off to Car'diff Castle. There his eyes were put out in the most cruel manner, and he was harshly treated until he died, twenty-eight years later.

After the battle of Tinchebrai, Henry took possession of all his brother's estates. But although he was now master of both England and Normandy, he was far from happy, for his conscience troubled him. Hoping to atone for the wrong he had done, he built a beautiful abbey at Reading (red'ing); but as this did not appease his remorse, he tried to forget his wrongdoing by keeping very busy. It was easy to find plenty to do, for the King of France had taken Robert's young son under his protection, and was trying to recover Normandy.

The war was therefore resumed, but even in one of the worst encounters, the battle of Brenneville (bren-veel'), the English lost but three men. All the rest escaped death, owing to their fine armour, which no weapon could pierce. The armour of those days, of which you can see fine specimens in the principal museums, consisted of a helmet, or steel hat, with a visor, or iron grating which could be drawn down over the face. This helmet fitted so closely upon the coat of mail, which covered the body, that there was no crevice through which an arrow, or the point of a sword or dagger, could be inserted.

Man in Armour.

The coat of mail was composed either of iron plates, of tiny steel links closely woven together, or of small plates like scales screwed together, and was hence called either plate, chain, or scale armour. Steel gauntlets, leggings, and shoes, a sword, a battle-ax, a shield, and a huge lance generally completed the outfit of a warrior.

As the armour was very heavy, the knights had to be very strong; and as the horses were also covered with armour, they were trained to bear great weights. But although it was hard to find a joint in the armour through which to wound a knight, it was possible for an adversary to unhorse him by riding hard against him and tumbling him over backward out of his saddle by a blow of a lance.

A knight thus unhorsed, and lying on his back, could not rise without help, owing to the great weight of his armour, and consequently he was at the mercy of his enemy. The latter could either kill him, or take him prisoner and keep him in captivity until he had paid a sum of money, which was called ransom.

XXX. THE "WHITE SHIP."

TO make sure that Normandy should continue to belong to his family, Henry went over there with his son Prince William, to present him to the nobles as their future lord. Henry was about to embark with all his followers, to go back to England, when a seaman came up to him, begging him to sail in his vessel, the *White Ship*. As William the Conqueror had once promised this captain the privilege of taking the royal family across the Channel, King Henry now bade his son William sail in it.

The king's vessel set out ahead, but the prince delayed, spending the last hours in Normandy in feasting. He sent plenty of wine to the boatmen, that they might drink his health, and when he finally set sail he bade the half-drunken sailors row fast, so as to overtake his father's ship.

Before the *White Ship* had gone very far, it ran upon a sunken reef, stove a hole in its bottom, and began to sink. The captain hurried Prince William into a small boat, and pushed away; but the prince heard his sister call for help, and insisted upon going back to save her.

As the small boat drew near the sinking vessel, so many frightened people crowded into it that it sank at the same time as the *White Ship*, with all its living freight. It was thus that Prince William died the death of a hero; but we are told that, although he did so noble a deed in the face of great danger, he was, on the whole, an unfeeling lad. Indeed, he is reported to have said that when he became king he would make Englishmen draw the plough themselves, like beasts of burden.

The *White Ship* went down, but three men were still afloat, clinging to a few spars which were tossing up and down on the waves. These men were the captain, a nobleman, and a Norman butcher. As soon as the captain could speak, he wildly inquired, "Where is the prince?" When he heard that William had gone down with the rest, he let go his hold and sank into the sea.

The nobleman clung to the spar all night; but when morning came he was too exhausted and cold to hold on any longer, so he also was drowned. The only person saved was the butcher. When the calamity became known, no one dared tell the sad news to the king. Finally a weeping boy was sent to him; and when Henry learned why the child's tears were flowing, his heart was filled with such intense grief that he never smiled again.

Henry's son was dead, and his sole living child was Matilda, the widow of the Emperor of Germany. She now married Geoffrey (jef'ry), Duke of Anjou (ahN-zhoo'), who was surnamed Plan-tag'e-net because he generally wore a sprig of yellow broom (*planta genistæ*) in his cap.

No woman had ever ruled over England then, but Henry wanted Matilda to be his successor, and to make sure that she should inherit his crown, he made all the barons swear fidelity to her. They did so reluctantly, because in those troublous times it seemed that the country could be safe only under an able-bodied man and a warrior.

Having taken these precautions, Henry fancied that he had made Matilda's succession certain. He reigned thirty-five years, lived to see his three grandsons, and we are told that he died from eating too many lampreys, a kind of fish of which he was very fond.

XXXI. MATILDA'S NARROW ESCAPES.

FOREMOST among the barons who had sworn to uphold Matilda was Stephen, her cousin, a grandson of William the Conqueror. Yet Henry was no sooner dead than Stephen took possession of the throne. He also had himself crowned at Westminster, and was recognized as King of England by the pope.

Stephen's manners were very pleasant, so he soon made many friends. As he knew Matilda would want to wrest the sceptre from him, he tried to gain both rich and poor by making many promises. He told the poor that he would give them a charter, or new set of laws, and he granted the barons more freedom, and permission to build as many castles as they pleased.

As the death of the king had been sudden, Matilda, who was then on the Continent, was not at once able to take any measures to defend her rights. But she soon sent over to claim the throne, and as Stephen would not give it up, she induced her uncle, David, King of Scotland, to invade England.

This monarch marched into England before Stephen could summon an army to oppose him. But a brave priest in the north of England, seeing the danger, collected an army on the spot and sent it to meet David.

As there was no king present to lead this army, the priest set up a standard in a chariot, and placed it in the midst of the army, telling the warriors it was their duty to defend their standard as loyally as their king. The battle which ensued has therefore been called the Battle of the Standard. The English were victors, but they bought complete peace from the Scots by giving them a large tract of land in the northern part of England.

Matilda, in the meantime, had been busy collecting an army, which, as she herself could not fight, and as her husband was dead, was commanded by one of her relatives, Robert of Gloucester (glos'ter). When this army appeared in England, many Norman barons joined it, because they were tired of Stephen, who had not kept his promises.

A civil war now broke out between Stephen's and Matilda's parties in England. The castles which were already standing were fortified and garrisoned, and many others were built on all sides. Under pretext of fighting for the king or the queen, as the case might be, the nobles living in these castles attacked one another, and burned and stole so freely that they are known as the robber barons.

Whenever Stephen found fault with these noblemen and tried to punish them, they joined Matilda's party; and soon the whole country was in an uproar. Stephen besieged Matilda in Bris'tol; but she escaped, collected another army, and met him again near Lincoln. Here Stephen was defeated and made a prisoner.

Matilda next rode in triumph to London, where she was named queen. But as she was haughty and violent-tempered, and kept pressing the people for money, which they were too poor to give her, they soon began to hate her. In their anger they drove her out of the city and forced her to take refuge in Winchester, where Stephen's brother came to besiege her.

Queen Matilda seems to have been fated to have narrow escapes, for she managed to pass out of this castle, and through the enemy's ranks, on the back of a fleet horse. But Robert of Gloucester, less lucky, was captured by Stephen's party, who refused to set him free unless Matilda would give them Stephen himself in exchange.

Stephen and Robert of Gloucester, therefore, changed places, and the war was renewed. Matilda, cornered again, now slipped through the hands of her enemies by pretending to be a corpse, and being carried out in a horse-litter.

Stephen, who had sworn never to give up until she was his prisoner, now besieged her in the Castle of Oxford, where, in spite of scant rations, the garrison held out until midwinter and until snow covered the ground. When Matilda saw that her brave defenders could not hold out much longer, she planned a bold escape. Clad in white from head to foot, so as not to be discovered against a snowy background, she crept out of the castle one dark night with three knights, crossed the river on the ice, and, walking six miles, came to a place of safety.

Here she met Robert of Gloucester, with Prince Henry, her eldest son, and the war went on for some time longer. But Matilda's energy was nearly exhausted, and, disheartened by the death of her chief supporter, Robert of Gloucester, she finally went back to Normandy. Then Prince Henry carried on the war alone; and in the year 1153, after eighteen years of civil war, he agreed, at the treaty of Wal'ling-ford, to leave the crown to Stephen as long as the latter lived, provided it should pass on to him at the king's death.

XXXII. THE STORY OF FAIR ROSAMOND.

STEPHEN, the last of the four Norman kings, died just one year after the treaty of Wallingford, leaving no children, so Henry had little trouble to get the crown. He is called Henry II., the Shortmantle, and is the first of the An'ge-vine or Plantagenet kings.

The new monarch was only twenty-one years old, and as he was handsome, graceful, and learned, he soon made many friends. Both the Saxons and the Normans were glad to have him reign, and as he dismissed the foreign soldiers whom Stephen had enlisted, issued good coin, and restored law and order, he became very popular.

Besides being one of the cleverest, Henry II. was one of the most powerful kings of his time. He inherited several French provinces from his father, and his wife El'ean-or brought him more land. Indeed, he was lord over more territory in France than the French king himself, so it is no wonder the latter was jealous of him.

Although his wife Eleanor was rich, she was so bad-tempered and cruel that Henry could not love her, and, if we are to believe one very romantic story, he neglected her in order to visit a beautiful young lady, called Fair Ros'amond. This made Queen Eleanor so jealous that she resolved to kill her beautiful rival.

It was not easy to find Fair Rosamond, however, for the king had built a maze for her at Woodstock, and her bower was in the centre of this labyrinth. Although the way to it could be found only by using a silken thread as clue, Eleanor suddenly appeared before Fair Rosamond one day, and told her she must die, sternly bidding her choose between the dagger and the bowl of poison which she held. We are told that the cruel queen forced Fair Rosamond to drink the poison. But all this happened so long ago that no one knows whether it is true; still, ever since then, when people have to take one of two evils, they are said to have no choice except between the dagger and the bowl.

During the long civil war in the last reign, the barons, as we have seen, had built many castles and waged many private wars. They had learned to do just as they pleased, to respect no one's rights, and to rob, murder, and burn. No one had been safe in the realm, except such as dwelt in the monasteries or convents, and it is no wonder that these were full, for people took refuge in the only place where they could dwell in peace.

Henry could not allow the barons to go on thus, and one of his first acts was to call them to order. He made war against all those who would not obey him, and had many of the fortresses pulled down, so that the robber barons could no longer take refuge behind their strong walls. To satisfy the people, he gave them the charter which Stephen had promised, and decided that criminals should be tried by a jury of twelve men. Trial by ordeal was not entirely abolished, but men were no longer forced to prove their innocence by conquering their accusers in battle.

The priests had hitherto been tried only by their own class, who inflicted very slight punishments upon them, but Henry now declared that if a priest or monk did wrong he should be tried and punished just the same as any other man. This change in the law was opposed for some time,

The First Trial by Jury.

and it was only after a long fight with the clergy, or church party, that the new laws were passed. They were carefully drawn up at last, and are known in history as the Constitutions of Clar'en-don.

XXXIII. THOMAS À BECKET.

IN the beginning of his reign, Henry was often helped by the good advice of a man named Thomas à Becket. A very pretty story is sometimes told about this man's mother. His father Gilbert, it seems, had gone to Palestine on a crusade or as a merchant. In some way he became the prisoner of a Saracen lord, and would have been obliged to remain in a dungeon all his life, had not the Saracen's daughter fallen in love with him. She helped Gilbert to escape; and then, thinking she could not live without him, she too started off for England, hoping to find her lover. She persistently said the word London over and over again until she reached that city. Then she changed her refrain and wandered up and down the streets, crying, "Gilbert!" which was the only other English word she knew. Strange to relate, Gilbert heard her cry, and, rushing to meet her, took her into his house, where she became his wife.

Thomas à Becket, the son of Gilbert and of this Saracen lady, received such a good education that he was asked to teach the king's children. Henry soon became very much attached to him, and he rose from rank to rank until he became chancellor of the kingdom, and keeper of the great seal, an impression of which was placed at the bottom of every royal decree.

Henry II. not only raised Thomas à Becket to a high rank, but also gave him great wealth. The chancellor delighted in fine clothes, had many followers, lived in beautiful houses, and spent his money freely. He was on such good terms with his royal master that they often had friendly disputes.

One day, when the king was riding out with Thomas, a beggar stepped up, asking for alms. Henry slyly asked Becket whether it would not be a very good deed to give the poor man a warm cloak. Becket answered that it certainly would; but when the king laid hands upon the beautiful mantle he was wearing, and tried to pull it off, he resisted. The result was a scuffle, and finally Henry gave so strong a tug that he tore the cloak off the chancellor's back. He then tossed it to the astonished beggar, and rode away, laughing at Becket's dismay.

In the first part of the king's reign, Becket, who was also a priest, helped him in his disputes with the clergy. Because of this, Henry decided that Becket should be named Archbishop of Canterbury. The priest of this cathedral was the *primate*, or principal clergyman, in the kingdom, and Henry fancied that when Becket was in this position he would go on helping him.

The king was mistaken, however, as he soon found out. No sooner had Becket become Primate of England than he suddenly changed. He no longer wore beautiful clothes or lived luxuriously. On the contrary, he wore the plainest garments, ate simple food, and, instead of leading a merry life, spent all his time in penance and prayer and in doing good.

Henry did not like this sudden change at all; but what made him most angry was that Thomas à Becket, instead of helping him subdue the rebellious priests, now became the most obstinate and resolute of them all. He bitterly opposed the Constitutions of Clarendon, refused to recognize any other master than the pope, and declared that Henry should obey the Church in all things, instead of trying to be sole master in his kingdom.

The quarrel between the king and his archbishop grew more and more bitter, until finally Becket left England and went over to France. Here he stirred up trouble for Henry by persuading the French king, Louis, to invade the English king's possessions there, and by threatening Henry with excommunication, or expulsion from the Church. Henry was, of course, very indignant when he heard this; but a meeting was soon brought about, and king and primate were publicly reconciled. To show the people that he and the priest were again good friends, Henry even held the stirrup of Becket's mule and helped him to mount it when Becket had once thrown himself at the king's feet.

XXXIV. THE MURDER OF THOMAS À BECKET.

HENRY and Thomas à Becket did not long remain on good terms, for the primate was as haughty as ever. During Becket's absence Henry's son had been crowned as his heir. The primate said no one had the right to perform such a ceremony without his consent. He therefore excommunicated the bishops who had done so. When this news reached Henry, he angrily cried: "Of the cowards who eat my bread, is there not one who will free me from this turbulent priest?"

These rash words were unhappily taken in earnest by four of his knights, who, leaving his presence, went over to Canterbury to murder Becket. They were so deter-

Martyrdom of Thomas a Becket.

mined to kill him that they forced their way into the cathedral, crying, "Where is the archbishop? Where is the traitor?"

"I am the archbishop, but no traitor," answered the primate, proudly, as he came forward to meet them. But they rushed upon him, weapons in hand, and in spite of his struggles struck him down at the foot of the altar.

Then, frightened by what they had done, they fled in haste, and, troubled by remorse, went to Palestine. They never dared come back to England, but died and were buried in the Holy Land, where these words were written on their tombstone: "Here lie the murderers of St. Thomas of Canterbury."

This murder, which the king had not positively ordered, excited great indignation among the people. They loudly mourned the archbishop, and buried him in the cathedral at Canterbury. Soon after, the pope declared that he was a saint and a martyr, so the pious began to visit his tomb in crowds. Before long the rumour spread that those who visited it were healed of any disease from which they happened to suffer, and that even the dead came back to life.

The result of this report was that pilgrims came from all parts of the world to pray at the shrine of St. Thomas à Becket. Every fifty years there was a special celebration, called a jubilee; and on one of these occasions no less than one hundred thousand pilgrims came to the grave of the murdered primate.

When the pope heard how Becket had died, he wanted to excommunicate Henry; that is to say, to forbid his entering a church or being considered a child of God. The people fancied that they need no longer obey a man who had been so wicked as to quarrel with a priest, and Henry saw that unless he did something to please the pope he would soon have no more power. He therefore went over to Ireland, conquered the country, and made the rebellious people obey the priests of the Catholic Church. Then he solemnly swore that he had not intended to kill Becket.

The pope consented to forgive him, but even then

Henry's troubles were not ended. His sons revolted; and Henry, hoping to gain God's help to subdue them, prepared to do public penance for his share in Becket's murder. He therefore walked to Canterbury barefoot, spent the night in prayer at the saint's tomb, bade the eighty monks there beat him on his bare shoulders, and by thus humiliating himself brought the monks and his subjects to think less severely of his sin. The same day his army won a victory, which the people claimed as another miracle worked by St. Thomas of Canterbury.

In the course of his reign, Henry had not only to oppose his rebellious children in Normandy, but also to fight their allies, the Scotch, Welsh, and Irish. He recovered the province which the Scots had won in the preceding reign, took their king captive, and became master of a large part of Ireland, which he said he would give to his favourite son, John, for at that time he fancied that John had always been a good son.

This was not so. All Henry's children were undutiful, because they had been badly trained by their mother Eleanor. When they first revolted, she tried to escape from England and join them; but by the king's orders she was overtaken and thrust into prison, where she staid as long as her husband lived.

Henry's public penance had made so good an impression on his people that they cheerfully helped him against his sons; but after some more fighting, Henry was compelled to make peace, submit to the terms of the French king, and swear to forgive all the rebels. As soon as he had given this promise, some one brought him a list of the men who had plotted against him; and Henry was stricken with grief when he saw among them the name of his youngest son, John.

This last sorrow proved too much for the poor king, who fell sick, and died at the foot of the altar, where he had asked to be laid. He had reigned thirty-four years, had extended the English territory, and had made many improvements in the condition of the inhabitants; so he is remembered as one of England's great kings.

XXXV. RICHARD'S ADVENTURES.

THE year before Henry died, all Europe was saddened by the news that Jerusalem, which had been in Christian hands for eighty-eight years, had again fallen into the hands of the Saracens. Another crusade was now preached, and the King of France, the Emperor of Germany, and a host of their best warriors joined it.

Henry's sons were anxious to take the cross, too, especially Richard Cœur de Lion (ker duh lee-awN'), or the Lion-hearted, who had won this surname by his remarkable courage. As their father refused to let them all go, they rebelled against him; and in the course of the war one of them, Geoffrey, fell very ill. Feeling that he was about to die, he regretted his unfilial conduct, and sent a pitiful message to Henry, begging him to come and forgive him.

The courtiers tried to persuade Henry that this was only a trick on Geoffrey's part. But although Henry did not go to his son, he sent him a ring in token of complete forgiveness. Geoffrey died lying on a bed of ashes to show his repentance, kissing the ring, and recommending his little son Arthur to his father's care.

When Henry died, Richard succeeded him on the throne, and, now that it was too late, he bitterly regretted having ever borne arms against his father. The remembrance of this sin made him all the more eager to keep his promise and go to Palestine; for people then supposed that one could be forgiven for any sin by visiting the grave of Christ at Jerusalem.

Before he could set out, however, Richard had to take possession of his new kingdom and arrange how it should be governed during his absence. He therefore crossed from Normandy to England, and went to London, where he was crowned with great rejoicings. All the people were invited to see the festivity except the Jews. In those days the Christians were always very cruel to the Jews, and besides forcing them to live apart, made them wear garments and hats of a dirty yellow colour, so as to recognize them from afar.

Hoping to make the new king kinder to them, some Jews came to offer him rich presents; but the people, seeing them, fell upon them, and after beating them began to kill them. This outrage became the signal for a series of massacres all through the kingdom. We are told that the York Jews, after holding out for a long time in a tower where they had intrenched themselves, killed their wives and children and set fire to the place, so as to die in the flames, rather than fall into the hands of the cruel Christians. Richard did not try very hard to stop this awful massacre, and no one was punished, except a few men who, in pursuing the unhappy Jews, injured some of their fellow-Christians.

Richard first released his mother Eleanor from prison. Then, to raise money for the crusade, he sold many offices to the highest bidders. For a certain sum of money he released the King of Scotland from his vassalage; he sold his castles and estates, compelled his subjects to lend him money, and declared that he would sell London itself, if he could only find a purchaser rich enough to buy it.

Then, having secured all the money he needed, Richard left the kingdom in the hands of two bishops, and set out for Palestine, where he was to play a brilliant part in the third crusade. He stopped twice before he got there, once at Mes-si'na, to await a favourable breeze, and once at the island of Cy'prus.

Here the king of the island was very rude to Richard's betrothed, the fair Be-ren-ga'ri-a, and unkind to shipwrecked sailors. This made Richard so angry that he took possession of all Cyprus and made the king a captive. We are told, however, that he was very polite to his royal prisoner, and that, when the latter objected to wearing iron chains like a common criminal, he had him bound with fetters of silver, a favour which was greatly appreciated by the fallen king.

XXXVI. RICHARD AND THE SARACENS.

RICHARD left Cyprus as soon as he had married Berengaria, and sailed on to A'cre, a stronghold on the coast of Palestine which the crusaders had vainly besieged for two years. There he was warmly welcomed by the Christian host; but he was so much braver than any of the other princes that they soon grew jealous of him.

Although the city of Acre was very strongly fortified, Richard made such daring attacks upon it that the inhabitants finally promised to surrender in forty days and to give back the cross to the Christians. But, hearing that their famous chief Sal'a-din had come with an army, and that he had hemmed in the Christians around the city, the people of Acre did not keep their word. When the forty days were over, and Richard saw that they had deceived him, he ordered the heads of three thousand Saracen prisoners to be struck off in the presence of their friends on the city walls.

When Saladin heard this, he had as many Christian captives slain, and the war was renewed more furiously than ever. Richard was very brave, but he was neither humane nor gentle, and he soon quarrelled with the King of France and the Duke of Austria. Although they remained with him, these two princes secretly hated him, and tried to hinder him in every way.

For months the fighting went on, and as Richard was always in the thickest of the fight, his name became the terror of the country. Saracen mothers used to threaten naughty children by saying, "Look out; King Richard will catch you;" and when a horse shied, the Saracen warrior would cry, "Dost think King Richard is behind yon bush?"

The Saracens, however, were worthy foes for the Christian knights; and their leader Saladin was just as brave, just as generous, and just as cruel, at times, as the famous

Richard himself. We are told that these two leaders once had an interview, in which each showed his skill in handling the sword. While Richard cut a huge bar of iron in two with one mighty stroke, Saladin deftly divided a down and silk pillow and a floating veil of gauzy tissue, which were equally difficult feats.

Once, during the war, Richard fell seriously ill with fever. When Saladin heard that his enemy was sick, he made a truce; and as long as the disease lasted, he daily sent Richard fresh fruit, and ice and snow which were brought down from the top of Mount Leb'a-non.

The Christians, however, were in the meantime sorely afraid of the Saracens, for the latter had the aid of the chief of the As-sas'sin tribe, called "the Old Man of the Mountain." The subjects of this chief were so devoted to him that they would obey him blindly, and he trained a number of the youngest and strongest among them to go among the Christians and suddenly stab them with poisoned daggers. Because these Assassins never appeared among the Christians except to commit murder thus, their name has become a common term for one who treacherously kills a fellow-being.

Acre was finally taken by the Christians, who now began to quarrel among themselves about the naming of a king for Jerusalem, which they hoped soon to win also. Richard sided with one party, the French king and the Duke of Austria with another. The man chosen by the latter party was murdered by one of the Assassins, but they accused Richard of having had a share in the crime.

The French king, angry and jealous because Richard was reaping all the honours, prepared to return home.

Before he left the crusaders he solemnly promised not to make any attempt to take Richard's lands or to do him any harm during his absence. But as soon as he arrived in Rome, he began to complain about Richard to the pope. The pope, however, would not listen to any of Philip's accusations, for he knew that without Richard the crusaders would soon have to give up all hope of taking Jerusalem.

Richard, in the meantime, had won a brilliant victory over the Saracens at Ar-suf', where many of the forty thousand slain fell by his powerful hand. He next wished to march on to Jerusalem; but his soldiers were weary of fighting, and refused to go farther.

Richard therefore retreated to As'ca-lon, where he helped the Christians rebuild their fortifications, carrying stone and mortar with his own hands. This conduct was viewed with scorn by the Duke of Austria, who insolently remarked that *his* father had not been a bricklayer. Some historians say that it was this remark which caused a final breach between the leaders, and report that Richard resented it by kicking the lazy and impudent duke. Others say that it was a dispute about a flag. However this may be, Le'o-pold of Austria left the army soon after this, and went home, vowing he would be revenged some day.

XXXVII. THE FAITHFUL MINSTREL.

WHILE Richard was busy fighting in Palestine, things were going on very badly at home. The offices, which he had sold to the highest bidders, were filled by men who thought only of growing rich, so law and order were very poorly maintained. Prince John, Richard's brother, who was surnamed Lackland because his father had left him no territory, was a very mean man, and he helped to make matters worse.

When Philip reached France, he became friendly with John, and proposed that they should invade Normandy together and take possession of King Richard's lands. John was quite ready to help him, but the French barons all refused to fight for Philip, because he had promised Richard not to act as he was doing.

Rumours of the troubles in England, and of the bad designs of Philip and John, came at last to the ears of Richard, who decided that it was useless to remain much longer in Palestine, and that he had better go home and take care of his people. He therefore staid only long enough to deliver the Christians whom Saladin was besieging at Jop'pa. Then, having again defeated his brave rival, he signed a truce with him, which was to last three years, three months, three weeks, three days, and three hours.

In spite of the bad season, Richard next embarked upon a vessel to return home. But the winds were against him, and after tossing about on the waves for many days, he was shipwrecked in the Ad-ri-at'ic Sea, and with much trouble managed to reach land.

Left thus without means and without followers, far away from home, Richard made up his mind to walk all the way across the Continent. As he had to pass through the lands of his enemy, the Duke of Austria, he put on a pilgrim's dress, hoping that no one would recognize him, and that he could thus cross the country in safety.

One day, in an Austrian village inn, one of Leopold's men recognized Richard by a ring he had always worn. This man told his master, who had the pilgrim seized and thrust into a prison, where he kept him for many months. Then Leopold sold his royal prisoner to the Emperor of Germany, who kept him in another dungeon.

The rumour that Richard was a prisoner spread all over Europe; but while John and Philip rejoiced, and planned how to divide his lands, some of Richard's friends grieved sorely. His favourite minstrel, a youth named Blon-del', anxious to find him, set out alone and on foot, and wandered all through Germany, it is said, singing as he went to earn his daily bread. Whenever he came to a castle, Blondel inquired what prisoners were kept there. Months had gone by in vain and weary search, when the minstrel came at last to Richard's prison.

He had no idea his quest was ended, and, sitting down under the castle walls, he sadly played a tune which was known only to him and to his master, and sang the first verse of the song. You can imagine his surprise and delight when he heard Richard's familiar voice floating out through the grated window, singing the second verse.

Richard was found. The poor minstrel, who could not free his master alone, now hastened back to England. Here Eleanor, helped by some of the English, made arrangements to have the king set free, and collected the large sum of money which the Emperor of Germany demanded for a ransom.

As the whole sum could not be sent at once, some German noblemen accompanied Richard to receive it; and when they saw the city of London, and the delight of the

English at recovering their king, they cried: "If our emperor had known the riches of England, your ransom, O king, would have been much greater."

XXXVIII. DEATH OF RICHARD.

WHEN it first became generally known that Richard was about to be released from the prison where he had lain in captivity about eighteen months, many people were terrified. The most frightened of all were John, the captive's brother, and Philip, King of France. The latter, finding he could not induce the German emperor to detain Richard any longer, sent this message to John: "Take care of yourself, for the devil is unchained."

When Richard arrived in England, he was recrowned, to efface the stain of his captivity. He found that many things had gone wrong in his absence, and that as the officers he had appointed had not done their duty, there had been much crime. The

Statue of Richard Cœur de Lion.

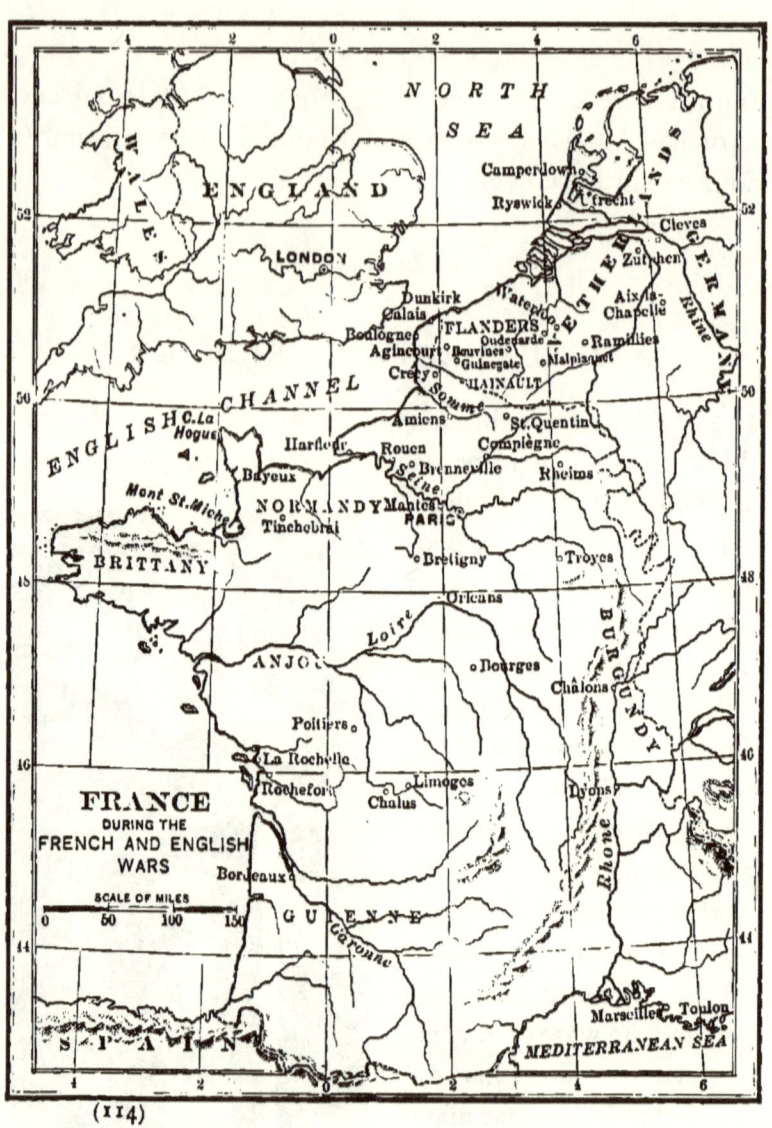

castles were occupied by robber barons, and the forests swarmed with bands of thieves or outlaws, headed by such chiefs as the famous Robin Hood.

This bold outlaw is said to have lived in Sherwood Forest, and such wonderful stories have been told about him in old ballads, that it is very hard to know what in his adventures was real and what was made up. From these old tales we find that Robin Hood was good to the poor and robbed only the rich. The spoil which he got he hid away in the forest. Hence the woods were known as Robin Hood's barn; and when people want to say that they took a roundabout road to get anywhere, they still exclaim, "I went all around Robin Hood's barn."

Although Richard tried to suppress the disorders in his kingdom, he was much greater as a warrior than as a statesman; so he did not stay in England long, but crossed over to Normandy to make war against Philip.

When John heard that his brother was coming, he did not dare fight, so he went to meet Richard, and, falling at his feet, begged his pardon for having tried to steal his kingdom during his absence. Richard generously forgave his brother, but showed that he did not believe John's penitence sincere by remarking soon afterwards: "I wish I may forget my brother's injuries as soon as he will forget my pardon of them."

During the next four years Richard was busy making war against his French rival; but at the end of that time both kings made up their minds to cease fighting and to sign a truce. Then, hearing that one of his vassals had dug up a treasure on his lands, Richard sent to claim it; for the law decreed that buried treasures belonged to the crown. The Lord of Chalus (shah-lüs'), however, would not give up the gold, so Richard besieged him in his castle.

As Chalus was a strong fortress, like those we have already described, Richard could not take it, in spite of all his bravery, and at the end of two months he was so angry at being detained, that he vowed he would yet hang every man in it. Because of this vow, he refused to accept the count's terms of surrender a few days later, and ordered a new assault. But in this attack Richard was wounded by an arrow; and although the hurt seemed trifling at first, the doctors, in cutting out the arrow, made the wound so much worse that the king soon saw that he must die.

While he lay in his tent, awaiting the end, his men took the castle, and, by Richard's order, they killed all its defenders, except the man whose arrow had wounded him. This archer was brought before Richard, who asked, "What harm have I done to you, that you should thus have attempted my death?"

"You killed my father and brother with your own hand," answered the archer, "and intended to kill me. I am ready to suffer with joy any torments you can invent, since I have been so lucky as to kill one who has brought so many miseries upon mankind."

When Richard heard this he ordered that the man should be set free; but, as the king breathed his last a few minutes later, his infuriated men fell upon the archer and flayed him alive. The dead king's body was buried in Rouen (roo-on'), and on his tomb you can see a full-length stone effigy of this man, who could be in turn gallant, brave, and generous, and mean, selfish, and cruel.

Many stories have been written about Richard and his

adventures, and there are writers who have made a hero of him. But a real hero would have thought more of the welfare of his people, and when called upon to fight would have acted just as bravely, but with less cruelty.

XXXIX. THE MURDER OF ARTHUR.

RICHARD THE LION-HEARTED, having no children, said that John should succeed him, although the crown belonged by right to his little nephew Arthur, the son of Geoffrey. A monarch not old enough to reign alone seemed very undesirable, so the English were at first very much pleased that John Lackland should have the crown. They soon found out, however, that he was cruel and miserly, and, worse than all the rest, very untruthful. He had been a bad son and a bad brother, and now he was going to prove also a bad king.

Philip of France, hearing that the people in Brittany were anxious to place Prince Arthur upon the English throne, soon excited them to declare war against John Lackland. But he did not give them so much help as they expected, and the result was that John defeated them and put his nephew in prison in Rouen.

Young Arthur now languished in a gloomy dungeon, very near the river, closely guarded night and day lest he should escape. But he was so good and gentle that even the grim jailers grew fond of him, and so John, fearing that Arthur might yet get free and take the crown, determined to rid himself of the young prince.

No one knows exactly how he did this, but there are awful stories told. Some writers say that little Arthur's eyes were put out with red-hot irons, in spite of his pitiful entreaties to be spared. Others aver that the jailers killed him by John's command. But it is generally believed that, cruel as they were, the jailers refused to harm the gentle child, and that John had to commit the murder himself. It is said that he came to the prison one night, led the child down to a waiting boat, pushed off into midstream, and there drowned the unhappy little prince.

When it became known that Arthur was dead, either by his uncle's hand or by his order, the people of Brittany clamoured to have John punished, and called upon the French king for aid. This monarch then said that as John owned provinces in France for which he was obliged to do homage as vassal to the French crown, he should appear before twelve other lords, his peers, and justify himself, or lose his lands in France.

John must have had an uneasy conscience, for he did not present himself before his peers. So the French king invaded Normandy, which became his property after belonging to Norman dukes for nearly three hundred years. John's other French provinces were also taken from him, and he soon had nothing left in France except Guienne (gee-en′).

Besides the troubles in France, John had worries at home; for when the Archbishop of Canterbury died, the monks and the pope selected one man, and John another, to occupy this position. The result was a religious quarrel, in which the pope showed his displeasure by putting John's kingdom under an interdict. That is to say, the churches were closed, no services were held, no bells rung, no baptisms, weddings, or funerals allowed, and all the people were under a ban. Four years later, seeing that John still refused to obey him, the pope declared that he should no longer be King of England, and bade Philip of France invade and take possession of the country.

XL. THE GREAT CHARTER.

NOW, although the English had no respect for John, they did not want to give up their country to the French king, so they began to rally around their monarch to help him defend the country. The pope then offered to forbid Philip to invade England, provided John would let Stephen Langton be Archbishop of Canterbury, do homage to the pope for the kingdom of England, and promise to pay a yearly tribute.

Promises were very easy to make, according to John's ideas; so he consented to everything. He made Langton archbishop, humbly laid his crown at the feet of the legate (the pope's messenger), allowed him to trample it without wincing, and received it from his hand once more, after solemnly promising to be the faithful vassal of the pope.

The interdict was recalled, Philip was forbidden to invade England, and John fancied that all was well. But the English barons were disgusted with him for having yielded to such shameful conditions. They had always prided themselves upon living in a free country, and they did not like to be considered the vassals of the pope. Besides, they were indignant at the way in which John governed, and at his methods for getting always more money, for you must know that John was as miserly as he was untruthful.

Whenever John heard that a Jew had become very rich by trading, he used to send for the unfortunate man and torture him until he promised to pay a large sum of money for his release. We are told that he imprisoned one wealthy Jew, and had one of his teeth pulled out every day. At first the man stood this very bravely, but when seven teeth were gone, he gladly paid a large sum to keep the rest and be set free.

The example set by the king was followed by the barons; and as a customary mode of torture was to drag the Jews over a bed of red-hot coals to make them give up their money, some people say that it gave rise to the expression "to haul over the coals," which is now often used to describe a severe and unsparing reprimand.

John, angry with Philip for taking Normandy and for being so ready to invade England, made an alliance with the Emperor of Germany and the Count of Flanders, and attacked France. But the English and their allies were defeated in the battle of Bouvines (boo-veen'), in 1214.

During John's absence, changes had been going on in England. First, the new primate, Langton, made some alterations in religious matters, besides dividing the Bible into chapters and verses as it is now. Then the barons found the charter granted by Stephen and Henry, and decided that its promises ought to be kept, and that their rights ought to be protected by a few more laws.

Battle of Bouvines.

Horace Vernet, Artist

The result of this was that the barons drew up a new code or set of laws, called the Mag'na Char'ta, or Great Charter, in which the rights of the king and of all the different classes of the people were clearly set forth; and when John came home, after the battle of Bouvines, they asked him to sign it.

The king angrily refused, whereupon all the barons left him and threatened to choose another king. Left with only seven followers, John concluded he must yield; so, going out to meet the revolted barons on Run'ny-mede (a meadow where the Saxons had often assembled), he reluctantly signed the Magna Charta, in 1215.

This code of laws is considered the foundation of English liberty, and has been very carefully preserved. It decreed, among many other things, that no man should be imprisoned unless he were tried and found guilty, and that girls of noble rank might marry without the king's consent.

From Runnymede John retired to the Isle of Wight, whence he sent a messenger to the pope, with a copy of the charter, a long letter of complaint against the barons, and a request to be freed from his promise, which he said had been wrung from him by force. The pope, knowing many of the barons were against him, sent a bull, or papal decree, excommunicating the noblemen and saying that John need not keep any of the promises he had made to his rebellious subjects.

This bull made the barons so angry that they vowed to fight for their rights. Some called a French prince into the country, offered him the crown, and hailed him as king in London. Others refused to accept him, and in the

King John.

midst of the civil war which ensued, the last remnants of John's army deserted him, and his baggage and all his treasures were swept away by the rising tide as he was crossing the Wash.

John himself barely escaped sharing the fate of his money, and he felt so badly over his loss that he rode on to a priory, where he fell ill and died. Some people say that he died of grief, others that he ate too many peaches and pears and drank too much cider, but a few declare that the prior poisoned him by order of the barons.

Although John was only forty-nine years old, the English were glad to be rid of him. They did not respect a king who, besides being mean and selfish, was always untruthful, and they gladly hailed as monarch his little son Henry, who was then only eight or nine years old.

XLI. THE WEAK RULE OF HENRY III.

HENRY III., called Henry of Winchester from his birthplace, was far too young to govern, so the Earl of Pembroke became regent of the kingdom. As the crown had been lost with the rest of John's treasures, the new monarch was crowned with a plain gold circlet. He was very gentle and merciful, but unfortunately very weak in character, and as untruthful as his father. This latter fact was the cause of many troubles.

Pembroke began his rule by ratifying the Great Charter. Most of the barons, hearing of this, now joined Henry, forsaking the cause of the French prince. But the latter had landed with an army, and would not give up all hopes of the English crown without striking a blow. So the civil war went on until the French troops were defeated at Lincoln, when they gave up the struggle and went home.

Pembroke, having rid the country of the French, now ruled so wisely that he was sorely missed when he died three years later. Other noblemen took his place, but they were not so able as he, and often made trouble.

Not long after the king was declared old enough to rule alone, he sent all his advisers away. He was so young and so far from clever that he made a very poor ruler. His foreign favourites were always asking for money, so he spent more than he should. Whenever he ran short of funds he called the barons together, and the assembly of these noblemen, called Par'lia-ment, supplied him with new sums in exchange for new privileges.

The barons finally became so angry at the greediness of the foreigners that the Archbishop of Canterbury advised Henry to dismiss them if he would not lose the confidence of his people and of the pope. Henry obeyed; but not long after he married a French wife, who brought many of her friends over to England. They soon won the favour of the weak king, and, seeing that all the money given to the king was spent foolishly, Parliament refused to let him have any more. Henry now tried to get it by borrowing, by extorting it from the Jews, by selling his plate and jewels, and finally by benevolences, as he called the gifts of money which he forced his rich subjects to bestow upon him. The priests also claimed a large part of the money in England, and sent it to the pope as the tax due to him as head of the church.

These heavy taxes grew so unbearable that the barons, headed by Simon de Mont'fort (a clever French nobleman who had married the king's sister and had become a good Englishman) marched into Parliament, arms in hand, determined to end this bad government. When the king saw their grim faces he was frightened, and tremblingly asked, " Am I your prisoner? "

" No; you are our sovereign," answered Simon de Montfort; but he went on to explain that they were ready to obey him and give him money, only if the kingdom were governed properly. New plans were made by the Parliament; but as they brought about greater confusion, it is known in history as the Mad Parliament.

XLII. A RACE.

AS Henry III. governed so badly, twenty-four barons were chosen to rule in his name; but as Simon de Montfort was by far the most powerful among them, he exercised all the authority. Although Henry had promised to abide by the decisions of the twenty-four barons, he soon failed to do so; and, supported by some of the noblemen who were jealous of Montfort, he collected an army and made war against this powerful subject. But in the battle of Lew'es (1264) Montfort defeated the royal troops and took Henry III. and his son Prince Edward prisoners. Then, hoping to win some more support, Montfort called a new Parliament, to which he admitted two knights from each county, two burghers from each city, and two men from each borough, or village of ten families. The new members of Parliament sat with the bishops and nobles, but later on they had an assembly of their own, which was called the House of Commons. Still, in 1265 the first real Parliament sat in England, and decided to meet three times a year, whether called by the king or not, to discuss the affairs of the realm.

The king's party, however, were not pleased with this new arrangement, so they began to plot against Simon de Montfort. One day when Prince Edward was out riding with some of the noblemen who kept guard over him, he made them ride races with one another until their horses were tired out. His own horse was still quite fresh, and when a single horseman appeared at the top of the hill and signalled to him, he drove his spurs into his steed and rode rapidly away, crying, "Farewell, gentlemen; I have enjoyed the pleasure of your company long enough."

The guards, of course, tried to overtake the runaway prince; but before their tired steeds had gone far, they saw him meet a troop of his friends and ride away with them. Many of the barons now went to join Prince Edward, who declared war against Montfort, although Montfort had forced Henry to issue a decree saying that any one who made war against him was a traitor.

The two armies met at Evesham (evz'um) in 1265, and the helpless king would have been slain in the fray had he not cried aloud: "Hold! I am Henry of Winchester, your king; don't kill me!" Prince Edward heard this cry of distress, and, rushing forward, rescued his father and brought him into a place of safety. But Simon de Montfort and his son were both slain in this battle.

Prince Edward now planned new warfare in the East. He joined the seventh and last crusade, and, like his great-uncle Richard, covered himself with glory by his brave deeds in Palestine. He was accompanied thither by his wife, Eleanor. She was as brave as he, and once, when he had been wounded by an assassin's poisoned dagger, she sucked the poison out of the wound at the risk of her life.

During the prince's absence Henry feebly tried to rule, until, finding death near, he finally sent a message to Palestine, to hasten his son's return. Henry had an inglorious reign of fifty-seven years, yet during that time there were grand changes in England: first, the beginning of the House of Commons, then the building of beautiful Gothic cathedrals by the Masons' Guild, and lastly the discovery of gunpowder and of reading-glasses, telescopes, and many other useful instruments, by a learned monk named Roger Bacon.

Because Bacon was so very much more learned than the rest of the people of his day, some of them foolishly accused him of being a magician, locked him up in prison for ten long, weary years, and deprived him of all his books and instruments. He is the author of Latin works on science, in which he set down all his wonderful discoveries.

XLIII. PERSECUTION OF THE JEWS.

THE news that Henry III. was ill took some time to reach Prince Edward, who thereupon made immediate arrangements to return home with his beloved wife,

Eleanor. But when they reached Sic′i-ly they met another messenger, who told them that their haste was unnecessary, as Henry had already breathed his last.

Hearing these tidings, Edward paused to rest awhile in Sicily; then, crossing over to France, he often stopped in the course of his journey to be entertained by the French noblemen. Wherever he went he was feasted and made much of, because the people knew he had fought like a true knight in Palestine.

When Edward came to Bur′gun-dy, he gladly accepted an invitation to take part in a tournament, or sham fight, in which he and a thousand of his knights were to test their skill against the Count of Châlons (shah-lawN′) and an equal number of Bur-gun′di-an knights. But when Edward came to the appointed place, he found that instead of a sham fight he and his followers would have to do battle if they would escape from the hands of the traitor. Dashing forward with his well-known courage, Edward called to his men to follow him, and, making good use of his great strength, he won a brilliant victory. This conflict is known in history as the Little Battle of Châlons.

Two years after Henry's death,—for travelling was very slow in those days,—Edward arrived in England, where he was received with loud cries of joy. At his coronation, which soon took place, the houses of London were hung with tapestry, the streets strewn with flowers, the fountains flowed with wine instead of water, oxen and sheep were roasted whole, and shows of all kinds and illuminations were given in his honour.

King Edward at once began to restore law and order in his kingdom. Hearing that some of the barons had taken unlawful possession of the land of their neighbours, he said that all those who could not show deeds for their estates should give them up. But when Edward asked one earl what instrument he could show to prove his claim to the land his family had occupied for many years, the nobleman proudly drew his sword and said: "This is the instrument by which my ancestors gained their estate, and by which I will keep it." This haughty answer showed Edward that it would be impossible to turn out the men who had held their estates a long time, so he changed the law.

Another thing that Edward did was to punish the people who had grown rich by "clipping the coin," or cutting off a little of the metal around each piece of gold or silver money. The money was also changed, and Edward said that pennies should no longer be cut into halves and quarters for halfpence and farthings, but that all coins, however small, should be round.

The Jews were very numerous in England in the beginning of Edward's reign. They did nearly all the trading and money-lending, and were very uncharitably hated by the Christians, who accused them of clipping the coin. Edward, who had been a crusader, fancied it was his duty to persecute all Jews; so, after illtreating them for thirteen years, he suddenly bade them leave England, allowing them to take only their gold and jewels with them.

Sixteen thousand Jews were thus unjustly driven out of the kingdom. In their stead the Lom'bards began to trade and lend money, and one of the important streets in London is still known by their name, because so many of them used to dwell there.

XLIV. THE CONQUEST OF WALES.

EDWARD'S great ambition was to rule over the whole island, so he soon began to plan how he could get possession of Wales and of Scotland. Now, as you know, Wales is a mountainous country in the western part of Great Britain. Hither the ancient Britons had fled when driven out of the southeast by the Saxons, and here they still spoke the old Briton language, sang about Briton heroes, such as Arthur, and proudly kept their old liberty.

Llew-el'lyn, one of the Welsh princes, had taken part in the barons' rebellion under Simon de Montfort, and had received the latter's permission to marry his daughter as soon as her education was finished. The young lady was then at school in France, but as soon as she was old enough to marry, she prepared to join her gallant lover.

Edward, knowing that she was coming over from France, had her captured and brought to his court, where he said that he would detain her until Llewellyn came and did homage to him as his lord. Llewellyn proudly refused, and a war ensued; but, for the sake of his betrothed, Llewellyn finally complied with Edward's conditions.

The Welsh were too proud, however, not to resent being under the English, and before very long they rebelled, under the leadership of Llewellyn and his brother David. The Welsh had been greatly encouraged by the heroic songs of their bards, and by an old prophecy, said to have been made by Mer'lin, in which it was foretold that a Welsh prince would be crowned king in London when all the money was round.

The Welsh seized the first good opportunity to make a raid into England, captured the Castle of Haw'ar-den, and killed all the English in it. Edward collected an army and marched into Wales to avenge this attack, but he lost many men in crossing Men'ai Strait, and could not get at the Welsh, who had taken refuge upon Mount Snow'don, whence they came down for sudden raids.

It was owing to a traitor that Llewellyn's brave little troop was finally conquered. Llewellyn's head was cut off and sent to London, where, to make fun of the Welsh prophecy, it was set up on the Tower and crowned with ivy or willow, or, some say, with a silver circle to make it look like a coin.

Six months later David also was taken prisoner. He underwent terrible torture before he was hanged. Then, as if this brutal treatment were not enough, his insides were taken out, and his body cut into four pieces, which were sent to the four most important cities to be exposed there. It was thus that by King Edward's order David was hanged, drawn, and quartered.

The Welsh were too exhausted to resist any longer, so the principal lords promised to be faithful to Edward, if he would give them as governor a prince born in their own land. Edward readily promised this; and when he added that the prince whom he intended to set over them did not know a word of French or English, they set up a shout of joy and clamoured to see him. Edward then stepped into the next room; but he soon came back, carefully carrying his infant son Edward, who had been born in the Castle of Car-nar'von a few days before, and who was thus a native Welshman.

P. R. Morris, Artist

The First Prince of Wales.

Of course the babe could not speak a word of French or English, but neither could he speak any Welsh. He was gladly welcomed, however, as "Prince of Wales." His elder brother soon died, so he became heir to the English crown, and ever since then the eldest son of an English monarch has borne the title of "Prince of Wales."

Some writers say that Edward ordered the massacre of all the Welsh bards, because he feared their exciting the people to new rebellion; but others deny this, and certainly some of these musicians must have escaped, for many of their songs have come down to us. The Welsh became loyal subjects, and it was a hundred years or more before they again rose up to fight against the English.

XLV. A QUARREL WITH FRANCE.

THE Welsh war was scarcely ended when trouble began with France. This war arose from a very slight cause. It seems that a Norman bark and an English ship once put in at the same port to renew their supply of fresh water. Two sailors began to quarrel while filling their casks, and soon came to blows. The crews of both vessels, instead of stopping the fight, joined in it, and a Norman was killed. A few days later the angry Normans took revenge by capturing and hanging an English merchant, and they added insult to injury by placing a dog at his feet. The news of this affront enraged the English seamen, and for some time after that, whenever Normans and Englishmen met, there were quarrels and fights.

Although both the French and the English king tried to avoid taking part in this contest, it soon grew so bitter that the French king summoned Edward to come to France, as Duke of Guienne, to answer for the damages done by his subjects. Edward, either unable or unwilling to go himself, sent his brother, who foolishly allowed the French monarch to occupy Guienne for forty days, upon his promise to give it back at the end of that time.

But when the forty days were ended, the French king refused to give up the province, and Edward, eager to regain it, began to raise an army. As he had no money to pay troops, he tried to levy a force in the same way as William the Conqueror. Calling the noblemen to help him, he bade them bring their vassals, and told the Earl of Her'e-ford to lead the army into Guienne.

The Earl of Hereford, however, flatly refused to obey; and when Edward angrily cried, "By heaven, Sir Earl, you shall either go or be hanged!" he retorted hotly, "By heaven, Sir King, I will neither go nor yet will I be hanged!" And having said these words, he coolly left the court and went home.

When Edward saw that he could not raise troops in this way, he began to tax the clergy to get money to hire men; and when they complained, he said he would not protect them unless they did as he wished, but would allow any one to take their property. In dismay the priests appealed to the pope, while the barons, banding together, sent word to Edward that he should have neither funds nor help unless he solemnly swore to ratify the Great Charter, and never again to attempt to raise money except through Parliament. Edward was forced to yield to these demands; and in 1295 was held the first English Parliament that was composed of a House of Lords and a House of Commons. Ever since then Parliament has exercised the right of taxing the people, whom it represents by bishops, lords, and elected members.

Edward himself now conducted his army into France, but before much fighting could be done the pope interfered. By his advice the two kings became friends, and then Edward went back to England.

Shortly before this good Queen Eleanor died. She had been Edward's wife for more than twenty years, and had borne him fifteen children. To show his affection for her, the king ordered that a cross should be erected wherever her body rested on its way from Lincoln to Westminster Abbey, where she lies buried. The best known of these interesting monuments is "Charing Cross" in London.

Charing Cross, London.

XLVI. THE CORONATION STONE.

HIS wife being dead, Edward now married the sister of the French king, and promised that Edward Carnarvon, the Prince of Wales, should marry a daughter of the same monarch. In all these years Edward had never lost sight of his principal ambition, to annex Scotland, and when the Scotch king died, a few years before, he had tried to make a match between his son and the baby queen of that realm. This little creature was called the Maid of Norway, because she had gone to live in that country; but on her way back to Scotland to be crowned, she was taken ill, and died on the Orkney Islands.

Thirteen different members of the royal family claimed the vacant throne of the Maid of Norway. Bruce and Ba'li-ol were the only ones who had any real right to succeed her, but as the Scotch could not decide which of the two should reign, they asked Edward to act as umpire and settle the matter.

After some consideration, Edward decided in favour of Baliol, but let him have the crown only on condition that Baliol should do homage to him for Scotland. The new Scotch king soon regretted having yielded to this demand, for several times, for mere trifles, Edward made him come to London to give an account of himself.

Annoyed by this interference, Baliol soon began to plot, and, helped by the Scots, who did not like to see their sovereign the vassal of an English king, he invaded England four years after he had been crowned at Scone. Edward made use of this attack as an excuse to make war against Scotland, and after defeating Baliol at Dun-bar', brought him a prisoner to London.

The Coronation Chair, Westminster Abbey.

All Scotland was soon reduced to obedience and annexed to England. Its great seal was broken, and its famous coronation stone was carried away to Westminster Abbey and placed in the seat of a throne. The loss of this stone was a great sorrow to the Scots. They said it was the stone that Jacob had used for a pillow when he dreamed that he saw the angels of God ascending and descending a wonderful ladder which reached from heaven to earth. Besides that, there was an ancient prophecy which said:

> "Should fate not fail, where'er this stone be found,
> The Scot shall monarch of that realm be crowned."

The Scots, who had always been independent, were not satisfied to send members to the new English Parliament; so one of their patriot princes, the heroic William Wallace, called them to help him free their country.

After defeating the English forces at Stirling Bridge, and ravaging the northern provinces of England, Wallace was named Guardian of Scotland. But, one year after his first victory, he was defeated by Edward at the battle of Fal'kirk, and Scotland was again forced to yield. During the next few years Wallace dwelt in the mountains and waged an incessant petty war against the English; but he was finally betrayed into their hands.

Then he was taken to London, tried, and condemned to death for treason. He was drawn and quartered in the most barbarous way, and his head was set up on London

Daniel Maclise, Artist.
Trial of Sir William Wallace.

Bridge. Yet, although he was dead, the Scots did not forget him; and when they heard how cruelly he had been treated, they rallied once more to fight the English.

Robert Bruce, a grandson of the Bruce who had disputed the throne with Baliol, was then a hostage at Edward's court. One day he received a purse of gold and a pair of spurs—a message which he readily understood; and, biding his time, he escaped on a fast horse whose shoes had been reversed so that he should not be tracked.

When Bruce arrived in Scotland, he met his ally Com'-yn, the son-in-law of Baliol, in a church. There they quarrelled, and Bruce, drawing his dagger, struck Comyn down, and then rushed out and told his followers what he had done. They cried that Comyn was a traitor, and went into the building, where they stabbed him again and again to make sure he should not escape. Bruce was crowned in 1306, and the Scots promptly rallied around him. But in spite of all his valour, and the devotion of his subjects, the English defeated him and forced him to flee to Ireland.

After this victory Edward showed himself very cruel to the Scots, whom he treated as rebels; and when they persisted in rebellion, under Bruce's untiring leadership, he was very angry. Although already so ill that he had to be carried in a horse-litter, he would not rest until he had seen his orders carried out. But when he reached Car-lisle', feeling that his end was near, he called his son to his bedside, bade him never rest until all Scotland was conquered, and asked that his body be carried ahead of the army which he had hoped to lead himself. Thus died Edward I., who, although brave and clever, was a very cruel king. He reigned thirty-five years, and was succeeded by his son Edward, the first Prince of Wales (1307).

XLVII. THE INSOLENT FAVOURITE.

EDWARD II. of Carnarvon brought many misfortunes upon himself and upon all his people by his weak character. He began his reign by breaking the promises he had made to his father. Instead of going on to Scotland, he journeyed back to London and buried the body of Edward I. in Westminster Abbey.

Even as a very young man, Edward had allowed himself to be governed by one of his attendants named Piers Gav'es-ton. This young man was handsome and clever, but not at all good or truthful. To get presents, he flattered the prince incessantly, and used to amuse him by making fun of all the greatest men in the kingdom.

When Edward I. perceived what a bad influence Gaveston had over his son, he sent this idle favourite out of the country, and, before dying, begged the prince never to recall him. As Edward II. had already broken two promises, he soon failed to keep the third, and Gaveston was not only invited back to court, but was loaded with honours and made principal adviser of the king.

Now if Gaveston had tried to influence the king for good, and had been modest and polite to the nobles, he might have remained in this position for a long time; but he was insolent, and greedy for money and honours, and he induced the king to treat the barons so badly that they al began to hate him with all their might.

Their dismay was great, therefore, when the king named his favourite Regent of England while he went over to France to marry Isabella, a daughter of the French monarch. Yet even the pretty young bride could not comfort Edward for his favourite's absence, so he hastened back to England. At the coronation feast, which followed his return, he bestowed new honours upon Gaveston, and this so exasperated both queen and barons that they threatened to rebel unless the king sent his friend away.

To make sure that Gaveston should never come back, the nobles made Edward and his favourite swear they would never see each other again; but the pope having

Edward II. and Piers Gaveston.

consented to absolve them both from this oath, Edward soon recalled Gaveston, who re-entered England only to show himself more worthless than ever.

As the king kept supplying his extravagant favourite with money, his funds soon gave out. He therefore called a Parliament at York; but the members declared they would not give him any more money so long as Gaveston was in England. The king in anger dissolved (dismissed) the Parliament, and called another at Westminster. As he had in the meantime sent his favourite abroad, this Parliament gave him funds, after making him promise to call a Parliament at least once a year.

The barons, who had come to Westminster determined to wrest this and sundry other promises from their monarch, looked so fierce that he did not dare to refuse. He therefore sent orders to Gaveston not to come back, and set out for Scotland, where his presence was needed. But even before he reached the border, his longing for Gaveston made him again break his word and recall his favourite for the third time.

This breach of faith roused the barons to action. Seeing that their king would be the tool of this bad man as long as the latter lived, they captured Gaveston, who was soon after executed at Warwick (wor'ik) Castle, by order of the king's cousin, the Earl of Lanc'-as-ter. Edward was so furious with the barons for putting his favourite to death that he wanted to make war against them; but trouble in Scotland soon forced him not only to make peace with the nobles, but to implore them to help him.

XLVIII. BRUCE AND THE SPIDER.

YOU remember, do you not, how Edward I. defeated Robert Bruce? Although this brave man had been driven out of Scotland, he was not ready to give up. Several times he tried to win back his kingdom, and several times he failed. An interesting story is told of how he gained the courage to persevere so patiently.

He was lying in a poor thatch-roofed cottage one day, wondering whether he had not better cease all efforts. Suddenly his eye rested upon a spider which was weaving its web. It climbed away up to the roof, but before it could fasten its thread there, it lost its hold and fell to the ground. A moment later, he saw the spider climb up and try again. Nine times the insect fell; but at the tenth attempt the thread was fastened and the web woven.

Bruce, who had watched the nine failures, gladly saw the patient spider succeed, and declared that the little creature had taught him a good lesson, and that he too would persist, in spite of repeated disappointments, until he should triumph at last. So, instead of giving up, Bruce tried again, and soon found that his luck had turned.

He and his faithful followers took one castle after another, and every day their little force increased, until they could boast of an army. Some of the strongholds garrisoned by the English were taken by force, and others by strategy.

For instance, when the Scotch were very anxious to secure Lin-lith'gow, they hid some of their men under a load of hay, and bade a farmer drive the cart for them. The castle gates were readily opened to admit the load of hay with its farmer driver. But the peasant pretended to be awkward, and turned the cart in such a way that the gates could not be closed. At that moment the hidden men sprang out, sword in hand; and as they were soon joined by their companions, who were hiding near there, they boldly attacked the garrison and took the castle.

The news of Bruce's earlier successes did not greatly trouble Edward; but when he heard that Stirling, the last great English fortress, would surrender if not succoured within a certain number of days, he set out for Scotland. He was at the head of an army of one hundred thousand men, while Bruce had only thirty thousand with whom to oppose him.

Nevertheless, knowing that a battle would be best, Bruce got ready to meet Edward. First he chose a good battlefield, and then he had his men dig pits which they covered with brush and grass, hoping that the English cavalry would tumble into them. Lastly, Bruce hid the camp followers and baggage wagons behind a hill, that they might not cause disorder in the ranks.

When all was ready, the Scots knelt in prayer, and the English army, coming up, fancied they were begging for mercy. An Englishman, impatient to strike the first blow, rushed forward on his battle steed before the signal was given, and attacked the Bruce. Although he had not yet mounted his war horse, and was riding a mere pony, Bruce boldly advanced, and, avoiding the Englishman's blow, cleft his skull in two with his battle-ax. The Scotch, who had trembled for the life of their king, now applauded him wildly, and, rushing forward, they fought with such courage that the English soon began to yield.

This advantage was no sooner gained than the Scotchmen managed to force the English cavalry towards the pits, where the fallen horses and riders increased the confusion. Just at this moment, either because they received the agreed-on signal or because they did not wish to miss their share of the plunder, the camp followers, who had supplied themselves with old armour and banners, came running over the hill.

When the Englishmen became aware of the approach of what they took for a fresh army, they broke ranks and fled. The Scotchmen pursued them, and we are told that they followed the fugitives ninety miles before stopping.

This victory of Ban'nock-burn (1314) terrified the English soldiers so sorely that many years elapsed before they again dared face their brave neighbours in pitched battle. Edward barely escaped with his life, and the fortress which he had intended to rescue fell into the hands of the Scotch.

Robert Bruce was now sole master of Scotland. He tried to conquer Ireland also, but soon gave up the attempt, and, returning to Scotland, took Berwick (ber'ik). You can imagine how happy he was to become master of this city, when you hear that members of his family had been prisoners there many years, as well as some Scotch nobles who had helped him in the days of Edward I.

Robert Bruce now began to think of governing his kingdom wisely; but he was not to enjoy his triumph long, for he was already suffering from a very painful disease, the result of the many hardships he had endured. When he saw that his end was near, Robert I., King of Scotland, called his friends around him and gave them his last instructions for ruling the land he loved so well. Then, having attended to his public affairs, he said that he was sorry to die before he had visited the tomb of our Lord at Jerusalem, according to a vow he had once made.

As he could not go himself, he begged Douglas, his best friend, to have his heart cut out of his dead body, and, after it had been embalmed and put in a golden casket, to carry it to the Holy Land. We are told that these directions were carefully carried out when he had breathed his last, and that Douglas set out for Palestine.

But on the way thither, he and his followers stopped in Spain to help the Christians there in one of their battles against the Saracens. In the midst of the fray, Douglas flung the casket forward, crying, "Go ahead, thou Bruce, as was ever thy wont, and I will follow thee." Tradition relates that when the battle was over the dead body of Douglas was found beside the casket.

In spite of Bruce's last wish, his heart was then brought back to Scotland, where it was buried in Mel'rose Abbey. This building is now a picturesque ruin, which strangers love to visit.

Melrose Abbey.

XLIX. DEATH OF EDWARD II.

AFTER Bruce's victory at Bannockburn, Edward lavished all his favours upon two noblemen, the Despen'sers, father and son. The barons had no objection to the old man, but they soon became displeased with the younger, who was as insolent and worthless as Gaveston.

So many lands and so much power were granted to the Despensers by the weak Edward, that the barons, led by Lancaster, again revolted. But, helped by the Despensers, Edward defied them, until, suddenly changing his mind, he yielded to them and banished his new favourites.

The Despensers were no sooner gone, however, than Edward planned to break his promises; and before long the two exiled noblemen were back at court, the most determined of the barons imprisoned, and Lancaster and twenty-eight other knights beheaded.

One of the captives, a baron named Mor'ti-mer, succeeded in escaping from the Tower in a daring way. After drugging his guards, he got out of his dungeon, and, finding his way into the kitchen, he climbed up its wide chimney. Once on the roof, he lowered himself by means of a rope ladder, and, gaining the river, embarked in a boat that was awaiting him. Protected by the darkness, Mortimer managed to board a vessel, which took him over to France. There he lived for some time, congratulating himself upon his escape from prison and death; for he had been sentenced a short time before his flight.

The King of France had repeatedly summoned Edward to come over and do homage to him for his French possessions; but Edward said he could not leave England, on account of his troubles with the barons. Instead he sent his wife Isabella and his eldest son to the French court, to present his excuses and make a treaty with the king.

Isabella, who was a Frenchwoman by birth, signed a treaty which gave all the advantage to the French. Besides that, she made the escaped prisoner Mortimer her favourite. In obedience to his suggestion, she even wrote to the king that she would not come back unless he sent the Despensers away. But as the king retained his favourites, she and Mortimer finally joined the angry barons in England, and entered London at the head of an army.

The Londoners warmly welcomed Isabella, but the king fled with his favourites. All the rebels he had sent to the Tower were released, and, joining the queen's army, besieged the city of Bristol. Here the elder Despenser had taken refuge, and when they took him, although he was a man of ninety years, they hanged him most cruelly and tore his dead body to pieces.

The younger Despenser fell into their hands soon after, and the barons avenged themselves for all the harm he had done them by crowning him with nettles and hanging him on a gallows fifty feet high.

Edward, deprived of his dearest friends, now wandered about from place to place, and finally surrendered to his enemies. They took him to Ken'il-worth, where they kept him a prisoner, while the queen called Parliament and proposed that he should give up his crown to his son. The barons welcomed this proposal, and forced poor King Edward to sign his abdication. The next day, Edward, the second Prince of Wales, began his reign as Edward III.

Edward of Carnarvon, who had reigned nineteen and a half years, was kept a prisoner and treated very unkindly by the barons, although his jailers pitied him. Taken from castle to castle, and deprived of all comforts, the king was once forced, we are told, to make his toilet out in the open fields. When the men brought him dirty water from a neighbouring ditch to shave with, the tears poured down his cheeks.

"See," he cried, "nature supplies the clean warm water which you would fain deny your captive king!"

After many wanderings, Edward was cruelly murdered in Berke'ley Castle, by Mortimer's and Isabella's orders.

L. THE MURDERERS PUNISHED.

EDWARD III. ranks as one of England's greatest kings; but as he was only fourteen years of age at the time of his coronation, the government was first carried on by a council of regency, composed of twelve lords. These noblemen, however, were ruled in their turn by Queen Isabella and her favourite Mortimer.

The wicked queen had not only taken possession of all the property of the Despensers, but after she had got rid of her weak husband, she tried to keep the authority in her own hands by surrounding her son with men who were her tools. The young king could not resist, and quietly bided his time.

Edward was a born soldier, and his greatest desire seems to have been to make conquests. Even in the beginning of his reign he joined his army and fought against the Scots, who were then still governed by Robert Bruce.

The English army was composed of heavily armed knights, while the Scots, led by Douglas, wore little armour, and rode small horses, which could scramble over the roughest ground. Instead of having immense trains of baggage, such as followed the English army, each Scotchman carried a bag of oatmeal and a flat iron plate on which he baked his cakes at the camp fire. Whenever the Scotch wanted meat, they caught and killed an ox. As soon as it was flayed, the skin was hung over the fire, filled with water, and thus served as a caldron wherein to boil the meat.

These simple arrangements gave Douglas and his men

a great advantage over the English, who could never overtake them. Sudden raids here and there, and very prompt retreats, formed the Scotch method of warfare; but they never engaged in a pitched battle with Edward's troops.

One night, when the English were fast asleep in their tents, Douglas broke into their camp with two hundred men. Edward would have fallen a victim to their blows, had he not been defended by his chaplain and chamberlain, who, by sacrificing their lives, enabled him to escape.

After carrying on this skirmish warfare for some time, the Scots discovered that the new king, although a boy, was a more formidable foe than his father, and agreed to make peace with him. In 1328, therefore, Edward III. and Robert Bruce signed the treaty of North-amp'ton, in which it was agreed that Scotland was to be independent.

That same year, young as he was, Edward married a good and beautiful princess, Philippa of Hainault (hā-no'). He also arranged a marriage between his own sister Jane and the son of Robert Bruce, who was then only a baby.

As soon as Edward was eighteen, he became his own master and began to reign alone. The very first use he made of his power was to punish the murderers of his father. Now, as you know, Isabella and Mortimer were the real authors of the crime. They were evidently afraid they might be punished, for they had withdrawn to the Castle of Not'ting-ham, which was closely guarded by their own men. Every evening the gates were securely closed and locked, the keys being brought to the queen, who kept them under her own pillow, to prevent treachery.

In spite of all this caution, Edward's followers got into the castle by a subterranean passage, of whose existence the queen was not aware. Before he could suspect his danger, Mortimer was seized and dragged away by the soldiers, while the queen, falling at the young king's feet, implored him to spare her " gentle Mortimer."

As he could not bring his own mother to trial, Edward had her taken to Castle Rising, where she spent the rest of her life a prisoner. Once a year he came to see her, but her imprisonment lasted nearly twenty-eight years.

Her accomplice Mortimer was taken to Westminster, where he was tried and sentenced to be hanged at Tyburn, the place where all common criminals were put to death.

LI. THE BATTLE OF CRÉCY.

ONE year after the treaty of Northampton, the brave King of Scotland died, leaving the crown to his five-year-old son David. But as the new monarch was a mere child, Baliol, the son of the former king of that name, drove him away and took possession of the crown. To make Edward his friend, Baliol offered to do homage to him for his kingdom, but this so enraged the independent Scots that they turned Baliol out and recalled David.

The result was that war began once more, with Edward and Baliol on one side, and David and his French allies on the other. No very great battles were fought, so Edward left his army to continue the war in Scotland, and prepared to go and fight in France.

Edward had been longing to make his kingdom larger, and he now thought he had a good chance, as he had three separate reasons for fighting the French. In the first place, he said they kept helping his Scotch enemy David Bruce; secondly, French noblemen often made raids into his province of Guienne; and thirdly, he claimed that, as the last French kings died leaving no sons, the crown really belonged to him. This last claim was hardly just, for Edward was the son of a sister of the last three kings of France; so, if the French crown could have passed on to a woman, it would have belonged, not to his mother, but to one of the daughters of the late kings. Nevertheless, it was on this threefold pretext that Edward III. began the Hundred Years' War, so called because about a century passed ere the quarrel was ended.

Calling his Parliament, Edward asked them for money, which they supplied him in exchange for new privileges. It was Edward's intention to sail for Guienne and begin the conflict with the French there; but, owing to contrary winds, he had to change his plans and land in the northern part of France. Hedged in between the Somme River and the sea, Edward saw that his position was unfavourable. Besides, many of his men became sick and died from eating too much fruit, so he was afraid the French army might get the better of him.

By offering a reward of one hundred pounds to any one who would show him a ford across the Somme, Edward cleverly secured a better position near the village of Crécy (crā-see'). Here he had pits dug, and provided his bowmen with sharp stakes to drive into the ground before them so as to form a fence which would prevent the French from riding them down. Then he commanded his men to eat and rest until they were needed.

It seems that one part of the army was then placed under the command of the Prince of Wales, a lad of sixteen. He was distinguished from the other knights by his coal-black armour, which won for him the surname of the Black Prince. Like most youths of his age and time, the Black Prince had been trained in all knightly exercises, but this was his first great battle, and he was very anxious to do some brave deed whereby he might win his knightly spurs.

The French army was about eighty thousand strong, but it was under the command of different French noblemen, who were all eager to press on ahead and strike the first blow. This lack of discipline in the French army, a sudden shower which wet their bowstrings, and the fact that they began fighting when tired by a long march, proved fatal to their hopes of victory.

The archers were in front, but, finding their bows useless, they turned to beat a retreat. As they were hired troops, the French knights fancied they were cowards or traitors, and, falling upon them with drawn swords, began to massacre them. The English took advantage of this confusion, and the Black Prince led a gallant charge into the midst of the French army.

Edward III., who was watching the battle from the top of a windmill on a neighbouring hill, was proud of his son's bravery, and when anxious courtiers pressed forward and begged him to send help to the fighting prince, he asked: "Is my son dead, wounded, or felled to the ground?"

"Not so, thank God!" answered the messengers; "but he is sore beset."

"He shall have no aid from me," exclaimed the king,

proudly. "Let him bear himself like a man; in this battle he must win his spurs."

These words, reported to the prince, nerved his arm to greater prowess, and when evening came he saw the whole French army routed. The battlefield was strewn with dead; for, owing to the steady fire of the English archers and the power of their great bows and "cloth-yard" shafts, armour proved but little protection. This battle, fought in 1346, showed the power of the men in the ranks as opposed to the mailed knights and their retainers, and with it began the fall of feudalism. It is interesting to read that cannon were used for the first time at Crécy, though they were not very effective. They merely threw "small iron balls" "to frighten the horses."

Thirty thousand Frenchmen were lying on the plain of Crécy, and on visiting the battlefield the next day, the Black Prince found there the body of the aged King of Bo-he′mi-a. This monarch was so brave that, although blind and almost helpless, he asked to be led into the thickest of the fray, so that he might strike a few blows.

Two of his knights fastened his horse to their own, and, dashing forward, enabled him to gratify his last wish. Their bodies lay close together, and by them stood the three horses, still tied together, but unharmed. When the young Prince of Wales saw the dead king's banner lying near him, he picked it up, and said he would adopt as his own crest the emblem of the three feathers it bore. He also appropriated the King of Bohemia's motto, "Ich dien" (I serve); and ever since then this motto and crest have belonged to the Prince of Wales.

LII. THE SIEGE OF CALAIS.

HAVING cut the French army to pieces at Crécy, Edward, who was anxious to secure a good seaport in France, set out to besiege Calais (cah-lā'), a strongly fortified city within sight of the Dover cliffs.

The town was bravely defended by a gallant Frenchman named Jean de Vienne, and in spite of the English ships blocking the port, and the English army surrounding it on all sides, the French held out stanchly. As no provisions were allowed to enter, the governor soon saw that the people would suffer from famine, so he sent out all the old men, women, and children. These were allowed to pass through the English ranks to join their friends elsewhere. But although the number of inhabitants was thus greatly diminished, and the food carefully portioned out, the famine became so great that the people of Calais ate cats, dogs, and rats, and even boiled old boots to make soup.

Month after month passed by, and although their sufferings grew greater every day, they still held out bravely, hoping the French king would send them help or drive away the English army. Once more the city gates opened, and a second troop of thin and haggard people came out; but Edward was now so angry at the obstinate resistance of Calais that he would not let them pass, and they died of hunger between the city walls and the English camp.

Finally the city was forced to surrender, but Edward declared that he would kill all the inhabitants unless six of the most prominent citizens came to him, barefooted and in their shirts, each with a rope around his neck, and bringing the keys of the city gates. When this message was delivered by the governor, the people of Calais groaned aloud, for they felt that their end was near. But St. Pierre, one of the wealthiest men in town, stepped forward, offering to be the first of the six required victims.

Two of his relatives immediately imitated him, and they were soon followed by three other noble-hearted volunteers. The six victims, in the prescribed attire, then went before Edward, escorted to the gates by their weeping kinsmen. When the Englishmen saw the Calais burghers appear, they were touched to the heart, all except Edward, who, in spite of the entreaties of the Black Prince and all his courtiers, ordered that they should be hanged at once.

The guards were about to obey, when good Queen Philippa knelt before her husband, imploring him to spare the lives of those six brave men. She spoke so movingly that all who heard her wept; then she gently reminded Edward that she had come over the sea to bring him the joyful news of the victory of Nev'ille's Cross, won over the Scots, whose king, David Bruce, was now her prisoner.

Her entreaties softened Edward's heart, and he gave her the six Calais burghers, to deal with as she wished. Philippa had them led to her own tent, where they were richly clothed, royally feasted, and, after receiving many gifts, were sent back unharmed to their rejoicing relatives.

As Calais now belonged to the English, Edward ordered all the Frenchmen to leave it and go and live elsewhere. He next peopled the city with his own subjects, and had it guarded by an English garrison. Hither English boats brought tin, wool, and other merchandise, to sell to the French merchants who came there to buy.

Philippa and the Burghers of Calais.

Although Edward had hitherto been so successful, he was now obliged to stop making war, and to conclude a seven years' truce with France. He was forced to suspend his conquests because a terrible pestilence, called the black death, had made its way into Europe from Asia, and was now carrying off thousands of people.

The black death raged for several years, and killed about one third of the population. It was so deadly because people in those days did not know that three things are necessary for good health: pure air, pure water, and great cleanliness, not only of the body, but also of all its surroundings—clothing, houses, and streets.

LIII. THE AGE OF CHIVALRY.

SHORTLY after the taking of Calais, Edward, who is regarded as one of the most chivalrous of the English kings, founded a new order of knights, which was called the Order of the Garter. It is said that at one of the court balls the Countess of Salisbury dropped her garter. The king saw her confusion, and, wishing to prevent any of his courtiers from being so rude as to laugh at the accident, he picked up the garter, put it on his own leg, and said aloud in French, "Honi soit qui mal y pense," words which mean, "Shamed be he who evil thinks."

He then declared that he was going to choose twenty-five of the most noble knights to belong to the new Order of the Garter, with him and the Black Prince. Each of the knights he chose wore a blue garter on his left leg, a blue sash across his breast, a medal with the effigy of St. George trampling the dragon, and a silver star with eight points.

The twenty-five Knights of the Garter have always been very proud of this honourable decoration, and in knightly days, when it was the custom to take solemn oaths, these men used to take pride in swearing by their "stars and garters." Hence, also, "to receive the blue ribbon" meant to have the greatest honour conferred upon one.

Some people, however, claim that the Order of the Garter was instituted by Richard the Lion-hearted. He, it is said, gave a leather garter to the knights who had distinguished themselves in fighting against the Saracens.

In the feudal ages, knights were men of noble birth, who, after undergoing a certain amount of training, were received into the order of knighthood or chivalry.

Until seven years old, boys staid under their mothers' care; then they were sent to the castle of some great nobleman, where they served as pages till they were fourteen. During pagehood the young noblemen learned to be courteous and gentle, to wait upon ladies, tell stories, sing songs, and play upon the lute, and they were daily trained to be strong, agile, frank, brave, polite, and truthful.

From the age of fourteen till they were about twenty they were called squires; they practised the art of fighting, and attended knights at war, to help them don their heavy armour or to raise them when they were overthrown. This term of apprenticeship ended, the candidate for knighthood spent twenty-four hours in fasting and prayer, and during the night knelt alone in the church, before the altar, upon which his armour was laid to be consecrated.

This time of meditation and prayer was followed on the next day by a solemn religious ceremony, in which the young knight vowed to protect the weak, the fatherless, and the oppressed, to honour all women, and to right the wrong wherever it was possible. Then a knight drew his sword and struck the kneeling candidate with the flat blade (this was called bestowing the accolade), calling him by name, and bidding him rise and receive his kiss of welcome into the order of chivalry.

Other knights, or fair maidens of high degree, then helped him don the different parts of a knight's armour. The fact that a knight had to undergo such a preparation, and take such solemn vows, tended to make him braver and better than he would otherwise have been; and a true gentleman nowadays is one who, like the knights of old, is strictly honourable in all things and gentle towards every one.

During the chivalric ages, the knights were in the habit of making strange vows, such as not to rest until they had fought a number of battles or won a certain prize in a tournament. When Edward started to make war in France, some of the nobles declared they would wear a patch over one eye until they had beaten the French!

Ladies also made queer vows, and we are told that when good Queen Philippa heard that Edward had begun the siege of Calais, she swore she would not change a certain linen kerchief she wore until he had taken the city. As the siege lasted ten months, the queen's kerchief had time to grow very yellow. Her ladies, to look as much like her as possible, wore unbleached linen, and thus écru became the fashionable colour.

LIV. THE BATTLE OF POITIERS.

THE black death no sooner ceased its ravages than the Hundred Years' War was renewed. This time it was carried on from the south, because the Black Prince had taken up his abode in Guienne and held his court at Bordeaux (bor-do'). The French king who had been defeated at Crécy was dead, but his son, John I., had collected a large army to drive the English out of the realm.

After four years of fighting, in the course of which no great battle occurred, the French hemmed in the English forces near Poitiers (pwah-tǐ-ā') in 1356. The English army was only about eight thousand strong, while the French were five times as numerous. The Prince of Wales, seeing the odds against him, cried, "God help us! It only remains for us to fight bravely!"

He felt so sure of defeat that he allowed a priest to try to make peace; but when he heard that the French king would consent only on condition that he surrender with one hundred knights, he haughtily answered that he would never be made a prisoner of war, except sword in hand.

Thus forced to fight, the Englishmen behaved so well that, in spite of the dashing courage of the Frenchmen, they not only won the victory, but took John and one of his sons prisoners. The Prince of Wales, like a true knight, treated his captives with the utmost courtesy, even waiting in person upon the king at table.

The royal prisoners were soon taken to England. They entered London in state, almost as if they were the victors, John wearing his regal mantle and sitting upon a magnificent steed, while his conqueror, plainly clad and riding a pony, escorted him with every mark of respect.

The captive king was lodged in the Savoy Palace, where he staid three years, while his son governed France in his name. At the end of that time, the treaty of Bretigny (brĕ-teen-yĭ') was signed, and it was agreed that John should return to France upon paying three million crowns of gold, and that Edward should renounce all claims to the throne of France. But the English king kept many provinces in France, which were all governed by the Black Prince from his court at Bordeaux.

John went home, but finding that the money could not be raised, and hearing that two of the princes whom he had left in England as hostages had escaped, he went back of his own free will, and staid in London until he died. The new French king, however, managed so cleverly that in ten years the French gradually recovered the greater part of their lost territory without fighting any great battles.

The Black Prince's health was so undermined by an unsuccessful war in Spain that he was no longer able to sit upon his horse, and had to be carried in a litter. The pain he suffered affected his temper, and instead of being gentle and courteous as of old, he became cruel and revengeful.

The people of Limoges (lee-mōzh') having revolted, the Black Prince went thither, and after taking the town he put all the inhabitants to death. But this act of cruelty did not prevent other cities from revolting too, and four years after the Black Prince finally left France, there remained only five cities that still belonged to the English.

The Black Prince died at forty-six, not long after his

return to England. He was buried in the Cathedral of Canterbury, where the armour he wore still hangs near the place where his body rests. All England mourned for him, and one of his friends died of grief at his loss.

The Normans and the Saxons, who had hitherto been rivals, had become friends while fighting against the French. These wars also had the effect of making France and England dislike each other, and the Norman nobles, who had hitherto spoken French, now considered it more patriotic to talk English. So, while there had formerly been three languages in England,—Latin for the church and for scientific writings; French for the court, for the nobility, for story books, and for lawsuits; and English for the common people,—there was now but one language for all practical purposes.

Much of this reform was brought about by the war, but it was also helped on greatly by the fact that some of the learned men now began to write in English. One of these men is the noted English reformer Wyc'lif, "the Morning Star of English prose," of whom you will soon hear more. Another is the poet Chaucer, who is called " the Morning Star of English poetry." He composed the delightful poems known as " The Canterbury Tales," in which he relates the stories told by a group of pilgrims on their way to visit the shrine of St. Thomas of Canterbury.

Edward carried on so many wars during his long reign that he had to depend upon the good will of Parliament to supply him with necessary funds. This body took advantage of these necessities to win certain privileges and to work certain reforms, which all tended to limit the power of the king and to extend the privileges of the people.

The end of Edward's life was very sad. He had lost his wife and favourite child, and for a time he became the dupe of a woman named Alice Per'rers, who pretended she loved him dearly. But she was only a vulgar and grasping woman, and when she had secured all the dead queen's jewels, and much money and land, she forsook the king on his deathbed, after stealing even his last finger ring. A priest, coming into the room, found the dying king all

Throne Room, Windsor Castle.

alone, forsaken by every one. He held his cross before the monarch's eyes, and staid with him until he breathed his last, and his fifty years' reign was ended.

Edward III. was a great warrior and very ambitious, but, as you have seen, he did not retain his French conquests very long. He built the palace of Windsor (win'zor) by levying troops of workmen, on the same plan as the Nor-

man kings raised an army in time of war. He was the last
king who did this, however, for the people were gradually
growing more independent.

Windsor Castle, from the Thames.

LV. THE PEASANTS' REVOLT.

EDWARD III. was succeeded on the throne of England by his grandchild Richard II., the son of the
valiant Black Prince. The new king was then only ten
years old, so his uncles wondered how he would behave
during the long coronation services. But he was so handsome and obedient that they had no trouble with him.
He did everything they bade him; still, the tedious ceremonies tired him so much that he had to be carried off to
bed. Little kings cannot take their ease and lie abed as
long as they choose; so the men soon roused Richard

again, to preside over a grand banquet, where his health was drunk, and where he had to listen to long speeches.

As the king was far too young to reign himself, his three uncles, the Dukes of York, Lancaster, and Gloucester, had all the power, but unfortunately they did not always agree.

The wars in France and in Scotland still required much money, and Parliament was called upon to supply it, and also to pay for the expensive coronation festivities. As the existing taxes were not enough to meet all these demands, it was decided that every person over fifteen should pay a shilling to the king. For the rich this was a mere trifle; but there were many poor who earned so little that it was impossible for them to pay it.

The news of this tax, therefore, caused great dismay and indignation among the working classes; and when the tax-collectors came, roughly demanding their money, they were received with scowls and threats. They finally came to the house of a blacksmith named Wat Tyler. He had a daughter of fourteen, who was so tall and womanly-looking that the men insisted upon her paying one shilling too.

In vain she protested that she was only fourteen. The tax-collector not only refused to believe her, but actually began to illtreat her. The girl's screams, however, were heard by her father, who rushed out of his forge, hammer in hand, and in his anger killed the collector.

When the tax-collector's friends came to arrest Wat Tyler, they found him surrounded by his poor neighbours, who swore they would protect him because he had killed the man in defending his child. Excited by this event and by the speeches of another workman, Jack

Straw, and of a poor preacher, John Ball, these men, with nearly one hundred thousand others from many parts of England, finally decided to march to London. They wanted to tell the king that they could not pay the tax, and to beg him to make new laws so they should no longer be forced to work for their lords without receiving wages.

The mob entered London, and after wandering about the streets helplessly, burned a few houses, and destroyed all the papers and records which the lawyers kept in the Temple. They also declared that strangers had no business in England; so they stopped all the passers-by, and killed those who could not pronounce "bread and cheese" with the proper English accent.

Their clamours terrified the Londoners, and for a while no one knew what to do. Strange to relate, the young king, who was but fifteen years old, was the only one who kept his presence of mind. As his uncles were all away, Richard made a proclamation, saying he would meet the rebels on a plain outside the city, on the next day, to hear their complaints.

LVI. RICHARD'S PRESENCE OF MIND.

THE greater part of the mob believed Richard and went out of the city to wait for him. True to his promise, Richard rode out the next day, and after listening to their grievances he promised that the tax should be removed, and that all serfs should be freed from their masters. Then he dismissed them, asking them to leave two men from each village, so he could give them his written promise.

The mob was quite satisfied, and disbanded, while the young king set thirty clerks to writing the promised papers. But while Richard was busy thus, Wat Tyler, Jack Straw, and a few others, thinking he meant to deceive them, forced their way into the Tower to find him. Their search proved vain, and in their anger they killed the Archbishop of Canterbury and several other persons.

The next day, as Richard was riding through Smithfield with the Mayor of London and sixty attendants, he met this division of the mob. Tyler now stepped forward to speak to the king. In his excitement he used a loud and threatening tone, and, laying his hand upon his sword, half drew it from the scabbard.

The mayor, fancying that Wat Tyler was about to strike the king, felled him to the ground with one blow. When the mob saw their leader fall, they advanced with angry cries; but Richard rode boldly forward, saying, "My friends, be not concerned for the loss of your unworthy leader. I, your king, will be your leader!"

Then, turning, he rode ahead, they blindly following him. His escort, in the meantime, had dashed off into the city in search of help, and soon came to rescue him with thousands of brave men. When the mob saw these soldiers coming, they fell on their knees, begging for mercy, and they scattered thankfully when the king assured them of his forgiveness and bade them go home.

The heads of Wat Tyler and a few of the men who had taken part in the murder of the archbishop were exposed on London Bridge, and the rebellion, which is generally known as the Peasants' Revolt, was ended. But, unhappily, most of Richard's promises were set aside by Parliament, and although the poll tax was stopped, the other grievances went on as before.

You see that Richard was fearless and generous at first. In spite of these qualities, he made a very poor king. This was principally owing to the bad bringing up he received. His uncles were proud of ruling, and, hoping to retain the power, they did not let him learn anything useful, but kept him amused by surrounding him with worthless flatterers and vain shows. They found him a wife when he was little more than a boy, but she was fortunately so gentle and lovable that she was called good Queen Anne.

Richard's uncles, in the meantime, were having much trouble with Rome because the pope did not like the teachings of Wyclif, a man whom the queen and the Duke of Lancaster greatly admired. Wyclif declared that many of the priests had grown rich and lazy, and that they took no pains to teach and help the poor. He therefore translated the Bible into English, so that the unlearned could read it as well as the learned. Then he preached so eloquently to his Oxford students that many of them travelled all through England and Europe, preaching the gospel.

The wandering teachers often sang hymns, so the people called them the singers, or Lol'lards, a name which was soon given to all those whose teachings were different from those of the Roman Catholic Church. The pope thought Wyclif was very wrong, and therefore forced him to go away from Oxford and to withdraw to a little village called Lut'ter-worth. But although Wyclif could no longer teach at Oxford, he had already sown the seed of the Protestant religion, so he is called "the Morning Star of the Reformation." He died at Lutterworth, in his little church;

and thirty years after his death he had won many converts. The Catholics considered his teachings so wrong that they had his bones taken out of their grave and burned. His ashes were cast into a brook, which carried them into a river, and finally into the ocean. But Wyclif's ashes were not scattered any farther than his writings and teachings, for, as you know, there are now Protestants in all parts of the world.

LVII. A TINY QUEEN.

THESE religious troubles were not all. War arose, and the king's uncles had to carry it on. But as they were quite selfish, you will not be surprised to hear that one of them, Lancaster, took the money which Parliament gave him for the war in France, and used it in securing the throne of Castile in Spain for his daughter.

Besides the war in Castile and France, there was a war with Scotland, the principal battle being won by Douglas and the Scots against the English under Percy Hotspur. This battle took place at Ot'ter-burn, and it gave rise to a ballad which was sung for several centuries—the "Ballad of Chevy Chase."

The Duke of Gloucester, one of the king's uncles, had used his power very unwisely, and had, besides, angered the king by putting to death his tutor, although Queen Anne knelt before Gloucester three hours, imploring him to spare the good man's life. Richard was naturally indignant, and shortly after this turned to his uncle in full council, and abruptly asked: "How old am I?"

"Your majesty is in your twenty-second year," answered Gloucester.

"Then I am old enough to reign," cried the king, and he dismissed the council.

Gloucester, deprived of the regency, now plotted against the king, who therefore sent him a prisoner to Calais. Here the duke died, and it is generally supposed that he was secretly put to death by Richard's order.

When good Queen Anne died, leaving no children, Richard decided to marry again, and after much thought he selected Isabella, daughter of the King of France. When he made this choice known, one of his courtiers objected that the princess was too young, as she was only eight years old. But the king answered, "The lady's age is a fault which every day will remedy," and sent an embassy to France to ask her hand in marriage.

Isabella was so little that every one wondered how she would behave. The men were brought before her, and when the ambassador had knelt and kissed her hand, he said: "Madam, if it please God, you shall be our lady and queen."

Baby as she still was, little Isabella gravely answered: "Sir, if it please God and my father that I be Queen of England, I shall be well pleased, for I am told I shall be a great lady."

The grandest outfit you ever heard of was made ready for this little queen, who was escorted to England by the embassy, and solemnly crowned at Westminster Abbey. She was so sweet and little that every one loved her; and the king used to visit her every day in her nursery, where he actually played dolls with her. He was so kind to the little queen that she loved him dearly, and she never forgot her playfellow, who was a good-hearted man, although a weak and worthless king.

The Duke of Lancaster was dead by this time, and his son, Henry of Bol'ing-broke, had been exiled by the king. Richard now thought it would be a good chance to seize this cousin's property; so he took possession of it, just before leaving for Ireland, where war awaited him.

Henry of Bolingbroke, or Lancaster, as he is called, now begged the Duke of Brittany to help him regain his estates. The duke consented, and while Richard was in Ireland, Henry landed in England. He was soon joined by a large force, and, seeing that the people were tired of their weak king Richard, Henry began to think of taking the throne himself.

Richard, hearing of his cousin's arrival, came back to England as fast as winds and waves would allow him; but he no sooner landed than his army deserted him. He then took refuge in Flint Castle; but Henry of Lancaster came there to get him, and by false promises persuaded him to go to London and there resign his crown.

The weak Richard offered no resistance to his cousin's entreaties, and after he had given up his crown to Henry, he withdrew to Pontefract (pom'fret) Castle, where he died in the year 1400, having been put to death, some say, by his cousin's order. Little Queen Isabella showed more spirit than he, for she refused to recognize Henry as king, and scorned to marry his son when she became a widow at twelve. After being kept a prisoner for some time, and being deprived of her attendants and jewels, she was finally allowed to go back to her father's court.

LVIII. HENRY'S TROUBLES.

RICHARD II. was the last of eight real Plantagenet or Angevine kings, and his successor, Henry IV., was the first ruler of the house of Lancaster. Although Richard had left no children, Henry could not claim to inherit the throne, because the seven-year-old Earl of March was next of kin. But Parliament then often gave the crown to any member of the royal family.

Henry IV. therefore became king through act of Parliament. His reign was not free from care, as you will soon see, for at first there were so many quarrels among the members of Parliament that as many as forty challenges were given and received in the House in one day. Besides that, a conspiracy was soon formed to depose Henry and replace Richard. To show that Richard's death was not owing to violence, his body was publicly exposed in London. But as only the face was visible, people never felt sure that his death had been natural.

Norman Gateway, Windsor Castle.

To prevent his enemies from trying to put the young Earl of March on the throne, Henry kept him a prisoner in Windsor Castle, and never allowed him to go out, except under safe escort.

As Parliament had elected him king, Henry was forced to respect its wishes and to grant many things it asked. He also tried to gain the friendship of pope and clergy, and to please them he allowed the Lollards to be persecuted, and even to be burned at the stake, as heretics or unbelievers.

Henry's conscience often troubled him sorely for the crime he had committed to secure the crown, and he lived in constant dread of seeing some one snatch the crown from him. He was also afraid of being murdered; for we are told that once, when about to get into his bed, he found in it a frightful instrument with many sharp blades.

Although Wales had long been part of the English realm, Henry IV. had to put down a rebellion of the Welsh, under Owen Glendower (glen'door), a descendant of Prince Llewellyn. This Welshman pretended to be a magician, and the people, excited by the bards' ballads, gladly rallied around him. For seven years Glendower baffled all Henry's efforts to capture him, for he and his followers used to retreat to Mount Snowdon, where they knew every foot of the ground and had secret hiding places.

A war with Scotland also kept Henry busy, although it was carried on mainly by Percy Hotspur and his father. They won a victory over the Scots at Hom'il-don Hill; but as the king would not allow them to sell their captives for a ransom, they revolted and joined forces with the Scots. Henry met the Percys and Scotchmen before they could join the Welsh army, and defeated them in the battle of Shrews'bur-y, where Percy Hotspur was killed. In this battle the king's eldest son, Prince Hal, showed great bravery; but the king himself, fearing to be recognized by his armour, had several noblemen dress like him. Strange to relate, all these knights were killed, while Henry escaped.

The Percy rebellion was scarcely quelled when Henry was called upon to put down another, led by Archbishop Scrope of York, who wanted to place the Earl of March upon the throne. His force, too, was defeated, and the priest himself was beheaded as a traitor, a punishment which had never yet befallen a member of the clergy. The common people fancied it was very wicked to execute an archbishop, even if he had sinned; and when Henry became ill soon after, they thought it was a punishment sent by Heaven.

Two years after the battle of Shrewsbury, Henry IV. succeeded in capturing the heir to the Scotch crown, who was on his way to France to be educated. By his order, this Prince James, the great-great-grandson of the famous Bruce, was brought to Windsor, and given so excellent an education that he afterwards became the best king who ever sat upon the Scotch throne, as well as a musician and a poet.

LIX. MADCAP HARRY.

AS we have seen, Henry IV. was often troubled by remorse. He suffered greatly, and had so many worries that, if the poet Shakespeare is to be believed, he once said, "Uneasy lies the head that wears a crown." Besides his remorse, his disease, and his wars, Henry had another source of anxiety, for his son, Prince Hal, was a very wild young fellow.

He was not altogether bad, for he had proved himself very brave as a soldier and had even shown a great deal of wisdom in his father's council; but the gay life of London was too tempting, and in the company of noisy, bragging companions, Madcap Harry, as the prince was often called, indulged in all manner of unprincely occupations. He even went so far, it is said, as to waylay and rob peaceful travellers. In doing this he was, of course, breaking the law, which, as prince, he should have been the first to respect.

After one of these highway robberies, so the story runs, some of his companions were arrested and brought before Judge Gascoigne (gas-coin'). He tried them, and, finding them guilty, sentenced them to the usual punishment. Prince Hal, who was present at the trial, strove to beg them off; and when the judge refused to grant his request, the indignant prince struck him.

The judge, knowing that the majesty of the law is greater than that of any prince, now ordered Madcap Harry off to prison. This made the young man realize how wrong he had been, so he apologized to the judge, and accepted his punishment submissively. When this was told to King Henry he joyfully exclaimed: "Happy is the king who possesses a judge who is not afraid to do his duty, and a son who is wise enough to submit to the law!"

In the end of Henry's reign troops were sent to France to side with one of the parties engaged in civil war there. But although the king had been a mighty fighter, he no longer took great interest in the war, for he was rapidly growing worse.

During one of his prolonged fainting fits it is said that Prince Hal came into the room, and, fancying he was dead, carried off the crown. As soon as Henry recovered, he asked for it, and when the prince brought it back, he said: "Alas, fair son! what right have you to the crown, when you know your father had none?"

"My liege," answered the prince, firmly, "with your sword you won it, and with the sword I will keep it."

A few days later the king had another fainting fit, while he was at prayers in Westminster Abbey. He was carried into the abbot's room; there he opened his eyes and asked where he was. They told him he was in the "Jerusalem Chamber." Suddenly he remembered an old prophecy that he should die in Jerusalem, and, refusing to be removed, he breathed his last in that apartment.

Perhaps the most famous man in Henry's reign was Whit'ting-ton, whose name you may have heard in nursery rhymes. He was the son of a nobleman; but as his father had lost all his money, he went off to London to make his fortune. He became the apprentice of a cloth merchant, but grew discouraged because he had no friends, and left London.

But, so runs the story, when he got outside the city and sat down to rest, his only friend, a cat, rubbing against his knees, he suddenly heard the Bow bells ring. The sound came to his ears, loud and clear, and the bells seemed to say: "Turn again, Whittington, thrice Lord Mayor of London." Encouraged by such prospects, Whittington picked up his cat and went back to London. There he tried so hard that he became a good and rich man, and was actually elected three times Lord Mayor of London.

When Whittington died, ten years after Henry IV., he left all his immense fortune to the poor, to found several charitable institutions.

Some people, however, say that Whittington's fortune was all made by a ship called the *Cat*, which brought coal from New'cas-tle to London to be sold at great profit. Others say that Whittington's cat was his old friend the real pussy, which he sent away to be sold in the East; there it brought a large price, and thus proved the beginning of his fortune.

LX. A GLORIOUS REIGN.

WHEN Henry of Monmouth, the wild Prince Hal, heard that his father was dead, he went into his own room, and there spent the night in meditation and prayer. He was very sorry for the past, and fully determined to do better in the future. When morning came he put these good resolutions into practice. First, he sent for his former companions and told them that he was going to reform and that he did not wish to see them again until they were willing to follow his example.

Next, he sent for the grave and learned men who had helped his father, and begged them to give him also their advice; and he told Judge Gascoigne—whom he honoured for doing right, regardless of rank—that he hoped his judges would always administer justice in the same way.

Having thus won his greatest victory by conquering himself, the new king set the Earl of March free, restored their estates to the Percys, and buried Richard II. and Henry IV. among the other kings.

Henry V. was able, energetic, and brave, as well as handsome and warm-hearted; so he soon won the affections of his subjects. His greatest fault was that he sorely persecuted the Lollards, whom he had been taught to believe very wicked. By his order, many of them were burned, among others old Lord Cobham, who, because he had once escaped from prison and joined some rebels, was accused of treason and heresy, and was consequently both burned and hanged.

The new king, however, was most anxious to conquer new lands. As the French king was insane, and as his two principal subjects, the Dukes of Or'le-ans and Burgundy, were warring against each other, Henry fancied that it was a good time to invade France. He therefore renewed the claim to the French crown which had already been made by Edward III., and landed at Harfleur (ar-fler') with an army of fifteen thousand men.

This city held out four months, hoping the French army would come to its rescue; but the troops could not leave Paris, as there was a quarrel about who should have command. Seeing no help coming, the people of Harfleur were forced to surrender; but by this time the English soldiers were nearly all sick.

Marching at the head of his army, and sharing all their hardships, Henry now set out for Calais; but on the way thither he was met by a French army of fifty thousand men. In spite of the great odds against him, the English king did not lose his presence of mind, and in his address to his troops he said that he intended to win great glory, either by victory or by death. When a soldier remarked that he wished some of his countrymen were there to help

Sir John Gilbert, Artist.
The Morning of the Battle of Agincourt.

them fight, the king cried: "If we are to die, I am glad we are so few; but if we are to conquer, our glory will be all the greater if unshared."

The French army consisted mainly of heavy cavalry, and as the ground was soaked with rain, the horses sank into the mud up to their knees. This fact told greatly in favour of the light-armed English bowmen, who, in spite of the bravery of the French, won a brilliant victory (1415).

Henry himself did wonders, and when the battle of Agincourt (ah-zhaN-koor') was ended, it was found that while the English had lost only forty men, the French slain numbered more than ten thousand. The next day the dead were buried; and when Henry went back to England, his people rushed into the water at Dover to meet him and give him an uproarious welcome.

Two years after this battle Henry went back to France with a new army. He besieged and took Rouen after ten months' effort, and finally became master of the greater part of France. The troubles in that kingdom had by this time grown so serious that many Frenchmen joined Henry, and a treaty was finally signed at Troyes (trwah) in 1420. It was then agreed that Henry should marry the French king's daughter, and that when the insane monarch died the King of England should reign in France too.

So Henry made a triumphal entry into Paris, where he first saw Catherine, his future wife. If you care to know

Wooing of Henry V.

how an English king who knew very little French could make love to a French princess who knew only a few words of English, you can read all about it in one of Shakespeare's plays.

During the next two years Henry and Catherine were very happy. But before their little son was a year old, Henry V. became very ill. He named his brother, the Duke of Gloucester, Regent of England, said the Duke of Bedford must rule France, and gave the guardianship of his little son to another nobleman.

Henry died in France, at the age of thirty-four, and his body was carried home to be buried. His funeral was the grandest that had yet been seen in England, and upon his tomb, in Westminster Abbey, tapers were kept burning constantly for more than a hundred years.

As Henry had to take so many troops over to France, he had many ships built; and he has hence sometimes been called the founder of the English navy. He was a very brave king, but although he won much glory, he burdened England with debt, and by his unjust wars caused the death of about one hundred thousand men.

LXI. THE MAID OF ORLEANS.

WHEN Henry V. died, his only child, Henry VI., was nine months old. The English crown was far too large and heavy for this baby monarch's head, and when the sceptre was brought, his tiny hand clutched it as if it had been a mere rattle. Fortunately for him, Henry VI.

had two very able uncles, the Dukes of Gloucester and Bedford, who governed England and France for him.

Two months after the death of Henry, the insane monarch of France breathed his last. According to the treaty of Troyes, Henry VI. was now King of France; but the Dauphin Charles, the eldest son of the mad king, also claimed the crown, which by right did really belong to him.

The northern part of France was now in the hands of the English, who in fun called the dauphin King of Bourges (boorzh), because they said he ruled only the province around a small town of that name. Charles had very few troops, but he often secured the help of the Scots, who hated the English because they kept the Scotch king, James I., a prisoner. The baby king's uncles now agreed to set James free, provided the Scots paid for his eighteen years' board, and promised they would not help the French or make war against the English for a term of seventeen years.

It now seemed as if all would go well for the English. The Duke of Bedford, who was as good a warrior as Henry V., declared that as soon as he became master of the town of Orleans, which he was then besieging, he would consider all France conquered. Just then, however, a poor peasant girl, Joan of Arc, fancied that she had been chosen by Heaven to save her country from the English. She was good and earnest, and spoke so convincingly that people finally believed her. A knight from the neighbourhood took her to Bourges, where the king and his advisers allowed her to do as she wished and lead an army to the rescue of Orleans.

The common soldiers, who were very superstitious, believed that Joan had seen visions and had spoken to angels, so they were ready to do all she told them. They felt sure they would win as long as she led them on. The rumour of her mission soon reached the ears of the English soldiers, who dreaded her appearance, and said that if Heaven had sent her, their resistance would be vain.

This state of feeling in the two armies grew much more marked when Joan actually fought her way into Orleans, bringing provisions to the famished inhabitants. They received her with rapture, and called her the "Maid of Orleans." But Joan was not yet satisfied, and she vowed she would not rest until she had driven the English away from Orleans and taken the dauphin to Rheims to be crowned in the same cathedral as all the kings before him.

Joan kept her word. The English fled as she drew near. Town after town opened its gates when she appeared, wearing a suit of armour like a man, and sitting astride a great battle steed. Advancing thus, she won back many of the lost provinces, and at last Charles VII. was formally crowned. Then she said that her mission was ended, and begged permission to go home and tend her sheep.

But the king would not let her go, and the generals, knowing the effect of her presence upon the minds of both armies, urged her to remain. Joan of Arc sadly yielded to their entreaties, but all her joyous confidence now forsook her. The result was that in spite of her courage the French soldiers ceased to believe in her. One day, when she had headed a sally from the town of Compiègne (cawn-pyān'), they even treacherously forsook her.

Poor Joan fell into the hands of a French knight, an ally

of the English, and he, seeing that her king had basely deserted her, sold her into their hands. Joan of Arc was then thrust into prison, treated with the most inhuman cruelty, and, after being accused of heresy and witchcraft, she was burned at the stake in Rouen, and her ashes were cast into the Seine! But the heroic Maid of Orleans died so bravely, on the very square where her statue now stands, that the English soldiers began to fear that they had killed a saint. Their dread, and the Frenchmen's indignation, gave the latter the advantage, and at each new defeat the English cried that it was a judgment against them for burning Joan.

When the Duke of Bedford saw that France was lost, he died of grief, and was buried in Rouen. Some time afterwards Charles VII. became master of that city, and his soldiers proposed to open the duke's tomb and scatter his ashes abroad; but the duke had fought so bravely that Charles would not allow this, and said: "No; let him repose in peace; and be thankful that he does repose, for were he to awake he would make the stoutest of us tremble."

The war between France and England went on several years longer, with occasional pauses. But the French steadily advanced, and the English finally found that the Hundred Years' War, which lasted from about 1338 to 1453, cost them no end of men and money, but brought them little besides the glory won in the three great battles of Crécy, Poitiers, and Agincourt. During the reign of Henry VI. they lost, in fact, all the territory they had won in France, except the city of Calais, which they were to hold for another century.

LXII. THE BEGINNING OF THE WAR OF THE ROSES.

HENRY VI. was carefully brought up by his great-uncle, Cardinal Beau'fort. But he was, unfortunately, not very clever. He was very quiet and timid, and as he had no will of his own and was easily flattered and directed, the people around him fancied it would be the best thing for him to marry a clever wife.

But Cardinal Beaufort and the Duke of Gloucester could not agree who this wife should be; and when Henry VI., at twenty-four, married the fifteen-year-old Margaret of Anjou, Gloucester was very angry. To obtain this bright young princess for his stupid nephew, the cardinal had to give up two French provinces, and to accept her without a dowry.

One reason that Gloucester had so far lost his influence was that he had fallen into disgrace with the king a few years before. His wife tried to harm the king by witchcraft, in the hope that her own husband might then come to the throne. With this object, she made a waxen image of Henry and set it before the fire, believing that as the wax melted, the king's strength would leave him. Of course this belief was the greatest nonsense, but it was very common in those days, and the duchess's intentions were no better for the fact that her way of carrying them out was so foolish. In punishment she was forced to do public penance by walking through the streets holding a lighted taper, and then was imprisoned for life.

Little by little the king's total incapacity became more

evident. Everything was going wrong, and the queen and her advisers made things worse. The people began to murmur, and some said it was no wonder that things were not right when the country was ruled by an idiot king, who, after all, had no real claim to the throne.

For the people now remembered that the Lancasters were descended from the third son of Edward III., while the Duke of York, on his mother's side, was the direct descendant of the second son. The Duke of York, moreover, was a very popular man, so the people said he ought to be king, or at least to govern instead of the queen and her adviser Suf′folk. They next accused Suffolk of having spent a great deal of money to no purpose, and of having lost France by his carelessness. He was tried and found guilty, but the queen pleaded so hard for him that he was merely exiled for five years instead of being condemned to death. This did not please his enemies, who overtook him at sea, and beheaded him on the side of a boat.

The nobles were, as you see, discontented with the state of affairs. So were many of the poor, who finally rebelled and came marching to London, led by Jack Cade. These twenty thousand men defeated the king's troops at Sevenoaks, and marched into London, where their leader proudly struck an old Roman milestone, called the "London Stone," crying, "I am master of London."

The mob was at first quite orderly, and only made a "complaint," in which the people said the king had bad advisers and asked that a few laws should be changed. After a while, however, they became excited and killed several prominent men. When they left the city, to spend the night in their camp at Southwark, the troops guarded

London Bridge, and would not allow them to return the next day. A proclamation was then made, promising pardon and redress if they dispersed. So they scattered; but their leader, Jack Cade, upon whose head a price had been set, was overtaken and killed, and his head was placed on London Bridge to serve as a warning to rebels.

The poor weak king became quite insane in 1454, so Parliament decreed that the Duke of York should govern in his stead as Protector. This decision made the queen very angry, and when the king recovered a gleam of reason, she made him send York away and give the power to her and her new adviser Som'er-set.

The result was that there were now two parties in the country. The one in favour of the queen and Somerset was called the Lancaster party and wore a red rose as badge. The party in favour of the Duke of York was called the York party and wore a white rose. These two parties, not content with quarrelling, soon began fighting, and the civil war they waged was called the War of the Roses.

LXIII. THE QUEEN AND THE BRIGAND.

THE War of the Roses began about two years after the Hundred Years' War ended. It lasted nearly thirty years, and in it twelve battles were fought and about one hundred thousand people perished. It was in many respects worse than the Hundred Years' War, because now the English were fighting against one another, and because they displayed great cruelty and showed no mercy.

In the first great battle of the War of the Roses, that of St. Albans, the Duke of Somerset was killed, and the Yorkists captured the poor wounded king. Then for a short time the Duke of York was again protector. But the party of Lancaster rallied around the queen to continue the struggle.

The Duke of York, finding that many people were opposed to the idea of his being king, now went off to Ireland, leaving his cause in the hands of his brother-in-law, the Earl of Warwick, who was one of the richest men in England. This nobleman had lands and castles, thirty thousand people were fed at his tables every day, and as he was well liked he could raise an army whenever he pleased.

Left at the head of the Yorkist party, Warwick collected troops, and defeated the Lan-cas'tri-ans at the battle of Northampton. Henry VI. was again captured, and was now forced to recognize the Duke of York as his heir. But Queen Margaret, at the head of a Lancastrian army, soon defeated the Yorkists at Wakefield, and in this battle the Duke of York was killed. By Margaret's order, his head was cut off and exhibited upon the walls of York, wearing a paper crown.

Margaret, encouraged by this victory, now marched on London to deliver the captive king. But she was met on the way by Warwick, and at St. Albans a second battle took place, in which the queen was victorious. Warwick was forced to flee, leaving the king in her hands.

As Margaret's followers had disgraced themselves by plundering all along the road, London refused to admit her when she appeared, and preferred to open its gates to the new Duke of York. Warwick, who entered with him, then asked the people whether they wanted a York or a Lancaster for king, and they clamoured for a York. So Warwick led his nephew to Westminster, where he was publicly proclaimed as Edward IV., King of England.

The new king was only nineteen, but he was handsome and clever, and would have made a good ruler, had he not been cruel and self-indulgent. As the Lancastrians would not submit, he fought against them at Towton, where he celebrated his victory by being even more harsh than usual. After this battle he was formally crowned as king, and he named his two brothers, George and Richard, Dukes of Clarence and Gloucester.

Queen Margaret fled to Scotland with her helpless husband and son, and, having secured new troops by journeying twice to France, she invaded England. But the Lancastrians were again defeated in the battles of Hedgeley Moor and Hexham. The deposed king, Henry VI., escaped only because he was well mounted; but after dodging his enemies for about a year, he was betrayed into their hands. Warwick tied his feet under his horse, made him ride around the pillory (whipping post), and, after many similar indignities, thrust him into the Tower.

As for Queen Margaret, she fled with her little son. In crossing a forest, she fell into the hands of a party of brigands. While these men were quarrelling over the division of her jewels, she managed to escape with her son. But she had not gone far before she met another robber. Stepping up to him boldly, she pushed her boy towards him, saying, "Protect the son of your king."

Thus appealed to, the brigand led the queen and prince to his retreat, where he hid them for a few days. Then

Margaret of Anjou and the Robber.

he helped them to cross over to France, where Queen
Margaret had many friends. It was well for her that she
managed to escape, for all the nobles who had sided with
her were now reduced to beggary. We are told that one
Lancastrian lord had to become a shepherd, and that the
Countess of Oxford had to support her family by doing
needlework and by begging in the streets.

LXIV. THE TRIUMPH OF THE YORKS.

WARWICK, not satisfied with reducing the Lancastrians to poverty and placing his nephew upon the
throne, now began to scheme to make the king marry
some great princess. But while he was trying to find a
royal bride for Edward, the latter suddenly married a
beautiful widow named Elizabeth Woodville. This step
made Warwick angry, and when he saw that the new
queen's father, brothers, sisters, and numerous other relatives had been given all the most important places at
court, and were behaving with great insolence, he was indignant.

The king's brother, the Duke of Clarence, now married
Warwick's daughter; and, helped by him and by Richard
of Gloucester, Warwick began to plan his revenge. He
formed a plot to place Henry VI. on the throne again, instead of Edward, provided Henry's son should marry
Warwick's other daughter.

Queen Margaret and her son gladly consented to this,
and in 1470 Warwick landed in England with a large

army to take the throne away from Edward. Many of the noblemen, who were jealous of the Woodvilles, now joined Warwick, and Edward IV., seeing it was useless to try to resist, made his escape on a fishing vessel. His wife, Elizabeth, was too ill to go with him, so she took refuge in a church, where her son, the future Edward V., was born.

As soon as Warwick reached London, Henry was dragged out of prison, and made king once more by the very man who had helped crown his enemy. But he was not to reign long, for the Yorkists, regaining courage and being led by Edward IV., won the victory of Bar'net. In this battle Warwick the "kingmaker," the last of the great barons who used to lead their vassals to war, was killed. With his death the age of chivalry was over.

The Duke of Clarence basely deserted Warwick at the last minute, and joined his brother, who forgave him for his rebellion. Warwick was closely followed by Queen Margaret with another army. When she landed, she heard of her ally's defeat and death; but, seeing it was too late to withdraw, she pressed onward.

The Lancastrians and Yorkists met for their last battle at Tewkes'bur-y, where the former were defeated, and where Margaret and her son both fell into the hands of Edward IV. King Edward then angrily asked the prince how he dared come into his kingdom in arms.

"I came to recover my father's kingdom," proudly answered the young prince. But these words made Edward so angry that he struck the youth. This was enough for the Dukes of Clarence and Gloucester; they immediately drew their daggers and murdered their captive.

Poor Queen Margaret was thrust into prison, but after lingering there five years, she was ransomed by her father, who sold all his estates to free her.

Edward IV., having won the battle of Tewkesbury, went back to London in triumph. On the next day, Henry VI., the last of the three Lancastrian kings, was found dead in his prison.

Although he had won back his throne, Edward IV. was not very happy. As he was always afraid lest some one should try to snatch the power from him, he hired ever so many spies to watch the princes and report all they said. Then, hoping to recover France, he collected a large army; but when he got over there, instead of making use of it, he concluded a disgraceful peace. When he came home, Gloucester, envious of his brother the Duke of Clarence, poisoned the king's mind against him. This was easy, for the behaviour of Clarence was such as to anger a king who liked to have his own way.

Some say that the king's suspicion of him came from an old prophecy that a man whose name began with G should kill the king's children. However this may be, George, Duke of Clarence, was soon arrested, tried by Parliament, found guilty of treason, and condemned to die. We are told that, being given his choice, Clarence begged to be drowned in a butt of malmsey, his favourite wine.

After Clarence's death, Richard, the Duke of Gloucester, was the most influential man at court, and he encouraged the king to be very cruel and tyrannical. Under the Lancasters, and indeed ever since the time of Edward II., Parliament had had much power, and England was what is called a constitutional monarchy, or a kingdom ruled by fixed laws. But under the Yorks the power of Parliament grew less and less, and the monarchy became almost absolute; that is to say, the king did just as he pleased.

Great changes were brought about at this time by the introduction of printing by Caxton. This man had learned

Daniel Maclise, Artist.
King Edward IV. visiting Caxton's Press.

printing on the Continent, and he brought the first press to London. Among the first books which he printed was "The Game and Playe of the Chesse," for people were then very fond of that game.

LXV. THE PRINCES IN THE TOWER.

BEFORE Edward IV. died, he foresaw that there might be trouble between his brother Richard and his wife's kindred, so he used his last breath to implore them to be friends. As soon as he was dead, two of the queen's relatives, Earl Rivers and Lord Grey, took charge of Edward V., the eldest son and successor of the king, while the queen withdrew into a sanctuary with her other children. Edward V. was on his way to be crowned at London, when his uncle Richard, Duke of Gloucester, came to meet him. During the first day's journey all went well, but on the second day Richard suddenly had Rivers and Grey seized by his guards. They were then dragged off to prison in spite of the little king's entreaties.

Having thus got rid of the queen's relatives, Richard, whose plan was to secure the throne for himself, led the little king to the Tower, where he was to stay until his coronation. Then, calling Parliament, Richard got from it the title of Protector, for Edward was too young to reign alone.

A few days later, Richard suddenly accused Lord Hastings, a friend of the late king, of treason. In proof, he showed his deformed arm, and told the assembled council that its shrunken appearance was due to the witchcraft of Hastings's friends. Now every one knew that this was not true, but no one dared oppose Richard. He therefore called the guards, and bade them immediately behead Lord Hastings, adding that he would not dine until he knew the traitor was dead.

The guards obeyed, and Lord Hastings was beheaded in the courtyard, on a convenient log of wood, without any further trial. Then some guards were sent off to Pontefract Castle, where Rivers and Grey were put to death, under the pretext that they also were traitors.

Thus rid of the men who would have been most likely

to oppose him, Richard, still pretending that he was devoted to the little king, sent for the latter's brother, Richard, Duke of York. The queen hated to let her second son go, but he joyfully entered the Tower to join his brother. As Richard now had both of these princes in his power, he made his friend Buck'ing-ham tell the people that they were not the dead king's own offspring, and that he, Richard of Gloucester, ought to be king.

Buckingham managed so cleverly that he persuaded a few persons to go and offer the crown to Richard. The latter pretended at first to be shocked and surprised; but finally he accepted the crown and the title of Richard III. Still, although he had a grand coronation feast, he felt that he should never be safe so long as his brother's sons were alive; so he resolved to put them to death.

Two murderers were therefore sent to the Tower, bearing an order to the governor, who was forced to give up his keys to them for one night. When the governor came back the next day, he rushed to the princes' room, but found it empty. A few days later it became generally known that the little princes were no more; but it was only after Richard's death that it was discovered how they had been killed.

It was then reported that the murderers, finding them asleep on their bed, clasped in each other's arms and with their prayer book beside them, smothered them under a big feather bed. Then they took the bodies and secretly buried them under one of the Tower staircases. Two hundred years later, a mason, in repairing some broken steps, found the bones of two children, and everybody now believes that they were those of the murdered princes.

The Princes in the Tower.

LXVI. RICHARD'S PUNISHMENT.

RICHARD III. bestowed many gifts upon his accomplice Buckingham, to reward him for so cleverly helping him to secure the throne. But a man who is not faithful to one master is likely to betray another; so the Duke of Buckingham, fancying that Richard did not do enough for him, soon began to plot to give the crown to the Earl of Richmond, Henry Tu'dor.

Henry Tudor was a descendant of the third son of Edward III., and also of a Welshman named Owen Tudor. Being thus the head of the Lancastrians, he made his claim to the throne stronger by promising to marry Princess Elizabeth, the eldest daughter of Edward IV., and hence the heiress of the house of York.

Buckingham proposed this marriage to Henry, and invited him to come over to England to claim the throne. But when Buckingham began his rebellion against Richard, a terrible rainstorm so terrified his adherents that they deserted, and Buckingham himself was betrayed into the hands of King Richard, who had him executed as a traitor.

During the next two years Richard governed England very wisely; but although he was an able king, he was a very unhappy man. His son, the only creature whom he loved, fell sick and died, and Richard mourned him sorely. Besides that, Richard was haunted by remorse, and in his dreams he saw the spirits of all his unhappy victims.

Hoping to win the people's affection and to have a child to inherit his throne, Richard now thought of marrying his own niece, the Princess Elizabeth. But when he saw that every one disapproved of this match, he gave it up. The rumour of his intentions, however, reached Henry of Richmond, who came over from Brittany with an army. Richard, who had taken part in the battles of Barnet and Tewkesbury, and who was very brave, collected an army and went to meet his rival, determined to conquer or die.

On the night of the battle, it is said, Richard, asleep in his tent, was, as usual, haunted by the ghosts of his victims. This seemed to him a bad omen, and on the next day, just as the battle of Bos'worth was about to begin, his commander in chief deserted him. Richard nevertheless called for his horse and dashed forward, hoping to meet and slay his hated rival. But in spite of all his courage, he was cut down, and fell head first, mortally wounded, into a brook. The crown, which a moment before sparkled so proudly upon his helmet, rolled under a hawthorn bush, and was picked up by Henry's soldiers, who crowned their leader on the battlefield.

Richard's body was carelessly thrown across a horse's back and carried to Leicester (les'ter), where it was buried. But the last of the York kings was not even to rest in peace in his grave. Some years later his body was torn out of its stone tomb, which from that time on served as a common watering trough.

Richard III., the last of the three York kings, was the last of the family of the Plantagenets, which ruled England for three hundred and thirty years. The battle of Bosworth (1485) marks the end of the Wars of the Roses, and also the end of feudalism, which had been introduced into England by William the Conqueror, at the battle of Hastings, four hundred and nineteen years before.

LXVII. TWO PRETENDERS.

HENRY VII., who was crowned King of England on Bosworth battlefield, was the first of the Tudor kings. He belonged to the house of Lancaster; and as he soon married Princess Elizabeth, daughter of Edward IV., of the

Marriage of Henry VII.

house of York, both parties were well pleased. But, fearing that the Earl of Warwick, Clarence's son, might claim the throne, Henry kept him a close prisoner in the Tower.

The new king was rather afraid of the few noblemen who had survived the Wars of the Roses, so he tried to restrict their power as much as he could. Knowing very well also that he had not the best right to the throne, and could keep it only as long as the people wished, he allowed Parliament more freedom than it had enjoyed under the preceding reign.

Henry was very fond of money, and as he fancied it would give him power, he tried to get all he could. With this end in view he encouraged commerce, and thus did much good to the whole country. His reign, however, was disturbed by two plots formed to drive him from the throne.

First, a priest named Simon trained a baker's son to make believe he was the Earl of Warwick. Now the Irish people had been very fond of Clarence, so they received this lad, Lambert Sim'nel, with joy, and proclaimed him king. But when Henry heard that a false Earl of Warwick was claiming the throne, he brought the real one out of the Tower and showed him to the people. In spite of this, the Irish still clung to Simnel, and, collecting an army, came over to England to place him on the throne.

Henry met and defeated the invaders at Stoke. There priest and pretender were both made captives. They were tried, and as Simon was found guilty of fraud, he was sent to prison for life. But, seeing that Simnel was not very intelligent, and had been forced to play his part, the king forgave him and made him a servant in the royal kitchen.

One of Simnel's stanch adherents, Lord Lov'el, is said to have ridden away in haste from the battlefield. Nothing was heard of him for a long time, so it was generally supposed that he had been drowned in trying to cross the Trent River. But more than one hundred years after the battle, some workmen, pulling down one of his massive stone houses, discovered there a secret chamber. In it they found the skeleton of a man seated on a chair, his head resting on a table, and near him stood an empty barrel and jar. Hence it has been thought that Lord Lovel, having escaped pursuit, hid himself in this retreat, where he probably starved to death.

The other plot which disturbed Henry's reign proved more serious. A rumour suddenly arose that little Richard of York had not been murdered in the Tower, as was popularly supposed, but that he had escaped to France, and was living there under the name of Perkin War'beck.

Many people believed this story; and when Perkin Warbeck, who was really the son of a merchant, was brought before the Duchess of Burgundy, she declared he was her long-lost nephew, and joyfully prepared to help him win the crown. Helped by the Duchess of Burgundy, the King of the Scots, and by several English noblemen who thought he was the real Duke of York, Perkin Warbeck invaded England, but was soon forced to retreat.

His friends then planned a second invasion from Ireland; but when Perkin landed in England, he was taken captive and put into the Tower, while his wife, a beautiful Scotch lady, became an attendant of the queen. It is likely that no further steps would have been taken against Perkin Warbeck, had he not made plans to escape with the Earl of Warwick. But this plot being discovered, both captives were condemned to death. The Earl of Warwick, being a nobleman, was beheaded on Tower Hill, but Perkin Warbeck was hanged like a common criminal at Tyburn.

LXVIII. A GRASPING KING.

HENRY VII., as you have seen, was rather a clever ruler, but he was so fond of money that he did many wrong things to secure it. For instance, he said that when people were not satisfied with the decision of the ordinary judges, they could come before a special court, held at Westminster, in a room where the ceiling was painted blue and decorated with gold stars. This tribunal was hence called the Star Chamber; and as people could sometimes bribe the judges, and thus get the verdict they wanted, it came to be regarded as a very disgraceful institution.

Two lawyers, Empson and Dudley, helped the king to get a great deal of money, and they made use of such dishonest means that their names are still used to designate bad men. Thus, by heavy taxes, and by asking for gifts from rich and poor, Henry contrived to save several millions, besides building for his own tomb the chapel which still bears his name in Westminster Abbey.

During his reign many great discoveries were made. Christopher Columbus, sailing across the Atlantic Ocean, opened the way for new and profitable trading. Henry VII., wishing to enrich himself, built a large ship, the *Great Harry*, and he too sent out expeditions. One of his captains was Cab′ot, who discovered New′found-land and the coast of the North American continent.

Henry VII. also tried to increase the wealth of his family by having his eldest son, Prince Arthur, marry Catherine of Ar′a-gon, the daughter of Ferdinand and Isabella of Spain. But soon after the marriage Prince Arthur died.

Rather than give up the dowry of the princess, Henry VII. now engaged her to his second son, Henry, although the latter was several years younger than his future wife.

Before dying, this money-saving king bargained that two thousand masses should be said for the rest of his soul, but should cost only sixpence apiece. Henry VII. was buried in Westminster Abbey, and his tomb is an example of a new style of building, first seen in his reign, and generally called the Tudor architecture.

Henry VII. was so severe, miserly, and unjust that his subjects gladly welcomed his successor, Henry VIII. The new king was eighteen, and as he was handsome, affable, well educated, and clever, many fancied he would make a very good ruler. But, as you will soon see, Henry was violent-tempered, wilful, conceited, and so fond of display that he soon spent all the money his father had saved.

In the very beginning of his reign he had his father's two wicked lawyers tried and sentenced to death, to show the people that he did not approve of their conduct. Then he pleased the people by marrying Catherine of Aragon, to whom he had been betrothed, by giving magnificent coronation festivals, and by holding gay tournaments in which he delighted in taking part himself.

He was so anxious to show what a great warrior he was, that although England was then at peace with France and Scotland, he stirred up war with them both. Then, crossing over to France, he easily routed the French at Guinegate (geen-gaht′), for their cavalry fled at the approach of the English. Because the enemy made more use of their spurs than of their swords, this encounter is known in history as the "Battle of the Spurs."

While Henry was winning this mock battle in France, his general, Lord Surrey, won a grand victory over the Scotch at Flod'den Field, where the beloved Scotch king James IV. fell, with ten thousand of his brave subjects.

These two battles ended the war, and peace was made with France, the king giving his own sister in marriage to the French monarch. But Louis XII. of France died soon after this wedding, so his widow was married to one of the king's friends.

LXIX. THE FIELD OF THE CLOTH OF GOLD.

HENRY VIII. was only twenty-four when the French king died, leaving his throne to his nearest male relative, Francis I. At that time Spain and Holland were both ruled by Charles V.; and as he too was young and clever, like the kings of England and France, there was great rivalry among the three rulers. When the Emperor of Germany died, the crown, being elective, was sought for by Henry, Francis, and Charles.

When the French king heard that Charles was elected, he felt angry and afraid, because his hated rival now occupied the land all around him. He therefore thought it would be a very good plan to make a friend of Henry, who could help him in case of war with Charles. So Francis invited Henry to come over to France and meet him near Calais, where they could enjoy a talk and indulge in games of skill, of which they were equally fond.

Henry gladly accepted this invitation, and got ready to go to France. But Charles, hearing of this plan, secretly crossed over to England, so as to see Henry first. His aim was to make himself so agreeable that Henry would not care to become the French king's ally. Charles won Henry's favour by calling him uncle, and secretly promised the king's minister, Wolsey (wŏŏl'zĭ), to help him become pope as soon as the present pope died.

Now you must know that Wolsey was a very ambitious man. Although only the son of a poor butcher, he had worked very hard to get a college education. Next he became a priest, and was so clever that Henry VII. engaged him as tutor for his children.

Little by little Wolsey won the king's confidence; and as he always did what he was told, and did it well and promptly, he soon rose in rank. Henry VIII. found him very useful, and as Wolsey flattered the young king, the latter liked him and made him Chancellor of State. Proud and even stern with every one else, Wolsey was always gentle and humble with the king, in whose name he really governed, although he pretended to be only a servant.

Henry was so generous that he is said to have given large estates to a lady who made him a good pudding, and to a gentleman who pushed his chair away from a too hot fire. You can understand from that how richly he would reward such a man as Wolsey, who soon lived almost as magnificently as the king, and owned the two palaces of Whitehall and Hampton Court.

Besides being chancellor, Wolsey was Archbishop of York and cardinal, and when the emperor promised to help him become pope in due time, he was greatly pleased. The visit over, Charles went home, while Henry and all his court went to France to see Francis I.

Sir John Gilbert, Artist.

Henry VIII. and Cardinal Wolsey.

Great preparations had been made near Calais for the reception of both courts. We are told that the camp was composed of nearly three thousand tents of silk and brocade, all decked with gorgeous banners. Both kings were fond of display, so there was seen a rare array of jewels, clothes, armour, horses, etc. In fact, there was such a glitter that the place was called the Field of the Cloth of Gold, and shows and diversions of all kinds were the order of the day. But while the kings and queens exchanged visits and viewed the gay tournaments, their ministers discussed matters of state. Every day the round of gaiety was more splendid than before.

Weary of the constant ceremonial, King Francis rode into the English camp alone one morning, and, entering Henry's tent, roused him from his morning slumbers by playfully crying, "You are my prisoner; behold your chains!" In saying these words, Francis took off his beautiful golden chain and put it around Henry's neck.

The English king then returned the compliment by giving Francis a costly bracelet; and when Henry rose, the French king helped him dress. The ice being thus broken, the kings freely rode in and out of each other's camp, and we are told they once enjoyed a wrestling bout together. But Henry's vanity was sorely tried when Francis threw him, and he did not feel comfortable until he had outshone his rival in archery.

When the gay doings on the Field of the Cloth of Gold ended, the kings parted and went home, without any decided alliance having been made. But shortly after this, Henry had a second interview with Charles, and became his ally.

LXX. THE NEW OPINIONS.

IN those days all Europe was in a state of excitement. The Reformation, begun so long before by Wyclif, had been steadily gaining ground; and although Wyclif's disciples, the Lollards, were sorely persecuted, their teachings had won converts in many parts of Europe.

Besides, the discovery of printing had brought into common use many books which had hitherto been in the hands of only a few learned men. The result was that people began to read more, and to form different opinions on all matters, especially on religion. These differences led sometimes to very serious disputes.

There was a man in Germany, Martin Luther, who had once been a monk, but who was now an ardent reformer; that is, he disagreed with the teachings of the Roman Catholic Church, and wrote in defence of his opinions.

This bold preaching by Martin Luther made a great stir in Germany, and while some of his hearers agreed with him, others thought he ought to be burned as a heretic, or man with wrong opinions. Among those who did not approve of Luther was Henry VIII. of England, who, after reading the reformer's book, wrote a treatise to show that he was wrong.

Priding himself upon his cleverness, Henry sent a copy of his work to the pope, who was so pleased with it that he bestowed upon the English monarch the name of "Defender of the Faith." This title is still borne by British sovereigns, and you can see it stamped on English coins to-day.

But although Henry thought it so very wicked of Luther not to obey the pope, you will soon see that he did not always do so himself. Henry had, as you remember, married his brother's widow, Catherine of Aragon. They had many children, but all died in infancy, except a sickly little girl named Mary.

As no woman had ever yet really reigned in England, Henry was afraid that if he died the crown would pass out of his family. He longed to have a son, was tired of Catherine, now that she was old, and wished he could marry one of her pretty waiting women, Anne Boleyn (bōōl'in), with whom he had fallen in love.

To get rid of Catherine, Henry first said he was sure God was displeased with him, because all his baby boys had died. Next he said that God must be angry because he had married his brother's widow, a marriage which the Catholic Church seldom allows.

When he had thus paved the way, Henry bade Wolsey send to Rome and ask the pope for a divorce. Wolsey obeyed, but although he tried very hard, he could not get the divorce. The fact was that the pope did not know what to do. He knew that the reformers were growing in numbers, and feared that if he refused, Henry VIII. would join their ranks. But if he granted the divorce he knew it would offend Queen Catherine's nephew, the Emperor Charles, who was master of all Italy, and who kept the pope almost a prisoner in Rome.

In spite of all Henry's urgings, therefore, the pope would not give a decided answer; but after a year of wavering, he sent his legate to talk over the matter with Wolsey. Now there was more delay, for the legate tried

Henry VIII. and Anne Boleyn.

to make Henry give up the divorce, while Wolsey tried to persuade Queen Catherine to withdraw into a nunnery. Neither would consent, and the king, angry at these delays, began to hate his former friend Wolsey. One day he asked the chancellor for the state accounts. By mistake, Wolsey brought the king his own private account book. Henry opened it, and, finding that the chancellor was far richer than he had ever supposed, grew jealous of his subject's wealth, and made up his mind to take back his presents. Wolsey was therefore forced to give up his two palaces, which became the property of the king, and to go and live at York.

LXXI. DEATH OF WOLSEY.

ALTHOUGH sent away from court in disgrace, Wolsey led so gay a life at York, and made such a display, that he won many admirers. This made Henry more jealous than ever, and as he needed more money, he suddenly sent officers to arrest his former favourite and bring him to the Tower.

This arrest broke Wolsey's heart, and as they journeyed on to London he became so ill that they had to stop at Leicester Abbey and lift him off his mule. Wolsey was by this time so feeble that he said to the abbot who came to greet him: "My father, I am come to lay my bones among you."

He was right; for, instead of getting better, he steadily sank, and died a few days later. His last words were: "Had I only served my God as diligently as I have served my king, he would not have left me alone in my gray hairs." You see, at the very end, Wolsey regretted that he had not always done what was right, regardless of the wishes of an ungrateful king.

All Wolsey's treasures fell, at his death, into the hands of the king, and the beautiful jewels he had collected became the ornaments of Anne Boleyn, who was the real cause of his sudden downfall.

In the meantime the king, who had not given up the idea of divorcing Catherine, overheard two of his officers discussing the matter with a clever young Oxford doctor named Thomas Cran'mer. This young man, who belonged to the Oxford reformers, frankly said that if he were in the king's place he would not wait for the pope's decision, but would ask the universities what they thought about it.

The eavesdropping king was so delighted with this suggestion that he hired Cranmer to write a book in favour of the divorce, gave him more and more of his confidence, and finally made him Archbishop of Canterbury. As soon as he became Primate of England, Cranmer declared that the king's marriage was against the law, that he had the right to take another wife, and that Princess Mary had no claim to the crown.

A few days after this, Henry, who had made a great pretence of being very sorry to part with Catherine, had Anne Boleyn crowned as his queen. But when the news of his divorce reached Rome the pope was very angry. He said that Cranmer had no right to decide the question, and that Catherine was still Henry's wife.

The pope's refusal to agree to the divorce made Henry so furious that he now called Parliament together, and made it declare that he was head of the church within his kingdom, as well as head of the kingdom itself. Henry also asked all his subjects to sign a paper to this effect, or take the oath of supremacy, as it was called.

Now, good Roman Catholics consider the pope head of the church, so some of them refused to sign the paper or take the oath. Among these were two great and good men, Fisher, the Bishop of Roch'es-ter, and Sir Thomas More, who had been named chancellor after Wolsey.

Besides being a good and noble man, Sir Thomas More was a man of genius. He had read the letters of A-mer'-

Sir Thomas More in Prison.

i-cus Ves-pu'cius as soon as they were printed, and had put his ideas about politics into a little story. In this book, he said that one of the companions of Vespucius had gone to the New World, where he had founded an ideal state called " U-to'pi-a " (Nowhere). Here all the people were equal, all were well educated, all were happy and healthy and good, and all had the right to worship God as they pleased.

The people of his time thought this story so absurd that Utopia was used—and is still—as we now use the word "fairyland." But since then a republic has been founded in the New World, where, as you know, people have the right to practise any religion they please, and we hope that some day it may become a real Utopia.

As Sir Thomas More and Fisher would not say that they accepted Henry as the head of the church, they were accused of treason, locked up in the Tower, tried, convicted, and sentenced to death. More was allowed a last parting with his favourite child, Margaret, who, after he had suffered death with great courage, bore away his remains to bury them.

LXXII. HENRY'S WIVES.

ALTHOUGH Henry had won his new wife with so much trouble, he was not long pleased with her. She was very beautiful, but two years after their marriage, and some time after the birth of her daughter Elizabeth, she was accused of a crime and sent to the Tower. Some writers say that Anne Boleyn was quite innocent, but that the king was tired of her and wished to marry another wife. Others insist that she was guilty, and deserved the death to which she was soon condemned.

However that may be, the fact remains that Anne Boleyn was led off to the block. She never complained about the king's cruelty, but merely said, with a sad smile, that she would soon be out of pain, for she had a very small neck. As soon as Anne had been beheaded, Parliament decreed that her daughter Elizabeth should not reign, just as it had already decreed with regard to Mary.

The very day after Anne Boleyn's death, the unfeeling king married a beautiful English girl, Jane Seymour (see'-moor). The new queen was gentle and good, and, happily for her, died before her fickle husband could get tired of her too. She left a little son named Edward, and the people were so glad to hear there was a male heir at last, that they celebrated his birthday with great rejoicings.

Ever since Wolsey's fall from power, the king had been helped by a man named Crom'well, who now held high office. Seeing that Henry was anxious to marry again, Cromwell suggested that he should choose some princess.

But none of the European princesses wanted to marry a king who had already had three wives, one of whom had been beheaded and another divorced. Indeed, one of the ladies who was asked to share his throne, refused, saying, "I have but one head; if I had two, one would be at his majesty's disposal."

As Cromwell was a reformer, he wished his master to marry a Protestant, and showed him the portrait of Anne of Cleves. Henry was so pleased with the lady's appearance that he sent for her to come and marry him. But when he saw her, and found out that her portrait had flattered her, he was very angry, and was rude enough to mutter, "I don't want to marry that Flanders mare!"

To avoid quarrelling with the lady's relatives, however, he did marry her; but as she was stupid, and could speak only Dutch, he soon decided to divorce her. First, he vented his displeasure by beheading Cromwell. Then he had Parliament declare his divorce from Anne of Cleves, who received a palace and a handsome income, and lived very comfortably all by herself.

A fortnight later Henry VIII. married a fifth wife, Catherine Howard. But when he discovered that she was a wicked woman, he promptly had her beheaded, and married Catherine Parr, a widow, who had the good fortune to survive him.

Ever since Henry had been named head of the church he thought that he knew all there was to know about religion. Whenever he argued about it, he was very angry if any one disagreed with him. He was so self-willed that if people had different opinions from his they were persecuted. Roman Catholics were put to death for considering the pope head of the church, and Protestants were treated in the same way if they did not accept certain Catholic doctrines which Henry still believed.

During his long reign Henry's opinions underwent sundry changes. For instance, he first ordered that an English Bible should be placed in every church, where people could come and read it for themselves if they chose. But when he found out that those who read the Bible often formed opinions different from his own, he decided that the books should be removed, and that none but learned men should have the right to see them.

Besides squandering his father's savings and Wolsey's property, Henry spent all the money he received as head of the church. He also sent men to examine all the churches and religious houses, and closed many of the latter, because, he said, the monks had grown rich and lazy and were not doing the good work they should among the poor. The only person who never felt Henry's anger was Cranmer, who, however, often disagreed with him. But Cranmer generally did as the king wished him to, and some say that whenever Henry wanted to do anything specially wrong he sent the archbishop away for a time, so that he should not try to oppose it.

It was owing to Cranmer that English came to be used in the services of the church. This marked him as a leader among those who favoured Protestant ideas. Both Cranmer and Wolsey were, like Henry, very fond of books, and encouraged learning as much as possible.

LXXIII. THE KING AND THE PAINTER.

HENRY VIII. was so fond of interviews that he once arranged one with James V. of Scotland. But either the Scots were afraid their king would be made a prisoner, or the Scotch king wished to please the Catholics. Anyway, Henry vainly waited for his fellow-monarch, and when he saw that James was not coming, he declared war against Scotland.

The troops of James V. were defeated at Solway Moss, and he felt so badly over the loss of his followers that he soon after died of grief, leaving the crown to his little daughter Mary, who became Queen of Scotland. Henry now proposed a marriage between this queen and his son Edward, which would unite the Scotch and English crowns. The nobles at first consented, to it, but it never took place.

Besides the French war mentioned in the beginning of Henry's reign, there was a second, in which the English won Boulogne (boo-lōn'), which, however, they promised to give back to France at the end of seven years.

As Henry waxed older he grew very stout, suffered a great deal from illness, and became so violent in temper that every one was afraid of him. We are told that even Parliament dared not disobey him, for he once said to one of the members: "Get my bill passed to-morrow, or else to-morrow this head of yours shall be off."

The queen once incurred his wrath simply because she differed from him in a religious argument. But when she found out that the king was going to have her tried for heresy, she disarmed his anger by saying that she loved to hear him argue because he was so clever.

Henry not only encouraged learning, but he was also very fond of painting, and engaged the German artist Hol'- bein to paint his portrait. He had great respect for men of talent, and when a courtier once complained that Holbein had insulted him by sending him out of the studio, into which he had forced his way, the king answered:

"It is I, in the person of Holbein, who have been insulted. I can, when I please, make seven lords of seven ploughmen; but I cannot make one Holbein even of seven lords."

Besides learning, Henry also encouraged commerce, which, under him, became very flourishing. But there was a new kind of trade begun in his reign which was not to his credit. This was slave trading, and it was many years before that wicked traffic came to an end.

Henry reigned thirty-eight years, and when his people saw that he was dying, they did not dare tell him so, lest they should be accused of high treason and put to death. Finally, however, a very old man plucked up courage enough to inform the king that he was nearing his end.

Instead of flying into a rage as every one expected, Henry took the news very calmly. He said that his son Edward should succeed him, and as the lad was delicate, he arranged that if the prince died without leaving any children, the crown should go to Mary, and after her to Elizabeth, and after them to his youngest sister, the Duchess of Suffolk. When all his arrangements had been made, Henry died; and all breathed a sigh of relief at the thought that the tyrannical ruler could frighten them no more.

LXXIV. A BOY KING.

EDWARD VI. was only nine years old when he was crowned King of England. His father, Henry VIII., had decided that until he was old enough to reign alone, the government should be in the hands of Cranmer and a council. But as soon as the king was dead, the Duke of Somerset was named Protector of England.

The little king was a gentle, lovable, and studious child. He had been brought up in the new religious ideas, and liked nothing better than to study theology or to listen to long sermons. As he was very delicate and needed a great deal of fresh air, his favourite preacher, the reformer Lat'i-mer, had a pulpit placed out in the garden under a tree, so that Edward could enjoy sermons out of doors.

All the little king's teachers were Protestants, and they said he was a remarkably studious lad. They must have been right; for some of his Latin exercises have been kept, and they are unusually good for a boy of his age.

Although Cranmer was not allowed to govern, he was given authority to make any changes he thought desirable in the religion of the country. He therefore, in accordance with his Protestant ideas, stopped all Latin services, and arranged a Book of Common Prayer, almost the same as that still in use to-day in the Church of England and in the Episcopal Church in America.

Although the king was so kind that he hated to pain any one, and shed tears whenever he was forced to sign a death-warrant, he became very angry with his sister Mary, because she would not change her religion. He forbade her to hear mass in public. But in spite of all he said, Mary continued firm and would never consent to listen to any of his favourite sermons.

While King Edward VI. was busy with his books and studies, the Duke of Somerset governed the kingdom; and as he was a zealous Protestant, he took the pictures and statues out of the churches, closed up many monasteries and convents, and told the monks and nuns to go out into the world and earn their living. The money he took from the religious houses was used to found schools and hospitals, or given to new lords.

Most of the monks and nuns had been so good to the poor people near them, that the latter grumbled sorely when they saw these holy men and women in need. Twice during Edward's short reign the peasants revolted, and twice they had to be put down by force.

But in spite of this resistance, the Protestant movement went on; and while under Henry VIII. the people had practised the Catholic religion, without a pope, they now had a distinctly Protestant form of worship. All had to worship as the king wished, or suffer punishment. Two important persons refused to obey; but while one of them, Bishop Gardiner (gard'ner), was imprisoned, the other, the king's sister, was allowed to hear mass in her own room.

The Duke of Somerset soon thought it time that the marriage between the young king and Mary, Queen of Scots, should take place. But as most of the Scotch were still good Catholics, they did not want their sovereign to marry a Protestant. Somerset decided to force them to obey; and, using the pretext that some of the border men had fought against the English, he invaded Scotland.

The English army marched almost to Edinburgh (ed'in-bur-ro), where it met a very large Scotch force. Somerset, frightened, offered peace; but the Scotchmen felt so sure of victory that they would not accept it. To their surprise, they were completely beaten, at Pinkie, and lost ten thousand men, while the English lost only three hundred.

Among the prisoners taken during the fight was a Scotch nobleman. Somerset asked him why he objected to the match between the English king and the Scotch queen, and he answered quickly: "I dislike not the match, but I hate the manner of the wooing."

Trouble having arisen in England, Somerset made peace with Scotland. But the little queen was sent over to

France, so as to be out of reach of the English, and to be brought up in a Roman Catholic country. In time she became Queen of France, for she married Francis II.

On coming back to England, Somerset discovered that his own brother had been plotting against him. Influenced by the bad advice of a son of the lawyer Dudley (who before long was made Duke of Nor-thum'ber-land), Somerset accused his brother of treason, and had him arrested, tried, condemned, and executed. Soon after this, Northumberland, taking advantage of the discontent among the poor, who were grumbling because the protector was building a new palace, accused Somerset of high treason. It was he who was now arrested, tried, sentenced, and executed, just as his brother had been.

Edward was only thirteen at the time, so the power was placed in the hands of Northumberland. The latter soon noticed that the king would probably not live long, and he became anxious that the crown should pass into his own family. With this purpose in view, he told the little king that he ought to make a will.

You know that Parliament had decreed, during the reign of Henry, that neither Mary nor Elizabeth should reign; but later on the same body had said that Henry could leave the throne to any one he wished. Henry had therefore said that the crown should pass in turn to Edward, Mary, Elizabeth, and then to the Suffolks if all his children died childless. To induce Edward to make a will, Northumberland said that if Mary became queen the Catholic religion would again be introduced. He added that if Mary were set aside Elizabeth must be also, although she was a Protestant, and coaxed Edward to make a will in favour of Lady Jane Grey, one of the Suffolks, who had married Northumberland's son Dudley.

Edward VI., who was failing fast, yielded to these entreaties, and made a will which was witnessed by Cranmer. Shortly after that, the doctors having vainly tried to cure him, Northumberland placed him under the care of an ignorant old woman, who vowed she could make him well. But instead of gaining strength, Edward soon died, praying that the reformed religion might continue in England. Some people believe that he was the victim of consumption; but others, who hated Northumberland, began to whisper that the latter had poisoned the prince, so that Dudley might reign.

LXXV. THE STORY OF LADY JANE GREY.

WHEN Edward VI. breathed his last, Northumberland tried to keep his death a secret until he could get possession of Mary and Elizabeth. He wanted to put them in prison, to prevent their opposing the coronation of his daughter-in-law, Lady Jane Grey. But the news reached Mary while she was on her way to visit her sick brother. She took refuge in a castle near the seashore, and merely sent an order to Parliament to proclaim her queen.

Northumberland, seeing he could not get the princesses into his power, now went to Lady Jane Grey with several members of the council, and did homage to her as queen. Lady Jane Grey, who was a most charming young lady of sixteen, was greatly surprised when she heard what he had to tell her, and gently answered that the crown ought to go to her cousin Mary, to Elizabeth, or even to Mary, Queen of Scots, before it could be hers. But her father-in-law insisted that she must be queen; and as young people in those days were taught to obey implicitly, and even middle-aged sons and daughters had to be as submissive

C. R. Leslie, Artist.
Offering the Crown to Lady Jane Grey.

as little children, she dared not resist. She was therefore forced to leave her quiet home, where her chief pleasure had been study, and go and dwell in the gloomy Tower.

She was led thither in state; but no one cheered as she passed by, for all knew that she had no right to the throne, and that Mary was the real queen. People were not very joyful, however, at the prospect of Mary's rule, for she was homely, sickly, and not very well educated, and the Protestants feared she would restore the Catholic religion.

Still, they would not oppose her, and Northumberland could secure only a very small army to uphold Lady Jane Grey. As soon as he had left London with it, the council went to Lady Jane Grey and persuaded her to return home, after a reign of ten days. You may be sure she was glad to give up the crown, which she had never wanted, and to return to her quiet house and her beloved books.

Meantime Northumberland's friends had nearly all deserted him, and he had soon fallen into Mary's hands. In spite of his humble entreaties to be spared, she sent him to prison and had him executed for high treason. Then, upon reaching London, she ordered that all the imprisoned Roman Catholics should be set free, and took Gardiner for her adviser. Mary opened her first Parliament with public mass, and sent a messenger to Rome to ask the pope to forgive the English for having said he was not head of the church. Then she forbade all the clergymen to preach until they had received a license from her. This permission was granted only to those who were willing to recognize the pope and be good Roman Catholics.

Many reformers were next whipped, fined, or imprisoned, and, knowing that Mary would soon do worse, some of them left the country. Latin services were once more heard in the churches, where pictures and statues again found a place, and many of the monasteries were given back to their holy inmates.

But while Mary was making these changes, she was haunted by the thought that if she died without children her sister Elizabeth would become queen and undo all her work. For that reason she took a Roman Catholic husband, Philip, the son of Charles V., King of Spain.

This marriage was allowed by Parliament, but only on condition that Philip should have no share in the government, and that if his wife died before him, and they had no children, the crown should go to Elizabeth. This made Philip dislike both the English and his homely wife.

Although Parliament consented to Mary's marriage, many of the English opposed it, for they had heard how cruelly Philip treated all Protestants in his lands. Some of the most indignant even rebelled and marched up to London, under the leadership of a man named Wy'att. Their intention was to dethrone Mary and give the crown to Lady Jane Grey; but they were defeated, and Wyatt and several others were executed.

To prevent any more plots of the same kind, Lady Jane Grey and her husband were sent to the Tower and sentenced to death for high treason. Dudley, who was as noble as his wife, begged that they might see each other once more before dying; but Lady Jane Grey said that an interview would only rob them of some of the courage necessary to meet their fate. She nevertheless sent him a last message, saying, "Our separation will be only for a moment, and we shall soon rejoin each other in a scene where our affections will be for ever united, and where nothing can have access to disturb our eternal happiness."

Dudley was led away to the block first, and from her window Lady Jane Grey saw his body borne to the tomb. A moment later, the jailer came to summon her to die in her turn. She calmly followed him to the scaffold, told the people she deserved death because she had not refused the crown more firmly, and, breathing a last prayer, laid her head upon the block.

LXXVI. THE DEATH OF CRANMER.

THE execution of Lady Jane Grey, and of those who were suspected of having sided with her, did not incline the people to love either Mary or Philip. The English disliked Philip because his manners were very bad, because he was so rude as to treat his wife with contempt, and because he urged her to persecute the reformers and make every one practise the Catholic religion.

The pope had consented to forgive the English, at Mary's entreaty, and had sent his legate, Cardinal Pole, to England. This man was very good and gentle, and he advised Mary and Philip not to illtreat the Protestants; but they would not listen to him.

In those days it was still the custom for those in power to persecute all who held opinions different from their own. When the Protestants were in power they had persecuted all who did not believe as they did. So now the Catholics began to persecute the Protestants. All who upheld the Protestant religion were very unkindly treated, and about three hundred were burned at the stake as heretics.

Among these were two good old preachers, Latimer and Ridley. They were hated by Mary's principal adviser, Gardiner, who was so anxious to have them die that he said, on the day of their execution, that he would not dine until he knew they were burned. As the two friends walked together to the place of torture, encouraging one another, Latimer said: " Be of good cheer, Brother Ridley; we shall this day light such a candle, by God's grace, in England, as I trust shall never be put out."

Latimer and Ridley were fastened to the stake, and some of their friends charitably tied packages of gunpowder around their waists, so that their tortures should not be too prolonged. But in spite of these precautions, the fire burned so slowly that the poor men suffered untold agonies. The cruel Gardiner was forced to delay his dinner four hours. But it is said he could not eat it then, for he was suddenly stricken by an illness from which he died.

Another who suffered death was the aged Cranmer, whom Mary hated, partly because it was he who had divorced her mother and had witnessed Edward's will. He was accused of high treason and of heresy, and on the latter charge was sentenced to be burned alive. Cranmer was, on the whole, a good man, but he shrank from bodily suffering. So, when told he would be forgiven if he would sign a paper recognizing the pope and giving up the Protestant religion, he had not the courage to refuse.

But Mary had no real intention of letting him go unpunished; and when Cranmer learned this, he became defiant and refused to read this paper at the stake. The queen's officers vainly tried to prevent his speaking to the assembled people; he cried aloud that he regretted his momentary weakness, and said that, as his right hand had offended by signing a lie, it should be burned first.

Saying these words, Cranmer thrust his hand into the fire, and firmly held it there until it was burned off. His courageous behaviour in the midst of awful torture greatly impressed the people. In fact, all these cruel punishments, which earned for the queen among her enemies the harsh title of "Bloody Mary," had, as the pope's wise legate had foreseen, an effect just contrary to that which she had hoped. Yet Mary thought she was doing right, for Philip urged her to be even more severe. She was always a very unhappy woman, for few people ever loved her. Her husband soon left her and went over to Flanders, where he did not even take the trouble to read the long letters she sent him. He was making war there, and needed a great deal of money; so Mary, hoping to win his affections, sent him all she could.

To supply him with funds, she loaded her people with taxes, and by his order she declared war against France. Parliament would not at first consent to this war; but Mary, it is said, got down on her knees to beseech the members to do as her husband wished. Then a force of ten thousand men was sent over to Philip, who won a victory at St. Quentin (saN koN-taN').

This success was soon offset by a great loss. The French, beaten at St. Quentin, but knowing that Calais was poorly defended, surprised two of the forts that protected it, and forced the city to surrender after a week's siege. It was thus that Calais, which had been taken by Edward III. after a ten months' siege, and had been in the hands of the English about two hundred years, became once more, in 1558, the property of the French.

The news reached England on New Year's day, and filled the country with dismay. Mary bewailed the loss of "the brightest jewel in her crown," and said that "Calais" would be found graven upon her heart after she was dead.

This loss, added to her other sorrows, so weakened her health that she died the same year. Few regretted her, and as she left no children, the crown passed on to her half-sister Elizabeth, the only living child of Henry VIII.

LXXVII. A CLEVER QUEEN.

PARLIAMENT was sitting when Mary, Queen of England, breathed her last; and when her death was announced, the members all sprang from their seats with shouts of joy, and cries of " God save Queen Elizabeth!" The news was received in the same way throughout the kingdom, and was no less welcome to the new queen, who had spent the last five years in captivity at Hatfield House.

Elizabeth now came to London, where she was joyfully welcomed, and where one of her first acts was to order the release of all who were prisoners on account of their religion. She selected Lord Burleigh (bur'ly), her brother's adviser, as her chief minister, and for the next forty years this able man ruled the country wisely.

At Elizabeth's first Parliament the Protestants came to beg her to release four important prisoners; and when the queen asked their names, they answered that these captives were Matthew, Mark, Luke, and John, who were bound fast in the Latin language. Elizabeth smiled when they said this, but soon answered that she would first inquire whether these prisoners wished to be set free.

She therefore assembled a council to discuss religious matters; and this council decided that it was best for the people to have prayers, hymns, and Scriptures in English. The Church of England, or An'gli-can Church, was therefore again declared the church of the country, and nine thousand priests were given their choice — to adopt the Anglican services and recognize the queen as head of the church, or to give up their positions. Only two hundred went away, and as their places were given to Protestants, the whole country was soon under the same teaching.

Thus the change was gradually made, but so gently that not one drop of blood was shed or one estate confiscated. As soon as this was known abroad, the exiled Protestants came flocking back. Some of them brought home from France and Germany what they called purer ideas of worship, so they were called Pu'ri-tans.

Elizabeth was twenty-five when she came to the throne. She was rather good-looking, very clever and well educated, generous, and forgiving. But she had also three great failings: she was vain, untruthful, and of a violent temper. She showed her forgiving nature by not trying to avenge any of her past injuries. Even to a jailer who had been very unkind to her, she only remarked that he should have the keeping of any prisoner whom she wished treated with great severity.

Queen Elizabeth.

Elizabeth was extravagantly fond of dress and display, and her coronation was a splendid affair. The streets were hung with tapestry and strewn with flowers; there were triumphal arches, shows, speeches, and presents without number; flags waved, bells rang, bonfires were lighted, and it seemed as if the whole nation had gone mad with joy.

Elizabeth had been so well taught by her tutor Ascham

(as'kam) that she was able to reign wisely. When she came to the throne the country was in debt, the money was bad, there was no good army or navy, and she saw that it would take time to make England what she wanted it to become—one of the foremost countries of the world.

Helped by her clever ministers, Burleigh and Wal'singham, Elizabeth began her reforms, and she went ahead so steadily that she soon saw great progress and in time reached her aim. By her order commerce and manufacture were encouraged, the army was properly drilled, and the navy was increased till she won the title of " Queen of the Northern Seas."

LXXVIII. ELIZABETH'S LOVERS.

IN spite of all her activity in state matters, Elizabeth's court was very brilliant and gay, and the people who gathered around her rivalled one another in the splendour of their garments, and in the fulsome compliments which they paid to the queen. Although so sensible when discussing business matters with her ministers, Elizabeth was often very silly, and chose her courtiers more for their good looks or skill in flattering her than for other talents.

She was at times very dignified, and made her courtiers address her only on bended knee; but at other moments her manners were very coarse. We are told that she used to swear very freely, slap her courtiers on the back, and box the ears of those who ventured to displease her. Her favourites were often changed; but there was one among them, a brother-in-law of Lady Jane Grey, whom she made

Earl of Leicester and treated with such marked favour that every one fancied she loved him.

Leicester himself thought that the queen would marry him, were he only free; and some stories say that he killed his gentle wife, Amy Robsart, to whom he had secretly been united, so as to marry Elizabeth. But while the queen took great delight in being admired and made love to by many suitors, she never accepted any of them, and is hence known as the unmarried, virgin, or maiden queen.

One of Elizabeth's first suitors was her sister's husband, Philip II., King of Spain. Although she never had the least intention of accepting him, she delayed giving him an answer as long as she could; for she was afraid that if she refused Philip he would make war against England before her army and navy were in good condition.

When she finally said no to him, she told him it was because she never meant to marry at all. But in spite of this decision, she afterwards allowed the Duke of Alençon (ah-loN-sawN') to court her for ten years. Finally a marriage contract was signed, but Elizabeth jilted this prince within a few weeks of the time fixed for her wedding.

Although Elizabeth never gave any special reason for not accepting one of her many lovers, people have said that it was because she wanted to keep all the power in her own hands. But because she had no brothers or sisters left, it was very important that she should either marry and leave the crown to her children, or decide who should have it after her death.

You remember, do you not, how angry the pope was when Henry VIII. divorced Queen Catherine, and how he said that she was still Henry's wife? Well, as soon as Elizabeth (Anne Boleyn's daughter) was crowned, the pope sent her a message saying that the crown did not really belong to her, but that if she would abide by his decision he would see whether she could be queen or not.

Elizabeth paid no attention to this message, for she had decided to act like her father and refuse to obey the pope. As she did not do as he suggested, the pope now excommunicated her, and wrote to Mary Stu'art that he gave the crown of England to her, as she was the next heir.

So Mary, Queen of Scotland and France, took the title of Queen of England also; and she sent a French army to Scotland to join the Catholics there in making war against Elizabeth. But when the French reached Scotland they found that matters had changed very much since Mary had gone to France. A great Protestant preacher named Knox had preached to the Scotch so persuasively

Mary Stuart.

that, instead of remaining Catholics, most of them had now become even stancher Protestants than the English.

As the Scotch knew that Mary and the pope wanted to restore the Catholic religion, they not only refused to help her, but actually sided with Elizabeth and forced Mary to give up her attempt. Shortly after this, the young French king died, and his nineteen-year-old widow sadly left France to return to her native country.

LXXIX. MARY, QUEEN OF SCOTS.

WHEN Mary reached Scotland, she was disgusted at the rude manners of the Scotchmen. She was beautiful and charming, loved dancing and music, dressed elegantly, and wished to have a gay court, such as she had seen in France. But the Scotch had become so strict that they looked upon dancing as a crime, and fancied that such a queen must be very wicked.

The Scotch Protestants tried to make Mary change her religion, and Knox fiercely reproved her for her gaiety; but she would not listen to him, and went on hearing mass, saying that her people might worship as they chose, provided they let her do the same. As Mary had no children, the Scotchmen soon urged her to marry again; and she, hoping to make Elizabeth her friend, begged the Queen of England to find her a suitable husband.

Elizabeth, who was jealous of Mary because the latter was younger and prettier than she, now proposed several husbands whom she knew Mary would not accept. Among these was her favourite Leicester, who, despairing of ever winning her, was willing to marry Mary.

But she would not accept him, and finally chose her cousin, Lord Darnley, a Roman Catholic and the next heir to the thrones both of England and of Scotland.

This marriage displeased the Protestants and Elizabeth, and Darnley proved so fickle and bad-tempered that Mary soon ceased to find pleasure in his company. To amuse herself she used to spend hours in her own room, with her ladies and her secretary Rizzio (rit′se-o), a gal-

Mary Stuart and Rizzio.

lant young musician who pleased her by accompanying her gay French songs on his lute.

Before very long Darnley became so jealous of Rizzio that he burst into his wife's rooms one day, accompanied by several nobles. There Rizzio was murdered, in spite of all her entreaties. This crime so angered Mary that we are told she soon dried her eyes, muttering, "No more tears; let's think of revenge."

But although she now hated Darnley, she pretended to be on good terms with him; and once, when he was ill with smallpox, and could not stay in Holyrood Palace lest he should give the disease to their little son James, she went to nurse him in a cottage. One day, when he was nearly well, the queen went back to the palace, to see the wedding of one of her servants. That same night, while Mary slept at Holyrood, the Edinburgh people were awakened by a terrific explosion. They ran outdoors, and soon found out that Darnley's cottage had been blown up with gunpowder, and that he and his servant were dead.

It was, of course, perfectly clear that Darnley had been murdered, and the people began to mutter that the crime had been committed by the Earl of Böth'well. As he had been a favourite of the queen, some of them added that Mary had had a share in contriving the murder.

But when the case was tried, a few days later, and Bothwell came riding into the city with a large body-guard of hired soldiers, no one dared accuse him openly, and he was acquitted. Shortly after, he suddenly appeared with a thousand men and carried off the queen to the Castle of Dunbar. There he kept her a prisoner until she consented to marry him, three months later.

LXXX. CAPTIVITY OF MARY STUART.

NOW, you must know that the story of Mary Stuart is perplexing. Some people say she was a very good but a very unfortunate woman, while others say that she was very wicked. The reformers thought she was so bad that she had killed Darnley so as to marry Bothwell, and they indignantly rose up against her.

Mur'ray, one of her relatives, headed the rebels, defeated her troops, and took her prisoner. Bothwell, however, managed to escape, and, knowing it would never be safe for him to come back to Scotland, he went to the Orkney Islands. There he became a pirate; but after some years spent thus he was captured and put into a Danish dungeon, where he died, a raving maniac.

Murray now took charge of the government, sending Mary to Loch-le'ven Castle, in the middle of a Scotch lake, whence he fancied she could not escape. The Scotch Parliament next decided that Mary ought to give up the crown to her son James VI., and that Murray should be regent until he could reign alone. So a paper was carried to Mary in Lochleven Castle, and she was forced to sign it and give the crown to her infant son.

Prison life soon became so irksome to Mary that she made several efforts to escape. Once she bribed a washerwoman to exchange clothes with her, and then left the castle in the boat which had brought the woman. But she was soon detected by the whiteness and delicacy of her hands, and was brought back to her prison.

Mary made several other unsuccessful attempts, but

finally escaped with the help of a boy called George Douglas. Friends were waiting to meet her, and Mary, having raised a small army, marched against Murray, who was coming to recapture her.

Although she commanded her troops in person, Mary was defeated. Fearing that the Scotch would again imprison her, she fled in haste from the battlefield. Without pausing once to rest, she rode sixty miles to the frontier, and, crossing Solway Firth, came into England.

Then she wrote a letter to Elizabeth, begging her protection. On receiving this message, Elizabeth pretended that she would be very glad to welcome Mary as her guest, but she said that she could not do so until the Queen of Scots was cleared from the charge of helping to murder Darnley.

Elizabeth therefore sent attendants to Mary, who was lodged in a castle, while a committee was appointed to try her. There were witnesses for and against her, but it was not settled whether she was innocent or guilty. Elizabeth said that as long as the matter was undecided she could neither receive her kinswoman nor allow her to leave England, and on this pretext kept her a prisoner.

At first the Queen of Scots was not kept in close captivity, for we are told that she was allowed to go out as much as she pleased, and to receive visitors. But when Elizabeth saw that Mary's beauty, intelligence, and patience won her many friends, she began to grow uneasy. Her uneasiness was increased by a plot which was made by the Catholics to kill her, free Mary, and place the latter on the throne of England.

This conspiracy was discovered in time, as well as two

others formed by Nor'folk and Bab'ing-ton, and most of those who took part in them were executed. After each attempt to set Mary free, her residence was changed, and at last she was taken to Foth'er-in-gay Castle. Here she was tried, found guilty of plotting against Elizabeth, and although she insisted that she was innocent of all crime, she was condemned to death as a traitor.

The news of this sentence was received with horror by the French and the Scotch, who both sent ambassadors to England to protest against its being carried out. But Parliament insisted that neither the queen nor the country would be safe so long as Mary lived, so Elizabeth reluctantly signed the death-warrant.

Mary calmly heard this paper read to her, prepared for death, wrote her will, and, after sleeping peacefully for a few hours, rose and dressed as richly as possible. At her request, a few of her most faithful servants were allowed to accompany her to the scaffold, which was erected in the great hall of the castle.

There, after freely forgiving the executioners who knelt before her to beg her pardon, Mary, Queen of Scotland, committed her soul to God, and, laying her head upon the block, gave the signal for her death. She had been a prisoner about nineteen years.

When she was dead, Elizabeth seemed to regret her execution. She even wore mourning for her, and sent away one of her ministers, on the ground that he had had the death-warrant executed after she had recalled it.

LXXXI. WRECK OF THE SPANISH ARMADA.

PARLIAMENT had fancied that when Mary was dead all trouble from the Catholics would be ended, because they would have no person of their faith to set upon the throne. Parliament was mistaken, however, for Mary in her will left her claims to the throne of England to Philip II. of Spain, the champion of the Roman Catholic Church, and a descendant of the English house of Lancaster.

Philip II. had several reasons for hating the English. First, he was angry because they had received him coldly and refused him a share in the government when he married Queen Mary; second, Elizabeth had refused to marry him; third, she had either secretly or openly helped the Protestants in the Netherlands when they revolted against him; fourth, Elizabeth—in order to punish him for training students in his universities to believe that any one who murdered her would do a good deed—had allowed many of her captains to capture his gold-laden ships on their way from America to Spain.

These reasons, added to Mary's will, gave Philip II. the excuses he wanted for making war against England. He therefore prepared an immense army at Dunkirk, under the Duke of Alva, his best general, and a huge fleet at Ca'diz. His ships were so large that he proudly fancied no one could resist them, so he boastingly called this fleet the never-to-be-beaten, or Invincible Ar-ma'da.

The news of the coming war and of Philip's vast preparations terrified the English. Elizabeth, however, did not seem to lose courage, and her noble example inspired all those around her with hope. Troops were drilled, vessels were manned, and arrangements of all kinds were made. Elizabeth herself rode through her army's camp, vowing that she wished she were a man, so that she might fight too.

Her greatest helper at this time was one of her bravest seamen, Sir Francis Drake. He had made many journeys to America, had captured several gold-laden galleons, and was the first Englishman to see the Pacific and sail around the globe. This man was bold, clever, and so daring that he actually made his way into the harbour of Cadiz and destroyed part of the ships and stores collected there.

Nothing daunted, Philip repaired his losses; but the Invincible Armada no sooner started out than it met a severe gale and had to put back into port. Finally, however, it sailed northward, and a Scotch pirate, who was the first to discover it, gave the alarm in England. There, as had been agreed, signal fires were lighted all along the shore to warn fleet and army of the coming attack.

The ships which composed the Armada were much larger than the English vessels, and twice as numerous. The English fleet was under the orders of Admiral Howard; but Drake, Hawkins, Frob'ish-er, Winter, and Raleigh (raw'ly), all noted English seamen, commanded a few vessels, and by their daring helped him greatly.

The Spanish galleys were so heavy that they moved slowly, and the English seamen took advantage of this to seize or sink all those which lagged behind the rest. They followed the fleet up the Channel, and when it anchored off Calais, sent into its midst boats filled with burning materials.

The Spaniards, fearing that their vessels would catch fire, cut their cables and scattered wildly, and many ships were captured, one by one, by the English. Seeing that he was worsted, the Spanish admiral wanted to return home; but as he did not dare run the gantlet by passing through the English Channel amid the English ships, he made up his mind to sail around the British Isles.

The English pursued him as long as their ammunition held out; and when they left him, a tempest arose, and many of his vessels were wrecked on the northern coast. Here the inhabitants murdered from five to seven thousand Spaniards; but a few were rescued, and made their homes among the Irish.

When the admiral came back to Spain with the battered remains of his Invincible Armada, Philip remarked that he had not expected him to make war against the billows. But the expedition was never renewed, and Elizabeth could pride herself upon having defeated a formidable enemy, thanks to her wise foresight in preparing for war ever since she had come to the throne. A medal was struck to commemorate the defeat of the Armada, and on it was the legend, "Jehovah blew, and they were scattered;" for the English rightly felt that the victory was not all due to their valour.

LXXXII. THE ELIZABETHAN AGE.

SIR WALTER RALEIGH was one of the men who distinguished themselves in the fight with the Armada. He was very clever; and after studying at Oxford, he fought for the Protestants in the Netherlands and in France.

Raleigh was fond of fine clothes and anxious to win the favour of the queen. So one day he dressed up in his best garments, and, placing himself in the queen's path, watched for her coming. Suddenly he saw her appear with her court, and pause in dismay at a muddy spot in the road. Rushing forward, the quick-witted Raleigh pulled off his elegant cloak and carefully spread it over the mire, thus allowing the queen to proceed without soiling her dainty shoes. This courtesy so pleased Elizabeth that she took Raleigh into favour, and soon after granted him an extensive tract of land in North America, which he called Virginia in honour of her, the Virgin Queen.

Another man highly esteemed by Elizabeth—Spenser, the author of a poem called the "Faerie Queene"—was introduced to her by Raleigh. But one of her principal courtiers was Sir Philip Sidney, who is noted for his goodness, his great talents as a writer, his beautiful manners, and especially for his truthfulness and generosity.

Sidney was also a brave general, and when he fell, mortally wounded, at the battle of Zut'phen, in Holland, his followers were in despair. One of them succeeded with great difficulty in bringing him a little water to drink. But Sir Philip, although he was longing for it, kindly gave it to a wounded soldier lying near him, saying, "Take it, friend; thy necessity is greater than mine." A few minutes later Sidney was dead. While he is honoured for his talents and courage, every one must feel that this unselfish action just before he died is the greatest of his deeds.

Raleigh, Spenser, and Sidney were not the only men of

Shakespeare at the Court of Elizabeth.
Ed. Ender, Artist.

(248)

letters, nor the greatest writers, of what is known as the Elizabethan Age. There were many other poets and prose writers whose works will some day interest you; but the greatest of them all was William Shakespeare.

This famous writer of plays came to London a poor young man, took a place as actor in a theatre, and often played before the queen. He soon discovered that he could also write plays, and he produced such fine tragedies and comedies that no other poet has ever been able to equal them, and they are now read and viewed with even more delight than in the days when he took part in them himself.

Besides the plays of Shakespeare and of the other writers of his time, Elizabeth delighted in pageants, or outdoor plays, and whenever she went to visit the great lords of her realm, they used to entertain her with such shows.

We are told that Elizabeth was very fond of making what was then called a "progress" through some part of her kingdom. On these state occasions she wore her richest garments and jewels, was carried in her litter by the noblest of her courtiers, attended by countless knights and ladies, and welcomed everywhere with music, fireworks, and festivities of all kinds.

One of the grandest of her progresses was made to the Castle of Kenilworth, where she went to visit her favourite Leicester, and where he spent a fortune

Ruins of Kenilworth Castle.

to please her. All this display was very agreeable to Elizabeth, who insisted upon seeing every one well dressed. She herself wore the most gorgeous apparel, but as she was afraid lest some one else should look better in one of her dresses than she, all her garments were carefully put away, and when she died three thousand discarded gowns were found hanging in her wardrobes.

LXXXIII. DEATH OF ELIZABETH.

WHEN Leicester grew too old to please Elizabeth, he presented to her his son-in-law, the handsome Essex. The queen lavished gifts of all kinds upon this favourite, and when Burleigh died, after serving her faithfully for forty years, she made Essex her principal adviser.

Trouble having arisen in Ireland, Elizabeth sent Essex thither to put down a rebellion headed by the Earl of Ty-rone'. But Essex had been spoiled by the favour shown him, and disobeyed the queen's orders. Hearing that she was angry, he came home without her permission, and forced his way into her presence all travel-stained.

The queen, who was already displeased, fancied that his soiled garments were a token of disrespect, and coldly bade him withdraw. This repulse was so unexpected that Essex fell ill; but when the queen heard he was suffering, she shed tears, and sent him soup from her own table.

Essex had made such grave blunders while in Ireland that a council was called to judge him; but he, thinking the queen had forgiven him, seemed not to fear a trial. He came about the court as usual, and when the queen refused to grant him a favour, he spitefully remarked that now she was an old woman she was as crooked in mind as in person. This speech was reported to Elizabeth, whose vanity was so hurt that she allowed the council to imprison and try her former favourite, and to sentence him to death for high treason.

But, according to one famous story, she fancied she could still help him, for she had once given him a ring, saying that if he should ever be in any trouble he need but send it to her and she would save him. Elizabeth felt sure Essex would make use of this ring to save his life, but it was not brought to her. Essex, on his part, could not believe that the queen would really allow him to die, and even on his way to the scaffold he kept watching for a messenger bringing his pardon.

Not very long after his death, the Countess of Nottingham begged the queen to come to her, as she wished to tell her something before she breathed her last. Elizabeth complied with this request, and then the dying countess confessed that Essex had given her a ring to carry to the queen, but that her husband would not let her do so. As she finished her confession she begged the queen to forgive her; but Elizabeth angrily shook her, saying, " God may forgive you, but I never can!"

Perhaps this romantic tale is true, and it was this confession she had just heard that embittered the rest of Elizabeth's life. Anyway, she soon became ill, took no food, and lay on the floor ten days, refusing to be moved. Her attendants supported her there with cushions, and when she became too ill to resist, they put her into her bed, where she died (1603).

Although Elizabeth was a tyrannical ruler for forty-five years, she had so many fine qualities that she was called, and is still known, as " good Queen Bess." She was the last of the five rulers of the Tudor line.

LXXXIV. A SCOTCH KING.

ONE hundred and eighteen years had passed since the Tudors first became masters of England on Bosworth battlefield. There were no Tudors left, and as Elizabeth had never before been willing to name a successor, her ministers, as she lay on her deathbed, begged her to appoint one. She was then too weak to speak, but nodded her approval when they suggested that the crown should go to her nearest relative, James VI. of Scotland, the only child of Mary Stuart and Darnley.

This monarch, who was already thirty-seven years old, therefore became King of England, which, with Scotland, is called Great Britain. But although the crowns were united, the parliaments were separate for about a century longer. James I. of England, as the new king was called, immediately set out for his new realm, and on his journey thither he gave the title of knight to many men. He had been born a Roman Catholic and brought up a Puritan; but he now favoured the Church of England, to the disappointment of both Catholics and Puritans.

A few of the former, seeing he would not restore the

Catholic religion, as they had hoped, now made a conspiracy to put his cousin Lady Arabella Stuart upon the throne. They failed, however; but as the poor lady had been merely their tool, she was at first kindly treated. When she escaped from prison and married, James had her captured again and closely guarded until she died.

Several noted Catholic gentlemen were accused of having taken part in this plot, among others the famous Sir Walter Raleigh. He was imprisoned, tried, and sentenced like the rest; but for some reason he was reprieved, and spent the next twelve years in the Tower. Here he was allowed to receive visitors and to write and study as much as he pleased.

In the reign of Elizabeth tobacco was first brought to England by Raleigh. It was such a curiosity that a new servant, entering Sir Walter's room and finding him smoking, fancied that his master was on fire, and hastily flung a pitcherful of water over him. As James did not approve of smoking, he wrote a book against the practice, pompously calling it "A Counterblast to Tobacco." He was so proud of this work, and of all his intellectual gifts, that the French wittily called him "the wisest fool in Christendom."

James I. was homely, vain, stupid, and so untidy in person and habits that even his friends compared him to the filthiest of all animals. He was also mean, untruthful, and so fond of eating and drinking that he has often been called a drunkard and a glutton. His principal amusement lay in hunting and cockfighting, or, as he prided himself upon being very learned, in arguing about religion.

Hoping to settle all church difficulties, and especially to

show his talent in argument, James soon called a religious conference. Although this meeting did not do all that he had hoped, it decreed a careful revision of the Bible. During the next four years, it is said, fifty learned men worked hard at this translation, and finally printed what is still known as "King James's Bible."

The Puritans, Independents, Sep′a-ra-tists, and Non-con-form′ists, as those who would not conform to the established religion were called, would not yield. Parliament refused to change the laws, so James boastingly said: "I will make them conform, or I will harry them out of the kingdom."

It was because James was so determined to have his subjects worship as he wished, that some of them resolved to leave the country. A small band of Separatists first went over to Holland; but, seeing that their children would soon forget the English language and their native country if they continued to dwell there, they came back to England, and, embarking on the *Mayflower*, set sail for the New World to make their homes there. These Separatists, who are known as the Pilgrim Fathers, landed on Plym′outh Rock in 1620, and founded the first colony in New England.

LXXXV. THE GUNPOWDER PLOT.

SHORTLY after the king's religious convention, some of the Roman Catholics, seeing they would never get what they wanted from the king, formed a plot to blow him up, with his eldest son and all the members of Parliament. With this purpose in view, they hired the cellars under the hall where Parliament sat, and stored away there great quantities of gunpowder and fuel.

One of the conspirators, anxious to save the life of a friend, wrote him a letter warning him not to go to Parliament on a certain day, as his life would be in danger.

The Present Houses of Parliament (built since 1840).

This letter seemed so suspicious that the man who received it showed it to the king. James, on reading it, cleverly discovered its hidden meaning, and immediately sent some officers to visit the cellars under Parliament House.

These officers, entering unexpectedly, found there a man named Guy Fawkes, and seized him. It was well they did so, for when they searched him, they found he had a lantern and slow-match all ready. Clearing away the fuel, they next discovered the barrels of gunpowder, and a train all ready laid to set them off.

When they asked Guy Fawkes why he had so much powder stored there, he gruffly answered that it was to blow the Scotchmen back to Scotland. He was taken off to prison, where, under torture, he revealed the names of his fellow-conspirators. Those who had taken part in the Gunpowder Plot were arrested, and hanged, drawn, and quartered.

The narrow escape of the king and Parliament was commemorated by a yearly holiday on the 5th of November. On that day there were bonfires everywhere, and after a straw effigy of Guy Fawkes had been duly paraded through the streets, it was publicly burned. This holiday, which is still celebrated in England, was observed also in America until the time of the Declaration of Independence.

Throughout James's reign there was a constant struggle between the Parliament and the crown. James fancied that a king reigned by divine right and could do as he pleased; so whenever Parliament opposed him, he dissolved it. Finding, however, that this did no good, and that each new Parliament was more or less against him, he tried to get along without any.

But as he was always in need of money, and as he could not raise it by taxes, except through Parliament, he was often forced to resort to strange means. Besides asking for benevolences, or gifts, from rich people, he sold titles and offices, and tried many other ways of raising money. The funds he obtained, however, were not wisely used, for James was both lavish and miserly.

Once, for instance, he ordered that £20,000 should be given to his first favourite, a worthless creature by the name of Carr. The treasurer, knowing that James would not willingly give away the money if he only realized how much it represented, made a heap of it and showed it to the king. James gazed at it in wonder, and when he heard that this glittering heap of gold was the sum he had promised Carr, he flung himself upon it and clasped it in his arms, saying he could not part with it.

To increase his own wealth, as much as for the good of the country, James encouraged commerce. This was a great advantage, and London grew rapidly, owing to the trade brought by the ships which came up the Thames (temz). Once, when angry with the lord mayor, who refused him funds, James threatened to leave London and establish his capital elsewhere, thinking such a measure would diminish the city's trade. But the lord mayor answered this threat by saying, "Your majesty hath power to do what you please, and your city of London will obey accordingly; but she humbly begs that when your majesty shall remove your courts, you would please leave the Thames behind you."

The mayor, you see, realized that it was owing more to the Thames than to the presence of king and court that London had become so thriving a city.

LXXXVI. SIR WALTER RALEIGH.

DURING the reign of Elizabeth, in the year 1600, some English traders formed the East India Company. Their charter was renewed in the reign of James, and at the same time a traveller named Cor'yat wrote an account of his visit to one of the greatest Indian rulers, and gave an enthusiastic description of the country, little suspecting that it would, in days to come, belong to the English.

James's eldest son, Prince Henry, was such a very good and clever lad that every one loved him. The prince was very fond of learned men, so he often visited Raleigh in the Tower, where the latter was busy writing a history of the world for his use. Henry greatly admired Raleigh, who had travelled so much, and who conferred an inestimable benefit on Ireland by bringing potatoes over from America to plant there.

Henry was sorry to see this able man languish in prison, and he was once heard to say: "No king but my father would keep such a bird in such a cage!" Unfortunately for Raleigh, the young prince did not live long enough to free him, but suddenly died from a cold caught after playing a violent game of tennis.

Some time after that, James, being short of money, and hearing that Raleigh knew where a gold mine was to be found, took him out of prison, and, giving him a vessel, sent him in search of the treasure. In this expedition Raleigh got into trouble with the Spaniards, and when he came home without any money, the king was so angry that he sent him back to the Tower to be executed.

Raleigh was a good and brave man, and, knowing he was innocent, he went to his death without fear. When he was on the scaffold, he gently ran his finger along the edge of the ax, and then, giving it to the executioner, he said: "This is a sharp medicine, but a cure for all evils."

James, having sent away his favourite Carr because the latter ceased to amuse him, now took up a young man whose principal attractions were his good looks and graceful dancing. He bestowed upon this new favourite the title of Duke of Buckingham, and soon no one could approach the king except through this "Steenie," whose only aim was to lead a merry life and get a great deal of money.

This vicious man spent much of his time with the king's son Charles, for whom he did not set a good example. He even went in disguise with the young prince to the court of Spain, for Charles was anxious to see the Spanish princess whom he was to marry. On their way, the two young men visited the French court, where they saw Henrietta Maria, the king's fair sister.

On reaching Spain, Buckingham was coldly received. This made him so angry that he soon influenced James to give up the Spanish match, and to bargain with France for the hand of Princess Henrietta.

James's daughter married the Elector Frederick V., so England was dragged into the war then troubling Europe, which is known as the Thirty Years' War. Here the English and the Spanish were opposed to each other; for since the marriage between Charles and the Spanish princess had been broken off, they had ceased to be friends.

Four very clever men lived in the reign of King James. The first was Lord Francis Bacon, one of Elizabeth's advisers. This man was very talented, but he accepted bribes, and was sent away from court in disgrace. The second, Ben Jonson, wrote so well that he came to be regarded as Shakespeare's successor, and was buried in Westminster Abbey. The third was John Na'pi-er, a man of science, who invented the tables of logarithms, which in higher arithmetic help as much as the multiplication tables in easier sums. The fourth was the Dutch artist Van-dyke', who first came over to England to paint the portrait of James I. Later on, he became court painter to

Ed. Ender, Artist.
Charles I. and Vandyke at Hampton Court.

Charles I., and his portraits of that unhappy king, of the beautiful queen, and of the royal children, now form the principal decoration of a room in Windsor Palace, which bears the artist's name.

LXXXVII. KING AND PARLIAMENT.

WHEN King James I. died of ague, in 1625, his son Charles became King of Great Britain in his stead. He was a most kind-hearted and amiable prince, devoted to his wife Henrietta Maria,—whom he married shortly after he became king,—and an excellent father. Unfortunately, however, Charles was a bad king. His father had taught him to believe in the divine right of kings, and Buckingham had taught him that a promise made to his people need not be regarded as sacred.

When Charles came to the throne, he found that his father had not only spent all the money in the treasury, but had left large debts. Moreover, money had to be raised to carry on the war against Spain; so Charles called a Parliament and asked it for funds. Now the members not only hated the queen because she was a Catholic, but were anxious to have the king dismiss his favourite, Buckingham. So they said they would do as Charles wished if he sent Buckingham away. The king refused, and as Parliament would not grant him as much money as he wanted, he dissolved it. Then the Catholics soon began to trouble him, because he did not give them all the privileges they wanted; so he listened to the advice of Buckingham, and, to punish the French king for helping Spain, decided to send aid to the Hu'gue-nots, or French Protestants. They were then closely besieged at La Rochelle (ro-shel'), a town on the coast of France.

The first expedition, under Buckingham, failed. To get money for a second, Charles granted Parliament the Petition of Right (1628), an enlarged edition of the Great Charter. The money secured, a fleet was made ready; but when Buckingham was about to take command of it, he was murdered by a man who fancied it would be well to rid the country of so vicious a creature.

Although Buckingham's death was no loss to the people,

the king missed him sorely. He needed an adviser, and, hoping to please every one, he selected a Puritan leader for his minister, and made him Earl of Straf'ford. At first the Puritans were well satisfied; but when they saw that Strafford used all his great talents to uphold the king, they were very angry. They showed this by refusing to do what the king asked, when the next Parliament met. Charles therefore sent them away in wrath, vowing he would govern without any Parliament, although he knew this was against the law.

During the next eleven years Charles ruled alone, helped only by his two ministers, Strafford and Laud. He raised a great deal of money by fines imposed by the Star Chamber; but as this did not prove enough, he finally sent out an order calling for ship money.

Until then, whenever the country was in danger, the people living along the coast had been called upon to pay a tax which, as it was used for the navy, was called ship money. Now Charles asked that all the people in England should pay this tax, a thing he had no right to do, for the right of imposing taxes belongs to Parliament only.

The result was that people grumbled a great deal, and one rich man, named Hamp'den, who did not like to see his countrymen treated unjustly, refused to pay it. He was promptly brought before the court, where only four men out of twelve had the moral courage to say that the king was doing wrong. Still, although people did not dare say so openly, and although the court forced Hampden to pay ship money, all were indignant and ready to revolt against a king who did not respect the laws he had solemnly promised to uphold.

LXXXVIII. CAVALIERS AND ROUNDHEADS.

LAUD, one of the advisers of Charles I., now told him that there would be less trouble if all the people were of one religion, and thus persuaded the king to say that everybody ought to conform to the Church of England. The result was that many Puritans and Catholics alike set sail for America to found new colonies, where they should have the right to worship as they pleased.

But when Charles bade the Scotch conform to the English Church, they resisted openly. One old woman even flung a chair at the preacher's head when he began to read the Anglican service; and the excited people, assembling in great numbers, drew up a "Covenant," or agreement, whereby they bound themselves to resist any religious changes. All those who signed this paper were called Covenanters, and as they were determined to fight rather than yield, they began to drill, and fortified their towns.

Hearing of this, Charles marched northward with an army, which he was obliged to dismiss before he reached Scotland, because he had no money with which to pay his soldiers or buy them food. As he could do nothing without funds, Charles called a Parliament which was so promptly dissolved that it is known as the Short Parliament.

A second Parliament soon assembled, and this time the members began by accusing Strafford and Laud of giving the king bad advice. They were so angry with the former that, in spite of all he could urge in his own defence, they sentenced him to death.

Charles, who was attached to Strafford, refused to sign

the death-warrant until the condemned minister wrote him a noble letter, saying that it would be best to do so, in order to pacify the House of Commons. The king then weakly yielded, and poor Strafford was beheaded.

Next, a law was made providing that Parliament could not be dissolved (which meant sent away for good and all) or adjourned (which meant sent away for a short time), except by its own consent. Parliament also put an end to the Star Chamber, and began to right various wrongs. But while these reforms were going on, a rebellion broke out among the Irish, who killed thousands of Englishmen in a few days.

As Parliament still refused to give Charles money and soldiers to put down this rebellion, the king tried to frighten the members by marching into their place of meeting with his guards, to arrest five of the principal men, among whom were the patriots Hampden and Pym. But they managed to escape, and the Speaker, or head of the House of Commons, refused to tell the king where they had gone.

Seeing that Parliament was using the money got by taxes to raise an army to oppose him, Charles soon withdrew to York, where he was joined by many noblemen and Catholics, who, on account of their gallant bearing, were called Cavaliers. As the opposite party was composed principally of Puritans who wore their hair cut short, they were soon dubbed Roundheads, a name which you will often hear.

The Royalists, or Cavaliers, were led by the king himself and by his nephew, the gallant Prince Ru'pert, while the Puritans followed the lead of Hampden and Pym in politics, and that of Fair'fax and Oliver Cromwell in war. The king gave the signal for civil strife by raising his standard on Nottingham Hill in 1642; and when it was blown down during a storm, people regarded this as a bad omen.

During the next six years the civil war raged; and while the Cavaliers fought with daring, they were not able to hold out against the steady discipline of the Roundheads. Although beaten at Edgehill, the Puritans won victories at Marston Moor and at Nase'by, where Charles vainly tried to rally his troops by calling to his men, "One charge more, and we recover the day!"

Oliver Cromwell.

Seeing that all was over, the king fled in disguise and surrendered to the Scotch troops, thinking that, although they too had rebelled, they would treat him kindly. His baggage fell into the hands of Cromwell, who, instead of imitating the conduct of the great Roman generals, read all Charles's private letters.

He not only read them, but had them published; and when, later on, the people saw that the queen had gone to Holland to pawn the crown jewels, and that the king still meant to have his own way, they began to quote these letters. The Scotch were indignant, too; and when Parliament refused to pay them for their services unless they gave up the king, they tamely yielded.

LXXXIX. "REMEMBER."

AT first Charles was treated with great respect, although closely guarded; but before it was decided what to do next, a quarrel arose between Parliament, which was mostly Puritan, and the army, which was composed of a very strict set of Roundheads, called the Independents.

The army was very determined to have things its own way, and, seeing that Parliament showed signs of coming to terms with the king, Cromwell sent his captain Joyce to seize Charles. The king, surprised, asked to see Joyce's warrant; but when the captain silently pointed to the men who formed his escort, he said: "Your warrant is indeed drawn up in fair characters and legible."

It was useless to resist, so Charles, who all through his trials behaved with great dignity and gentleness, quietly allowed himself to be taken to Hampton Court. Then, seeing that Parliament was inclined to forgive the king, Cromwell placed soldiers at the door to prevent any but Independent members from going in. It was thus that the Rump Parliament, so called because it was only a small part of the state body, voted that the government should be placed in its hands, and that Charles should be tried as a traitor for taking up arms against the law.

The king was therefore brought before his judges, who addressed him as Charles Stuart. But he refused to answer their questions, saying they had no right to try him. When they accused him of treachery, in the name of the people of England, a voice in the audience boldly cried out: "No; not a tenth part of them."

But although many were still ready to defend the king, although the French and the Scotch protested against his arrest, and although Prince Charles, the king's eldest son, promised to do anything Parliament wished if it would only spare his father, Charles was condemned to death.

The king heard his sentence calmly, and asked only that he might take leave of two of his children, who were still

F. Goodall, Artist.
The Children of Charles I.

in England. This wish was granted; and when Charles had his little son on his knee, he kissed him and said: "Mark, my child, what I say: they will cut off my head, and will want to make thee king; but thou must not be king so long as thy brothers Charles and James are alive. Therefore I charge thee not to be made king by them."

Little Prince Henry, who was too young to understand what was going on, was, however, so impressed by what his father said, that he looked up into Charles's face and solemnly said: "I will be torn in pieces first!"

This parting over, Charles got ready to die, with the help of his chaplain Juxon. He slept peacefully the last night, and, hearing that it was cold out of doors, he put on two shirts, lest the wind should make him shiver on the scaffold and the people should think he was afraid to die.

The scaffold had been erected just outside of Whitehall, so the king was led out to it through one of the windows of the banquet room. There was a great throng present, but the people were kept at a distance, and drums were beaten when the king began his last speech. But even on the scaffold Charles behaved in the same gentle way, and after saying that he had always done what he considered right, and that his only crime was to have consented to Strafford's execution, he prepared to die. The last word the king uttered was, "Remember," which he addressed to Juxon. A few moments later the executioner held up the king's head, saying, "This is the head of a traitor," and all the people burst into tears.

No one has ever known exactly to what the mysterious word "remember" referred, because Juxon would never tell; but it is generally supposed that Charles reminded his chaplain to be sure to tell his son never to avenge his death, but to forgive the men who had condemned him.

As most of the king's family were abroad, they suffered no harm. But the two children who had seen their father just before his death were sent to learn a trade. One of them, the little princess, died of grief for her father, but Cromwell finally took pity upon little Prince Henry and sent him over to his mother in France.

XC. THE ROYAL OAK.

A FEW days after the execution of Charles I., Parliament said that as there was no king in England, there should be no nobility, and therefore no House of Lords. England was now a republic instead of a monarchy, and the new seal of the state, or Commonwealth of England, bore the inscription: "The first year of freedom, by God's blessing restored, 1648."

But while all the Puritan party said the monarchy was at an end, the Royalist party claimed that since Charles I. was dead, his son Charles II. was King of England. The Scotch Parliament, which had had no share in the king's execution, promised to be true to Charles II. if he would only swear to respect their Covenant.

In Ireland, also, all the Catholics were in favour of Charles. They rebelled against the Commonwealth, but Cromwell immediately set out to subdue them. He carried on the war with such cruelty, sparing neither man, woman, nor child, that the mere name of Englishman became a terror to the Irish.

While Cromwell was thus busy in Ireland, Charles II. had come over to Scotland, where the people rose up to help him recover his throne. Cromwell, hearing of this, left his chief officer, Ireton, in Ireland. Then, crossing the Irish Sea, he marched over the border, defeated the Scotch troops at Dunbar, and moved on to Edinburgh.

The Royalists, taking advantage of this, boldly invaded England, where they expected that many people would join them. But Cromwell, marching rapidly southward again, surprised their army at Worcester (woos'ter). The Cavaliers were routed, and King Charles sought safety in flight. He was in great danger, for Cromwell's soldiers were scattered all over the country, looking for him. Charles's few followers soon saw that their only chance of safety lay in separating and escaping in disguise.

The young king, therefore, went to the house of a farmer named Penderell, at Bos'co-bel, and, telling the man who he was, begged his help. Although this farmer knew that he was risking his life in befriending the king, he gave Charles a suit of his own clothes and cut off his long hair. Then, hearing that search parties were in the neighbourhood, he led the king through a forest to a field in the midst of which grew a very bushy oak tree.

Penderell helped Charles to climb up and hide in the branches of the oak. Here they staid all day, the weary king resting against the farmer, who, seeing his royal charge had fallen asleep, held him tight lest he should fall. While they were thus concealed in the Royal Oak, a party of soldiers rode directly under the tree, talking of Charles and of the reward they soon hoped to win.

During the next six weeks Charles wandered about from place to place, in different disguises, trying to reach the seashore and find a boat in which to escape to France. All through those weary weeks the royal fugitive was helped first by one person and then by another.

We are told that more than forty persons, and most of them very poor, knew who he was and helped him, although they ran great risks and could have earned a large reward by betraying him. After much tramping and many adventures, Charles came to the house of a Royalist named Lane. Here he assumed the livery of a servant, and soon rode away as the attendant of Miss Lane, who had a permit to journey to Leith with her servant.

In this disguise Charles passed right through the Parliamentary troops, and came to an inn, where the hostler recognized but did not denounce him. In another inn, the king roused the cook's suspicions because he did not know how to turn the meat to roast it properly; but he disarmed this man's anger by saying they were too poor at his house to have any roast meat.

A landlord once recognized him, and begged that he and his wife might receive the titles of lord and lady as soon as the king came to the throne. Thus wandering from place to place, Charles finally reached Shoreham, where, embarking upon a little vessel, he bribed the captain to take him over to France.

XCI. THE COMMONWEALTH.

WHILE Charles was thus making his escape, General Monk subdued Scotland, General Ireton reduced Ireland, and Admiral Blake began to punish the Dutch, who had made trouble for the English vessels. You see, Parliament had decreed that no ships of other nations should bring the products of foreign countries to English ports. The Dutch, who had long made much money by carrying goods to England, did not like this Navigation Act; so they declared war, and their admiral, Van Tromp, after sundry checks, won a victory over Admiral Blake and forced him to retreat. The Dutch admiral felt so proud of this victory that he sailed up and down the Channel with a broom tied to the top of his mast, boasting that he had swept the seas clean.

But for all his boasting, he was soon defeated by Blake, and a treaty was made in which it was settled that all foreign vessels should recognize England's power by lowering their flags thrice in salute when they met an English ship.

In the meantime the affairs of the state were not going on satisfactorily. Cromwell, seeing that the Long Parliament, after sitting thirteen years, had not done much good, thought it time to dissolve it; so he arose in the hall one day and suddenly cried: "For shame! Get you gone! Give place to honester men. You are no longer a Parliament. The Lord has done with you. He has chosen other instruments for carrying on his work."

At a stamp of his foot, his soldiers came filing in to drive the members out. Then Cromwell bade them remove the mace, the emblem of Parliament's power, and, locking the doors, he carried away the keys. Shortly after that he called a new Parliament, composed mainly of Independents, and as the principal orator was named Praise-God Barebone, this Parliament is often called Barebone's Parliament.

This new assembly gave Cromwell the title of Protector of the Commonwealth. He decided that in the present state of affairs England was best under military rule. So he dismissed Parliament, raised taxes whenever he pleased, and had all the power of a king, although he refused to accept the crown when it was offered to him.

Cromwell dissolves Parliament.

Benjamin West, Artist.

But although Cromwell proved so able a ruler that he forced all the foreign countries to respect England, and made the country very prosperous, he was not happy. He knew that the Catholics and Royalists hated him, and was in constant dread of being killed. He wore armour under his clothes, never slept two nights in succession in the same room, always had loaded pistols at hand, and never came back to Whitehall by the road by which he left it. Besides, he knew that the people he loved most, his wife and daughters, did not approve of his having allowed Charles I. to be killed, or of his refusing to give back the throne to Charles II.

During his short rule Cromwell won the city of Dunkirk and the island of Ja-māi′ca from Spain; he subdued the

Westminster Abbey.

pirates at Tu′nis and Trip′o-li; and, best of all, he insisted that every one should have the right to worship as he chose.

The Jews were therefore allowed to come back into England, whence they had been driven by Edward I.

Other great improvements which took place during the rule of Cromwell were the circulation of the first newspapers and the development of a better postal service. Letters were now carried from point to point on certain fixed days, instead of waiting until the postman thought there were enough to make it worth while; and all members of Parliament were allowed the right of sending as many letters as they chose, free of charge, a privilege which was called "franking."

Although Oliver Cromwell was Protector of England for only five years, he is one of the most famous men of the country whose welfare he had close at heart. He did so much for England that he was granted the right of naming his successor. He therefore said that his son Richard should govern after him. Soon after this he died of ague, in 1658, and was buried in Westminster Abbey, among the bodies of the kings whose power he had wielded without ever bearing their title.

XCII. THE RESTORATION.

OLIVER CROMWELL was, as you have seen, a very remarkable man; but great as he is in history, his secretary Milton is even greater than he. This man was a Puritan of great genius, and so very diligent that he spent all his time in study. When only a college student, he wrote a beautiful poem called "Ode on the Nativity," and after a busy life and much hard work, he spent his old age in writing "Paradise Lost," one of the greatest poems in the English language.

Although he had become blind, Milton would not cease to work; so his daughters sat by him, reading aloud learned works in Latin and Greek. But they could not understand these books, for their father said that "one tongue was enough for a woman," and would not let them study more. Milton's poem was published about nine years after Cromwell died, and about seven before the poet's death.

Richard Cromwell was very unlike his father, and unwillingly accepted the office of protector. Seeing that the people were dissatisfied under his mild rule, he resigned at the end of a few months, leaving the country in a very bad state, for both Parliament and the army wanted to rule.

As Cromwell's strong hand was no longer there to hold the reins of government, General Monk, the most capable man in the country, decided that England would be better off under the rule of her rightful king. He therefore came down from Scotland with his army, dismissed the Parliament, and called for a new election.

Most of the members of the new Parliament were so strongly in favour of law and order that when General Monk proposed that Charles should come back, the plan was greatly approved not only by the House of Commons, but also by the House of Lords, which was now assembled for the first time since the death of Charles I. A message was sent to Charles in Holland, and he immediately set out for England, where he landed in May, 1660. General Monk came to Dover to meet him, and escorted him to London, where he was crowned in Westminster Abbey.

This return of the royal family is known as the Restoration; for now the crown was restored to the rightful heir.

All the people received the pleasant-mannered, good-natured king with great delight, and as he encouraged them to resume amusements which the strict Puritans had considered sinful, he is known as the Merry Monarch, and the country was again called " Merry England."

Charles pleased everybody, at first, by promising that every one should be pardoned, except the sixty men who had taken it upon themselves to sentence his father to death, and who were known as the regicides, or king killers. Some of these were already dead, and others had left the country; so only a few were captured and put to death.

Next, the body of Cromwell was taken out of its grave and hung at Tyburn, with those of a few other dead regicides. But Richard Cromwell, who had left England, was soon allowed to come back and end his days in peace there.

With the return of the king the Church of England was restored; but Charles did not follow Cromwell's wise example and allow every one to worship as he pleased. Charles generally allowed his friend the Earl of Clarendon to govern for him. He tried, however, to force even the Scotch to become members of the Church of England, although he had once promised to respect their Covenant. They resisted fiercely, held secret meetings in the mountains, and, when surprised by the king's troops, died like martyrs rather than give up their mode of worship. Exasperated by the cruel treatment inflicted by Clav'er-house, commander of the king's troops, the Covenanters finally rebelled, and for many years stoutly resisted every attempt to force them to worship as the king wished.

XCIII. PLAGUE AND FIRE.

WHEN Charles came to the throne he was already thirty years old. During his exile he had met and loved a woman whom he secretly married. This marriage, however, was not according to the law, so it was decided that the king's son, the Duke of Monmouth, could never inherit the crown.

The legal heir to the crown was the king's brother James, a Roman Catholic, and it was feared that he would try to make England a Catholic country. As many of the people had not forgotten the troubles which such an attempt had brought about in the days of Queen Mary, they begged Charles to marry again, hoping he would have a legitimate son to succeed him.

After much hesitation, Charles finally chose Catherine of Bra-gan'za, daughter of the King of Portugal. She was very rich, and besides a great deal of money, gave her husband the city of Tan-gier' in Africa, and that of Bombay' in India, where the English had been trading ever since the year 1600. The new queen was a strict Catholic, brought up in a convent, and she was so shocked by the free manners of the ladies and gentlemen at her husband's court that she lived a very quiet and retired life.

It was not the same with Charles II. He lived a gay life, and set such a very bad example for his people that he did a great deal of harm. The Puritans were shocked by his lack of principle, and those who had fought for him were pained by his ingratitude. For, out of all who at such peril and self-sacrifice had aided him in his escape, the only person whom he ever rewarded was the farmer who spent a day with him in the Royal Oak.

Throughout Charles's reign there were many troubles about religious matters, and soon there came a calamity which the Puritans said was sent to punish the king for his sins. This was the plague, a disease which started in the East and spread rapidly over Europe. It raged everywhere, but nowhere worse than in London. Whole families died in a few days; and while the rich fled into the country, hoping to escape contagion, the poor had to stay in the city, where many who did not die of the plague perished of hunger. No trading was done, grass grew in the streets, and almost every house bore a cross and the words, "God have mercy upon us," rudely marked on the door, to show that it was plague-stricken. Twice a day heavy carts rumbled along the deserted streets to bear away the dead. Their passage was heralded by the ringing of a bell, and the dismal cry, "Bring out your dead, bring out your dead."

It is estimated that two thirds of the inhabitants of London died of this plague. The houses, mostly built of wood and badly ventilated, could not be properly cleaned; so a second calamity, a great fire which destroyed thirteen thousand houses the next year, proved a blessing in disguise by destroying the germs of the plague.

The flames swept onward so fast that people barely escaped with their lives, and a great deal of property was lost. In spite of the efforts made even by King Charles and his brother, the flames raged on and on, until they consumed the old Church of St. Paul's.

When the fire was finally put out, a large part of the

city had been burned down and had to be entirely rebuilt. This led to a great improvement; for the streets were now made wider, the houses more comfortable, and the great English architect, Sir Christopher Wren, made plans for thirty-five new churches and entirely rebuilt St. Paul's.

XCIV. THE MERRY MONARCH.

THE Puritans, who did not approve of any kind of amusement, said that the plague and the fire had been sent to punish the people for following the king's gay example. For a time, therefore, the calamity had the effect of sobering both people and king; but the latter soon

Sir Edwin Landseer, Artist.
King Charles Spaniels.

resumed his merry life, and thought more of his pet dogs than of his duty.

All the money voted by Parliament was spent for pleasure; and as those sums were not enough, Charles sold Dunkirk to the French, three years before the great plague.

This made the people so angry that they accused Clarendon of being a poor minister, and had him exiled.

Clarendon gone, the power was placed chiefly in the hands of five ministers, who formed a committee called the Ca-bal', and, strange to say, the letters spelling this word were also the initials of their names. The Cabal made England begin a war with Holland, and closed a secret treaty with the French king, who paid large sums to Charles to get his help against the Protestants. But when it had ruled six years, better ministers took its place, and called a new Parliament, to restore order.

The new Parliament found out that Charles favoured the Roman Catholics; and as he and Catherine had no children, and his brother James (a firm Catholic) was his heir, they again began to fear that an attempt would be made to force all England to return to the old faith. The majority were so opposed to this that they made a law that no one should hold a government position until he swore to uphold the reformed faith.

Many Catholic officers consequently gave up their positions; and as the Quakers refused to take any oath, because their religion allowed them only to say " yea " and " nay," they too could hold no offices. In fact, many of them were thrown into prison, while others left the country and went to settle in the New World.

The same Parliament also made the law, still called by the Latin words *ha'be-as cor'pus*, whereby no man could be kept in prison unless he had been tried before a judge and found guilty. This was a great improvement; for until then the king had sometimes imprisoned people without any trial, and kept them captive as long as he pleased.

At this time the whole country was divided into two large parties. One was composed of fierce Protestants, called Whigs. They were willing to let Charles reign as long as he had Protestant ministers, but said that his brother James, the Duke of York, should never come to the throne. It was to please this party that Charles married his two nieces, Mary and Anne, the daughters of James, to Protestant princes. But, while the Whigs approved of these marriages, the Catholic or royal party, who were called Tories, did not like them.

The quarrels between the Tories and the Whigs led to sundry plots. One of them, the Rye House Plot, was discovered, and many people were executed, because they were accused not only of wishing to prevent James from ever being king, but also of wanting to murder Charles. As the discontent in the country still increased, James now proposed some harsh measures. But Charles, knowing the English would rebel, quietly answered: "Brother, I am too old to go again on my travels; you may, if you choose."

Things might have grown worse had not the Merry Monarch suddenly been stricken with apoplexy, and died at the age of fifty-five. His reign is famous on account of the writings of the poets Milton and Dryden, and of Daniel De-foe', who, as you may know, wrote an account of the plague, and the story of "Robinson Crusoe."

Though very good-tempered, Charles was neither a good nor a great man. He was far more fond of pleasure than of work, and his promises were easily made and broken. One of his courtiers, who knew his character perfectly, once showed him the following verse which he had written, as a joke, for the royal tombstone:

> "Here lies our sovereign lord the king,
>   Whose word no man relies on;
>   Who never said a foolish thing,
>   Nor ever did a wise one."

Charles, having read these lines, handed them back to the author, saying with a smile, "The last part may be very true; for my words are my own, but my doings are my ministers'." This, however, was no real excuse; for Charles, being king, was responsible for his people, and should at least have tried to do his best for them.

XCV. JAMES DRIVEN OUT OF ENGLAND.

CHARLES was succeeded by his brother James, who, as you know, was not very welcome to many of the English, because he was a Catholic. Still, they allowed him to reign, for they hoped he would not rule long, as he was already more than fifty years of age, and they knew that his daughters, Mary and Anne, who would succeed him, had both married Protestants.

James was very different from his brother, and, although earnest, was so far from clever that a courtier once said: "Charles *could* see things if he *would;* James *would* if he *could.*" The new king had wandered about a great deal during his youth, and at the Restoration he had become an admiral. We are told he did good service at sea, and that he invented the system of signalling with flags. In reward for his services in the Dutch war, he had received the province and city of New Am'ster-dam, whose name he changed to New York.

When James's first wife died, leaving two daughters, he married a young and beautiful Italian princess called Marie d'Este (däs´tĕ). She was much younger than he, a very ardent Catholic, and greatly disliked by the English because she tried to meddle in state affairs.

On coming to the throne, James II. promised to support the Church of England and to govern the country by the laws of the realm. But, three days later, he broke both these promises by sending a messenger to the pope and by raising money without the permission of Parliament. The people, seeing that he could no more be trusted than the other Stuarts, were very angry, and many of the Protestants joined the Duke of Monmouth, who landed in England to demand the throne.

Monmouth claimed the throne as Charles's son, and accused James of setting fire to London, of poisoning King Charles, and of many other crimes of which he was not guilty. Some of the English pretended to believe what Monmouth said, and joined in the rebellion. It burst out in Scotland under the Duke of Ar-gyle', and in England under the Duke of Monmouth. Both dukes were defeated, however. When Monmouth fell into James's hands, after the battle of Sedgemoor, he begged pitifully for mercy, but he and Argyle were both beheaded.

James was very revengeful, so he sent a cruel officer named Kirk, and a still more heartless judge named Jef´freys, to try and to punish all the rebels. Kirk and his "lambs," as he jokingly called his soldiers, massacred all who had borne arms, while Jeffreys sentenced to death men and women who had only given water or food to fugitive rebels. He was so cruel that he condemned both innocent and guilty, and his rule has been called the English Reign of Terror, or the Bloody Assizes.

Urged by the queen and by other bad advisers, James not only showed no mercy to the rebels, but rewarded Jeffreys for his cruelty by making him chancellor. Then he began to remove Protestants from their offices, so as to put Roman Catholics in their places. When six of the bishops refused to read a declaration which annulled all the laws against Catholics, he sent them to the Tower. But, owing to the Habeas Corpus Act, he had to let them go when the judges said they were guilty of no crime.

All these things were borne rather patiently by his subjects, who comforted themselves with the thought that as oon as James died his Protestant daughters would succeed him. But all their hopes were blasted when they heard that the queen had given birth to a son, who would, of course, be brought up a Catholic and inherit the crown.

This was more than the Protestants could bear, so they sent word to William of Orange, the husband of Mary, to come over and deliver them from a Roman Catholic rule. The nobles and Princess Anne joined in this petition; and when James heard that his favourite daughter was against him, he cried: "God help me! My own children have forsaken me!"

The people were so angry that the queen hastily fled with the baby prince, and King James, fearing lest he should lose his head like his father, soon prepared to follow them to France. He slipped out of the palace unnoticed, rowed over the Thames, into whose waters he flung the great seal, and went to Fav'er-sham, whence he hoped to sail across the Channel. But he was recognized by some

E. M. Ward, Artist.
James II. receiving the News of the Landing of William of Orange.

fishermen there, who brought him back to London. The king was more frightened than ever; but his daughter Mary, thinking it best that James should seem to flee from England of his own accord, gave orders that the soldiers should guard him carelessly. James then contrived to escape, and joined his wife and son in France, where the king gave him the palace of St. Germain (saN zher-maN′) for his abode.

XCVI. A TERRIBLE MASSACRE.

JAMES gone, the crown was offered to William and Mary by Parliament. A new charter was made, in which, besides the laws of the Magna Charta granted by John, and those of the Petition of Right granted by Charles, were those called the Act of Settlement. Among other things, this act decided that the crown could belong only to a Protestant ruler, and that if Mary, Anne, and William all died without children, it should go to Sophia, a granddaughter of James I., and to her Protestant descendants.

The change of government which gave the crown to William and Mary is called the "glorious revolution of 1688;" and it was glorious not only because it took place without costing a drop of blood, but also because England, instead of being ruled by a tyrant, was to be governed by its own laws, and thus to be a constitutional monarchy.

William of Orange was the great-grandson of a famous Dutch hero of the same name, and grandson of Charles I., King of England. Although weak and sickly, he was a great fighter and a very determined man. The English did not like him much at first, because he was cold and reserved and spoke English badly; but they all loved the virtuous Queen Mary. Her excellent example was soon followed by other women, who, instead of gambling and thinking of nothing but dress and amusement, now began to delight again in needlework and study.

Although most of the Protestants had warmly welcomed William and Mary, all the Catholics had remained faithful to James; and as his name in Latin was Ja-co'bus, they were called Jac'ob-ites. Besides, the Highlanders, as the Scotch who lived in the northern and mountainous part of the island were called, were so loyal to the old royal family that for a time they refused to obey William and Mary.

After these Highlanders were defeated, an edict was published, promising full pardon to all rebels if they would only take, before a certain day, an oath to be faithful to the new rulers. One of the Highland families, or clans, the MacDon'alds, by mistake failed to take this oath in time; so their enemies, the Campbells (kam'elz), got an order to put them to death. Coming to the valley of Glen-coe' as if they were friends, and tarrying there twelve days, the Campbells suddenly fell upon the MacDonalds and began to murder them. A few escaped to the mountains, but it was only to perish of hunger and cold, not far from the ruined homes where they had once been happy.

William wanted the whole kingdom to be of one religion; but finally he granted full freedom in religious matters to all the people. The church was therefore mainly Anglican in England, Presbyterian in Scotland, and Roman Catholic in Ireland, and so it still remains to-day.

In England the population had been increased by the arrival of many French Protestants, the Huguenots, who had been driven out of France in 1685, when the king recalled a law allowing them to worship as they pleased. These industrious Huguenots began to work at their trades, and at Spit'al-fields they set up the first English silk manufactory.

XCVII. WILLIAM'S WARS.

ALTHOUGH the Whigs had welcomed William III. and Mary II., King James had kept some friends in England. These did not believe, as did most of the Protestants, that his child was an adopted one which he passed off as his own merely to make sure the crown should not go to his Protestant daughters. As they wanted James back, he came with a small French army, and landed in Ireland, where most of the people were Catholics and Jacobites. He first tried to take Lon'don-der-ry, one of the few Irish towns which were in the hands of William's party. The siege lasted one hundred and five days; but although the people suffered untold agonies from famine, and ate cats, dogs, rats, and old leather, they would not yield.

Finally an English vessel with provisions was sent to Londonderry's relief, and forced its way through the enemy's fleet. Shortly after this William himself came over to Ireland, and met James on the banks of the Boyne. Here William's best officer, General Schom'berg, was killed, and William himself narrowly escaped a like fate.

The battle raged fiercely, and James, who was watching it from afar, kept wringing his hands and crying, "Oh, spare my English subjects!" William, having already taken part in many battles, showed such coolness and courage on this day that he won a great victory. He also won the admiration of the Irish; for when taunted by an English soldier, an Irish captive promptly said: "Exchange kings with us, and we will fight you again."

James in the meantime fled from the battlefield of Boyne, and did not draw rein until he came to a place of safety. Here, in answer to a question put to him by an Irish lady, he pettishly said: "Madam, your countrymen have fled." "Yes," she answered promptly; "but I see your majesty has outstripped them all!"

As there was no hope for him in Ireland, James went back to France to collect new troops. The French fleet had won a slight victory at Beachy Head, but it was defeated later on by the Dutch and English at La Hogue.

The rebellion in Scotland and Ireland being quelled, William left Mary in England to govern with the aid of her council, and went back to Holland, where war awaited him. For while James was trying to recover his throne in Ireland, his allies, the French, were making war against the Protestants in Germany, the friends of the Dutch.

This war between the French and the English extended even to America, where it was known as King William's War. It was concluded, however, a few years after the battle of La Hogue, by the treaty of Rys'wick (1697), wherein Louis XIV. recognized William and Mary as rulers of England and promised never to help the Jacobites again.

Queen Mary having died of smallpox, William now became sole king. One of the first acts of Parliament in his reign was to give the newspapers full freedom and allow them to say anything they pleased, a privilege which had been denied them until then.

When James II. died, the French king broke the promises made in the treaty of Ryswick; for he at once proclaimed James's son to be King of England, under the name of James III. But the English remained faithful to William, and always spoke of the young prince as the Pretender, under which name he is best known in history.

The English soon declared war against France; for not only did the French support the Pretender, but they had also placed a French prince upon the throne of Spain, in spite of an agreement they had made not to do so. Parliament voted large sums of money for this War of the Spanish Succession, and William was eagerly looking forward to taking part in it, when he was thrown from his horse, and died a few days later from his fall.

XCVIII. THE DUKE OF MARLBOROUGH.

WILLIAM III. reigned five years jointly with Mary and eight years after her death. Under his wise rule English law and liberty made great progress, and while he was never greatly loved, he was much respected. He was a stern, silent, but good and earnest man. He loved his wife dearly, and after his death a ring containing a lock of her hair was found tied to his arm.

Besides helping the country to become strong and prosperous, William founded two great institutions — the Greenwich (gren'ij) Hospital for sick and disabled seamen, and the world-renowned Bank of England.

It had been decided by Parliament that if William and Mary died without children the crown should pass to Anne, the second daughter of James II. A good, gentle, and kind-hearted woman, the new queen was not well educated, nor clever, nor handsome. She had married a very insignificant Protestant, Prince George of Denmark, but although they had many children, all died when babies, except one son who lived to be eleven.

When Queen Anne came to the throne, in 1702, all the preparations had been made to carry on the war which in Europe was called the "War of the Spanish Succession," and in the colonies "Queen Anne's War." In this contest the English, Dutch, and Germans banded together in the Grand Alliance, to punish the French king, Louis XIV., for placing his grandson upon the throne of Spain.

The Germans were commanded by Prince Eugene; but the Dutch and English forces were in charge of the Duke of Marl'bor-ough, who had already fought under James and William. This general, who never lost a battle or failed to take a town, was always calm and deliberate, forming a great contrast to the impetuous Prince Eugene.

One day, we are told, when a council of war was called, Prince Eugene and the other officers were all in favour of attacking the enemy on the morrow, but Marlborough would not consent. Prince Eugene argued for a while, then flew into a passion, taunted Marlborough with cowardice, and finally challenged him to fight a duel. But the duke remained perfectly cool, refused the challenge, and allowed the prince to depart in anger. Early the next morning, however, Marlborough came to Prince Eugene's tent to awake him and bid him prepare for battle. The prince sprang up joyfully, saying, "But why would you not consent to this last night?"

"I could not tell you my determination last night," answered Marlborough, "because there was a person present who, I knew, was in the enemy's interest and would betray us. I do not doubt we shall conquer, and when the battle is over I will be ready to accept your challenge."

Prince Eugene, like a true gentleman, seeing that he had been in the wrong, now promptly apologized for his passion on the night before; and when he and the duke parted amicably, the latter said: "I thought, my dear prince, you would in time be satisfied."

This strangely assorted couple of commanders was very successful, and although the French tried to make the duke ridiculous by writing a long ballad about him, they were thoroughly beaten in the four battles of Blen'heim, Ramillies (rah-mee-yee'), Ou'den-ar-de, and Malplaquet (mahl-plah-kä'). The news of these victories was received with joy in England, and after each new triumph the queen bestowed some new reward upon her brave general.

It was thus that Marlborough received the Woodstock estate, where the grateful English people built him a palace which is still called Blenheim, in memory of his greatest victory. He also received the Garter, which was generally given only to kings or princes, and large sums of money. It is said that the greater part of these gifts were bestowed at the suggestion of his wife, Lady Church'ill, who was Anne's most intimate friend. This woman was very clever and imperious, and had a great influence over the gentle queen; but she became so proud that at last she treated even the queen with scorn.

After patiently submitting to all Lady Churchill's caprices for a long while, Anne finally grew very tired of her. She therefore made a friend of her lady of the bedchamber, Mrs. Masham, and sent the Duchess of Marlborough away. The gifts bestowed upon the duke now became fewer; but those he and the duchess had already received have belonged to their family ever since.

The Duke of Marlborough, who was one of the greatest generals that ever lived, and one of England's military heroes, was nevertheless a strange mixture of all that was great and noble, and, alas! of all that was mean and small. The great qualities which make every one admire him were spoiled by the fact that he was so fond of money that he would do the meanest things to increase his fortune. Besides, he was not always faithful to his king, and did not consider his promises sacred.

XCIX. THE TAKING OF GIBRALTAR.

WHILE Marlborough was winning glorious victories for his country in the north of Europe, another English commander, Sir George Rooke, carried on the war in Spain, and by a bold move became master of Gibraltar, one of the strongest fortresses in the world. The fort stands on a huge rock at the entrance of the Mediterra-

Gibraltar.

nean Sea; and although many efforts have since been made to recapture it, the British flag still floats proudly over it. But at first the English so little knew the value of this glorious possession that Parliament did not even send a vote of thanks to the gallant Sir George Rooke.

Shortly after the taking of Gibraltar, the union between Scotland and England was completed by arranging that there should be only one Parliament for both countries. Since 1707, when this change took place, Scotchmen have had seats both in the House of Lords and in the House of Commons.

All through the reign of good Queen Anne the two political parties, Whigs and Tories, were constantly quarrelling, yet England steadily prospered. The queen herself took very little part in the government, which was left almost entirely in the hands of her ministers. But while all England was rejoicing over the victories won abroad, Anne was very sad; for her husband, George of Denmark, became ill and died. He had taken no part in the government, and he was so uninteresting that Charles II. once cried in jest: " I have tried him drunk and sober, and there is nothing to him."

Five years after his death, the War of the Spanish Succession came to an end, and peace was signed at U'trecht (1713). Louis XIV. again promised not to uphold the Jacobites, and in America he gave up all claim to Newfoundland, A-ca'di-a, and the land around Hudson Bay.

Although Anne herself was not a clever woman, her time is almost as famous in literature as that of Elizabeth, because so many noted men lived then. Among them were the poet Pope, the satirist Swift, and Ad'di-son and Steele, the great writers of the " Tatler " and " Spectator," the first two English magazines. That is why in literature you will find this epoch called the Age of Queen Anne.

Parliament, you know, had decided that if Anne died without leaving children, the crown should go to Sophia, the granddaughter of James I. This princess had married the Elector of Han'o-ver, and had always hoped to be queen; but she died before Anne, so the crown, which she never wore, was placed upon her coffin.

When Queen Anne grew very ill, and her ministers saw she was about to die, they sent word to Sophia's son George, the Elector of Hanover, to be ready to come over to England at any moment, to take possession of the throne. Then, as soon as Anne breathed her last, Parliament proclaimed George King of Great Britain.

The new monarch came over as quickly as possible, though this was not very fast, for travel was very slow in those days. He was met and welcomed by Marlborough and by the Whigs, who were then in power. George I. was a plain-mannered, middle-aged German who could speak only a few words of English. He was a good business man; but when he wanted to talk with his prime minister Wal'pole, he had to use the help of an interpreter, or else speak Latin, the only language that they both knew. The English, however, were so anxious to have a Protestant ruler that they welcomed George and applauded him greatly when he said: "My maxim is never to abandon my friends, to do justice to all the world, and to fear no man."

C. THE SOUTH SEA BUBBLE.

WHEN the English saw that George I. was more attached to his German friends than to any one else, they were not pleased. The Tories, many of whom had been satisfied as long as a Stuart reigned, were indignant at being turned out of their offices to make room for Whigs. They began to side with the Jacobites, and said that the crown ought to be given to the Pretender.

This party in favour of the Pretender even went so far as to proclaim him James III. of England, and to invite him to come over and join them. Provided with a small army by the French king, the Pretender started out; but he was of so timid a disposition that he inspired his followers with no confidence. The Jacobites were already disheartened by the battle of Sher-iff-muir', and James soon gave up the contest and returned to France.

The Scotch, ever faithful to the Stuarts, had been the first to fight for the Pretender, and it was they who suffered most sorely. A few of the nobles were beheaded, although their friends tried to save them; but many were merely banished to America, where the colonies were steadily growing in importance.

As there was not much to amuse him in England, George made long and frequent visits to Hanover, leaving the government in the hands of his ministers, who did all they could to make Great Britain a great and free country. Little by little, through the king's neglect of his duty and through his absence from the meetings of his ministers, his power grew less while theirs grew greater. The ministers came to be very important officers of the government, and the king having let slip his control over them, his successors could never fully recover it.

For several years England was greatly excited over the South Sea Company's plan for trading with Spanish America. People were eager to get rich without working, so they gave all their money to speculators, who promised them ten pounds for every one they invested. A great many of the English foolishly believed this, and rashly gave their savings, although Walpole constantly warned them that the plan could not succeed. At that time there was no end to the wild schemes in which money was invested, for companies were even formed for making salt water fresh, and for changing all metals to gold! As Walpole had predicted, the South Sea scheme swelled like a bubble and — burst. Many people lost all they had, and complained bitterly, but ever since then the English have not been by any means so ready to rush into wild speculation.

The reign of George I. was short and uneventful. He was king for thirteen years, and died of apoplexy in his carriage, on his way to Hanover, whither he was hastening back, as usual, after a short sojourn in England. His eldest son, who had been named Prince of Wales at his coronation, now became king, under the title of George II.

George II. had the simple tastes of his father, but was less clever and of a violent temper. He, too, preferred Hanover to England, and therefore left the government to Walpole.

The French and the Spaniards, meantime, had made a secret or "family compact" to help each other. The Spanish now boarded English ships under pretext of searching for their countrymen or goods, and acted very insolently. This, added to a quarrel about the boundaries of Georgia and Florida, made bad feeling between the two nations. One day a Spanish captain roughly tore off the ear of an Englishman named Jenkins. Then, flinging the fragment in the man's face, he bade him carry it to King George and tell the latter that the Spaniards would treat him in the same way if they caught him.

This rude message proved the "last straw," and started the "War of Jenkins's Ear," as it is sometimes called. But although the fighting began between England and Spain, a quarrel about the crown of Austria soon involved all Europe in the "War of the Austrian Succession." Great Britain, Holland, and Austria were on one side, France, Spain, Prussia, and Bavaria on the other, and the war spread even to the colonies. You can read in your United States histories how it was conducted in America, where it was called "King George's War." In Europe it was carried on by George II., who took part in and won the battle of Det'ting-en. But the British did not win any very great advantage, and after eight years the War of the Austrian Succession was ended by the peace of Aix-la-Cha-pelle' (1748).

CI. BONNY PRINCE CHARLIE.

TAKING advantage of the general confusion during the War of the Austrian Succession, Prince Charles Edward, the son of the Pretender, tried to recover the Stuarts' throne.

Aided by a French fleet, he attempted to land in England. Then, undismayed by a first failure, he made a second venture, and, in spite of a tempest, set foot on the shores of Scotland. Here he and his seven followers were quickly joined by Highlanders, who, as the king and army were on the Continent, got possession of Edinburgh.

Next, the gallant Young Pretender, whom the Scotchmen affectionately called "Bonny Prince Charlie," won a victory at Pres-ton-pans', and, having secured the artillery, began to march towards London. The English, in terror, set a price of £30,000 upon the head of Prince Charlie, and quickly collected troops.

In the meantime most of Scotland had fallen into the hands of the Jacobites. Perceiving, however, that the brave Highlanders could not fight in England so advantageously as in their wild mountains, and seeing that the English force was three times greater than his own, Prince Charlie retreated. He was finally overtaken and beaten at Cul-lo'den. Flight saved him from death or captivity, but during the next five months he had to wander from place to place. He had many narrow escapes during that time, and suffered greatly from cold and hunger, although the brave Highlanders did all they could for him.

At last, after many adventures, Prince Charlie put on the dress of a servant girl, and pretended to be the maid of a young Scotch lady, Flora MacDonald, who volunteered to help him. With her aid, he passed through an English squadron and reached a vessel which brought him safely to the Continent.

At the peace of Aix-la-Chapelle it was again agreed that the French should no longer uphold the Stuarts. The Pretender, therefore, left France and went to Rome, where he and his two sons led unworthy lives. Bonny Prince Charlie, who had been so brave and energetic in Scotland, now became an idler and drunkard, and thus forfeited the esteem of all respectable people. These last three members of the Stuart family claimed in turn the titles of James III., Charles III., and Henry IX. They were buried in Rome, where their tomb, the work of the celebrated sculptor Ca-no'va, bears these pompous names.

Alexander Johnstone, Artist.
Flora MacDonald's Introduction to Prince Charlie.

The Highlanders who had so bravely helped and screened Prince Charlie were punished sorely; for the victor of Culloden, the Duke of Cum'ber-land, killed so many of them that he is known in history as the "butcher."

The War of the Austrian Succession was barely ended when a new conflict broke out. This was known in Europe as the "Seven Years' War," and in America as the "French and Indian War." Once more the English and the French were opposed, and fought wherever they met.

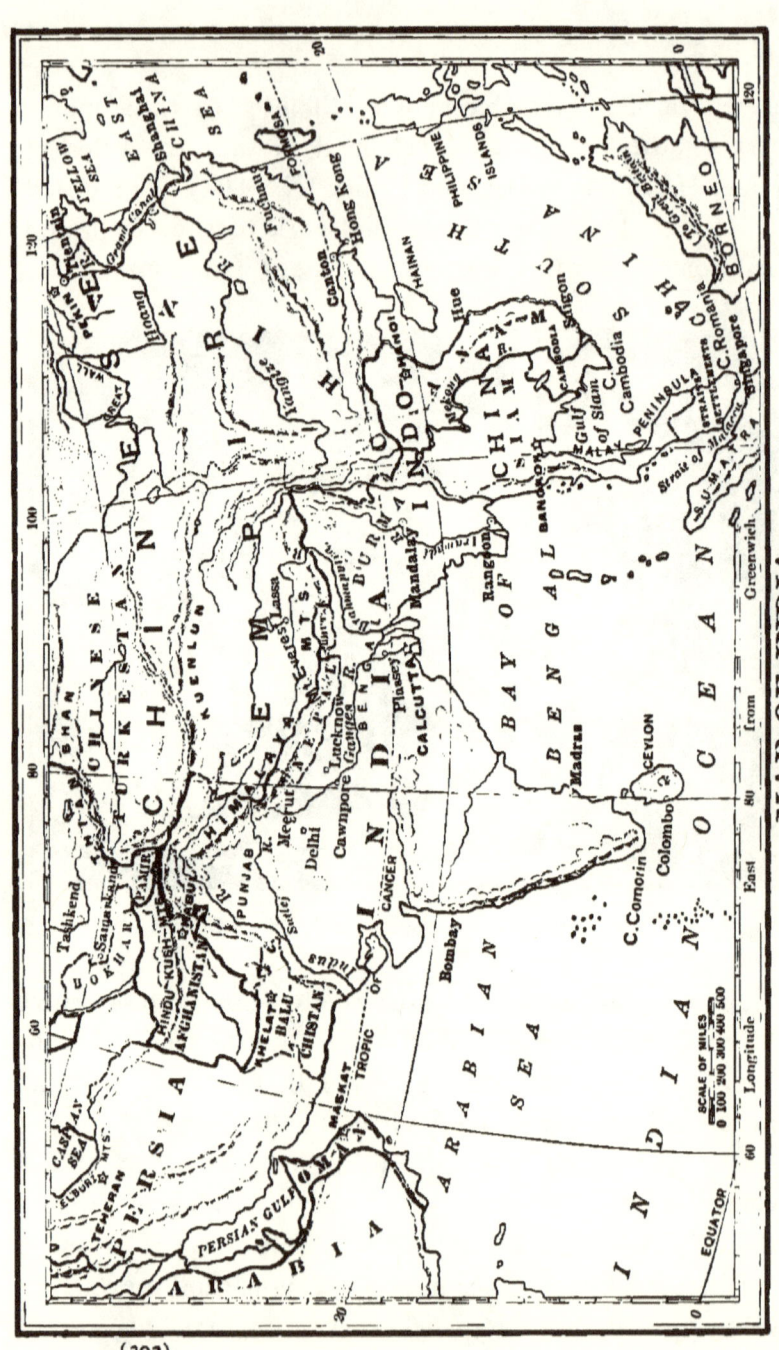

MAP OF INDIA

The British minister was now William Pitt, who is called the "Great Commoner;" and he took such wise measures that victory remained with the British. You know how they took Fort Duquesne (doo-kān'; which was afterwards named Pittsburg, in honour of Pitt), Forts Ni-ag′a-ra and Ti-con-der-o′ga, and the city of Que-bec′.

Thus the British gradually became masters in North America. At the same time their men and money helped win the battle of Min′den, and Admiral Hawke bravely destroyed the French fleet, although at the risk of losing his life and ships on the rocky coast of Brittany.

CII. THE BLACK HOLE OF CALCUTTA.

THE war which thus raged in two parts of the world was also extended to a third. In the days of Queen Elizabeth, the English had formed the East India Company and had begun to trade in Asia, where the French had preceded them. By this time the East India Company had several trading posts, besides the city of Bombay, which had belonged to the English ever since the marriage of Charles II. Whenever there was war between France and England, the French and the English traders in India took part in the quarrel.

Now, when the Seven Years' War began, the English had a small station at Cal-cut′ta, besides their settlements at Ma-dras′ and Bombay. The Viceroy of Bengal (ben-gawl′), an ally of the French, suddenly attacked the Calcutta station with a large force of natives. Of course the place fell into his hands, and he ordered one hundred and forty-six English prisoners to be locked up under the fort in a small, dark room, known as the Black Hole.

There was barely standing room for the prisoners in this small place; but they were driven in at the sword's point and the door was closed. Now you know that people cannot live without plenty of air; and as soon as these captives were shut in they began to gasp for breath, for there were only two very small windows.

It is frightfully hot in India, and this was in the month of June. The English knew that they must die in a few hours if they were not released, so they implored the sentinels to go and ask the viceroy to put them elsewhere. But the soldiers did not dare disturb their master, who was resting; and, besides, they were so heartless that they laughed as they watched the Englishmen struggling to reach the window for a breath of air, and heard them clamour for water. This was given to them in very small quantities, but only in exchange for large sums of money.

The suffering of those poor people cannot be described; and when the door was finally forced open, the next morning, only twenty-three were still alive! All the others — one hundred and twenty-three — had perished from want of air!

When this news reached the ears of the English traders, one of them, Robert Clive, set out with a force of about one thousand Englishmen and two thousand natives, whom he had drilled until they made good soldiers. With this small army, he defeated the Viceroy of Bengal's sixty thousand men at Plas'sey (1757), and recaptured Calcutta.

Since that day Calcutta has belonged to the British, who have made of it a great and flourishing city. The whole of Bengal soon came under their rule, and little by little they extended their conquests, until in 1760, the year of the death of George II., they drove the French out of India.

During the reign of this monarch a change was made in the calendar. The English had hitherto kept to the length of the year adopted by the Romans in the days of Julius Cæsar. But it had long been known that according to this system the year was, on the average, about eleven minutes too long; and these eleven minutes in each year had by this time amounted to eleven days, so all dates were eleven days wrong.

On the Continent this error had been corrected by the pope in 1582; but the English had clung to the "Old Style," and they dated their letters September 3 when people elsewhere wrote September 14. This difference made correspondence very awkward, so, by decree of Parliament, the date was changed in the year 1752. Not only were the eleven days provided for, but it was also decided that the year should thereafter begin on January 1, instead of on the 25th of March, as had been the custom until then.

CIII. LOSS OF THE THIRTEEN COLONIES.

GEORGE'S son having died before him, he was succeeded by his grandson, George III. The new ruler was not a native German, like the two Han-o-ve′ri-an kings who preceded him, but prided himself upon being "born a Briton."

As his grandfather and his mother were not on friendly terms, George III. had been brought up far from court, and in such quiet surroundings that he was always rather timid and awkward. It was only when called upon to make public speeches that he appeared well; for he had been carefully taught this art by an instructor who proudly cried, after his first speech: "I taught the boy!"

George III. was a good man, and so gentle and unassuming that he is often called Farmer George. He was very kind to every one he met, and a better father, husband, and son has never been seen. He and his family were so happy and united that they were an example to the whole nation, and Queen Charlotte is always spoken of as a very good woman.

The only great defect in the character of George III. was that he was narrow-minded, obstinate, and anxious to rule by himself. Still, the English were all very fond of him, and the Jacobites, seeing the worthlessness of the Stuarts, now became loyal subjects, and accepted public offices from the king.

The Seven Years' War was still going on when George III. came to the throne; but the British were tired of supplying money for what they called "German quarrels." Still, although the national debt already amounted to many millions, they could not make peace, for Spain had joined forces with France against England.

As a result, the war was carried on in the southern as well as in the northern part of Europe, in the colonies, and on the sea. There were numerous engagements, the British gaining the advantage everywhere, and in 1763 Spain and France were anxious for peace. In the Peace of Paris it was decided that almost all the French possessions in North America, east of the Mississippi River, should belong to the British, who also received Florida from Spain.

Great Britain was now the foremost country in the world, having the largest colonies and the most trade. This prosperity was greatly owing to able ministers, among whom one of the best-known is Pitt.

The war had cost a great deal of money, so heavy taxes were laid upon the people. Not only were these taxes laid upon England, the "mother country," but Parliament decided to impose them upon the colonies also, although Pitt was strongly opposed to this. The most prosperous of all the colonies were located in what is now known as the United States of America; and these refused to be taxed unless they were allowed either to send members to Parliament to protect their interests, or to decide in their colonial assemblies how much they could afford to pay. A good many in Parliament thought the colonists were right, and spoke and voted in their favour; but the greater number —who did not at all represent the common people of England—insisted that the colonists had to obey any law they chose to make. They therefore began by imposing taxes under a law called the Stamp Act. But the American colonists resisted it so strongly that Parliament withdrew the Stamp Act, and insisted only upon a small tax, laid principally upon tea.

Now it was not unwillingness to pay the money that caused the colonists to resist, but it was the thought that the British would not allow them the same freedom as the people of England enjoyed. First, they refused to buy tea; then, seeing that the British wanted to compel them to obey, the colonists took up arms, and at the battle of Lex'ing-ton, in 1775, began the Revolutionary War, which lasted about seven years. The American forces were ably led by Washington; and the British, although they came over with hired German troops and won several victories, were gradually compelled to yield.

The colonies proclaimed their independence from Great Britain on the 4th of July, 1776, and were soon recognized as the United States of America by France, Holland, and Spain. In 1781 Corn-wal'lis, the British commander, surrendered; and Parliament, which had fancied there would be no great trouble in putting down the American rebellion, soon after had to acknowledge the independence of the United States.

The great statesman Pitt, who had first opposed the taxation of the colonies, made his last and most brilliant speech to protest against their separation from the mother country. He was then so ill that he fainted before his speech was ended, and had to be carried home, where he soon died. His son, the Younger Pitt, who shared his views, was elected member of Parliament in 1780. For the next twenty-six years he was one of the ablest British statesmen, and he too served his country nobly.

The independence of the United States being acknowledged in England, John Adams was sent there as ambassador; and to him George III. frankly said: "I was the last man in the kingdom, sir, to consent to the independence of America; but now it is granted, I shall be the last man in the kingdom to sanction the violation of it."

CIV. THE BATTLE OF THE NILE.

THE French, who had helped the Americans fight, and who had been the first to recognize the independence of the United States, had in the meantime grown very much dissatisfied with the state of affairs in their own country. Their king, Louis XIV., had laid heavy taxes upon them to supply money for his wars and for his pleasures. His successor, Louis XV., did not care how much the people suffered, as long as he was comfortable, and carelessly said that after him the deluge might come.

This selfish, hard-hearted king was followed by Louis XVI., a blameless and gentle monarch, who had to suffer for the sins of those who came before him. Seeing that his people were about to rebel, he made arrangements to have the foreign powers help him. The French found this out, and were so exasperated over it that they killed the king's guard, bore the royal family off to prison, beheaded Louis XVI. and his beautiful wife, and, in imitation of the Americans, set up a republic.

But there were cruel and selfish men at the head of the French republic. They pretended that all the nobles were dangerous, and while they were in power they imprisoned and beheaded all those that they could seize. This awful time is known as the Reign of Terror, and Great Britain was first to express indignation at this behaviour and to refuse to recognize so barbarous a government (1793).

With the help of other European nations war was therefore begun against France. The French fleet was defeated by Lord Howe, but the French army soon conquered Holland, which became a republic. France now wanted to do the same with Ireland; but the British put an end to this plan by the naval victories of St. Vincent and Cam'per-

P. de Loutherbourg, Artist.

Lord Howe's Victory.

down. To prevent Ireland from again joining the French, it was united to Great Britain, and since 1801 there have been English, Scotch, and Irish members in both Houses of Parliament. Then, too, George III. gave up the empty title of King of France, which had been claimed by English kings ever since the time of Edward III.

When the war began, France was alone against all Europe; but she won many allies, owing to the bravery of her troops and to the military genius of Na-po'le-on Bo'-na-parte. The Dutch helped the French at Camperdown, and the Spaniards lent their aid at St. Vincent.

Napoleon, who had recovered Toulon (too-lawN') from

the English and had become a general in the army, meanwhile carried the war into Italy. Here he won many victories over the Austrians, forcing them to give up the country to him and sign a treaty at Cam'po-for'mi-o.

A great thinker once said that he who was master of Egypt would be master of the whole East. Napoleon, hating the English, determined to destroy their power in India, and set out for the Nile with an army. The battle of the Pyramids made him master of all Egypt, but his plans were spoiled by the bravery of Admiral Nelson. This great English hero came up with a smaller number of ships, and completely destroyed the French fleet (1798).

It was in this naval encounter, the battle of Aboukir (ah-boo-keer'), or of the Nile, that the little son of a French officer named Ca-sa-bi-an'ca died an heroic death. His father had told him to stay at his post until called away, so the brave little fellow staid there, amid shot and shell, until the ship was all wreathed in flames. Casabianca had been killed in another part of the ship, but the boy, true to his promise, stood on the deck until the powder magazine exploded and the vessel sank. His courage and obedience were so beautiful that Mrs. Hemans wrote a poem about him, which you will like to read.

After the battle of the Nile, Napoleon vainly tried to take Acre in Syria, but could not do so without a fleet. His had been destroyed by Nelson; so, seeing that he would not be able to carry out his plan of fighting the English in India, he now suddenly decided to go back to France. Passing boldly through the British fleet, he escaped capture by miracle, as it were, and, arriving in Paris, began to rule France, under the title of First Consul.

CV. NELSON'S LAST SIGNAL.

AFTER Napoleon left Egypt, the British gained possession of it, and brought back to the British Museum the large collection of antiquities which had been gathered by the French men of science.

Soon after, in 1802, a short peace was made between France and Great Britain at Amiens (ah-mĭ-aN′). On this occasion, when Napoleon and the English statesman Fox met, some one pointed to a globe, and remarked that England occupied a very small space upon it. "Yes," retorted Fox, promptly; "our island is indeed a small country—that island in which the Englishman is born, and in which he would fain that his bones should repose when he is dead. But," added he, advancing to the globe and spreading his arms round it, over both oceans and both Indies, "while the Englishmen live, they overspread the whole world and clasp it in a circle of power."

A peace between England and France, two nations then so jealous of each other, could not last long. It was barely a year, indeed, before Napoleon reopened hostilities. In 1804, being now Emperor of the French, he planned to invade England. He had an army of over one hundred thousand men encamped at Boulogne, ready to cross the Channel. But how were they to be taken across, in the face of the vigilant Nelson and his fleet? Napoleon knew that all depended on that, and said: "Let us be masters of the Channel for six hours, and we are masters of the world." Fortunately for England, he never gained this mastery of the Channel, for the French and

Spanish fleets, with which he had hoped to control it, were defeated by Sir Robert Calder, and soon afterwards were almost destroyed by Nelson in the battle of Traf-al-gar′ (1805), one of the most famous of sea fights.

It seems that Admiral Nelson had cornered the French and Spanish fleets at Cadiz. Although the enemy had seven vessels more than the British, Nelson took his measures so carefully that he hoped to succeed. He finally bade his officers signal to the fleet these famous words: "England expects every man to do his duty."

Then the men set up a deafening shout, and began the fight bravely. Nelson soon fell, mortally wounded; but he covered up his face, lest his men, seeing he was dying, should lose courage. He was carried below, where he lived long enough to hear that the victory had been won, and died saying, "Thank God, I have done my duty."

Daniel Maclise, Artist.

Death of Nelson.

This great English hero had already been in many battles, and had won many victories. On one occasion he lost an eye; on another he was shot in the arm. As none of the medicines now used to deaden pain were then known, he suffered greatly while the doctors were cutting off his arm. Having found that the pain was made keener because the instruments were cold, Nelson ever after had them put in hot water before they were used on his men; for he was as thoughtful of their comfort as he was brave.

The glorious victory of Trafalgar is commemorated in London by Trafalgar Square, in the centre of which there is a tall column surmounted by a statue of Lord Nelson. The hero himself is buried in Westminster Abbey, where England's greatest warriors, statesmen, men of letters, and men of science have beautiful monuments, as well as most of the English kings.

Monument in Trafalgar Square.

CVI. THE BATTLE OF WATERLOO.

AFTER the failure of his plan for crossing the Channel, Napoleon plunged into new ventures. He suddenly marched off to attack Austria and Russia, and won battle after battle in central Europe. Then, hoping to make Great Britain poor, he declared that none of her vessels should be allowed to come into any port on the Continent, to buy or sell any merchandise. Of course, such an order made the British angry; and when they heard that Napoleon intended to seize the fleet of Denmark and use it against England, they bombarded Co-pen-ha'gen and seized the Danish ships.

Spain and Portugal, indignant at the treatment they received from their French conquerors, now declared war against Napoleon. They asked the help of the English, so Wel'ling-ton, the "Iron Duke," immediately set out for the south. With a force of ten thousand men, he won the battles of Ta-la-ve'ra, Sal-a-man'ca, and Vi-to'ri-a. This war, which lasted from 1808 to 1814, is generally known as the Peninsular War, because the principal battles were fought in the peninsula formed by Spain and Portugal.

Although it seemed as if Great Britain had already enough to do in fighting the greater part of Europe, she was soon called upon to fight against the United States also. In this War of 1812, about which you can learn in your American histories, King George took no interest; for he was now both blind and insane, and his son George was acting as regent in his stead.

Napoleon, having failed to conquer Russia, was obliged to face all the European powers. They defeated him at the battle of Leip'zig, or the "Battle of Nations," in 1813, and drove him back to France, where, in 1814, they forced him to give up the crown to Louis XVIII., a brother of the beheaded Louis XVI. Napoleon was then sent to the island of Elba, in the Mediterranean Sea. But while the

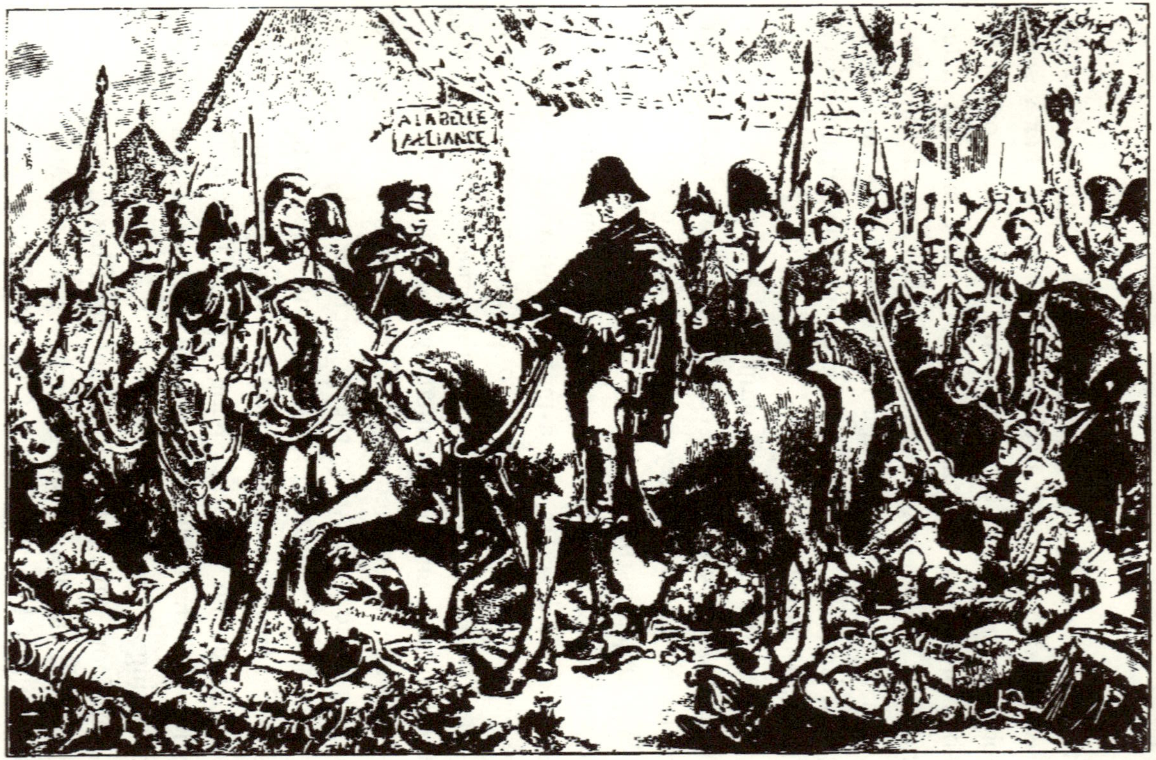

Daniel Maclise, Artist.

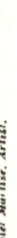

The Meeting of Wellington and Blücher.

different nations were assembled at Vi-en'na, trying to decide how to divide his conquests, he suddenly escaped. Landing in France, he was joined by a large force, and for nearly one hundred days was again supreme.

The European powers, however, were determined not to allow him to reign long, and prepared for war. The British under Wellington, and the Prussians under Blü'cher, were first in the field. Napoleon met them at Wa-ter-loo' (1815), and there, in spite of all his genius and the great courage of his soldiers, he was completely defeated.

"It is all over; we must save ourselves," said Napoleon, who had been in the midst of the fight, but was still unwounded. He was right; all was indeed over for him. He went back to Paris, and thence to Rochefort (rōsh-for'), intending to escape to America. But the British fleet blocked the port; and, being assured of honourable treatment, he went on board the *Bel-ler'o-phon*.

Napoleon had been so dangerous a foe that, in spite of all the promises made to him, the British rulers finally decided that it would be best to exile him to the island of St. He-le'na. Here, in the middle of the Atlantic Ocean, closely watched by soldiers who allowed him no privacy, Napoleon spent six lonely years. He died of a painful disease in 1821, and the British vessels which had cruised around the island to prevent his escape then returned home.

It will probably interest you to hear that it was Wellington, the victor of Waterloo, who put an end to duelling in the army, by telling his soldiers that it was far more cowardly to accept a challenge than to refuse one. Since then, British soldiers have ceased to fight, except when in the presence of the enemy.

Napoleon on board the "Bellerophon."

W. Q. Orchardson, Artist.

CVII. THE FIRST GENTLEMAN IN EUROPE.

EVEN before Napoleon surrendered, the British and Prussian armies marched on to Paris, where they were joined by the Austrians and Russians, and placed Louis XVIII. again upon the throne. The war was now ended; but the British national debt was larger than ever, and the heavy taxes caused great discontent.

Besides, the regent was very extravagant, and spent such large sums of money upon his pleasures that the poor people began to be very indignant. They were especially angry because, owing to the corn laws,—laws that almost prevented the bringing in of grain from abroad,—they could not themselves get enough to eat. The regent had also treated his wife so unkindly that his unfeeling conduct had greatly added to his unpopularity. Still, when George III. died, at the age of eighty-two, after a reign of nearly sixty years, his son quietly succeeded him as George IV.

George IV. was handsome, well educated, and had such elegant manners that his courtiers called him the "First Gentleman in Europe." But he was a gentleman only in outward appearance. He is regarded as one of the worst of the English kings, because he never tried to do what he knew to be right, and because he was very selfish.

Fortunately for the English nation, he had two very able ministers, Peel and Canning, who had charge of public affairs during much of his ten years' reign. They opposed him when he tried to get a divorce from his ill-used wife, Caroline, and gradually brought about many important improvements in the laws.

For instance, Parliament changed a law which had been in force ever since the time of Charles II., and justly decided that Roman Catholics as well as Protestants should be allowed to have seats in Parliament and to hold office. This was demanded by the Irish, who had chosen one of their great men, O'Connell, as a member of Parliament. This new law, which is called the Catholic Emancipation Act, was soon followed by others; for the British were tired of old abuses, and the time, or era, of reform had begun.

During this reign, the British, who were now the first naval power in the world, joined France and Russia in protecting the Greeks from the Turks, and helped win the famous battle of Na-va-ri'no (1827). Byron, one of the great English poets, took part in this Greek war. But he fell ill of fever at Mis-so-lon'ghi, and died before he had been able to do much for the country which he loved because it was once the home of many heroes, and of the great poets of antiquity.

CVIII. THE CHILDHOOD OF QUEEN VICTORIA.

GEORGE IV. left no children, so his crown passed on to his brother, William IV. As he was once in the navy, he is often called the "Sailor King." He was a good and able man, although somewhat rough in manner, and he was much liked because he was in favour of reform.

During his short reign England prospered greatly. With the building of the first English railway, in 1830, the way was opened for making travel much more rapid and easy.

A change was also made in the mode of elections, and when a new House of Commons assembled, there were members from all parts of the country, and all the nation was at last fairly represented.

By the efforts of a man named Wil'ber-force, slavery was abolished in the colonies. Parliament also made many laws in favour of the poor, and reduced the rate of letter postage.

William IV. and good Queen Adelaide had no children, so their niece Victoria was considered the future Queen of Great Britain. But the crown of Hanover, which had been worn by five kings of England, could not be inherited by a woman; so when William IV. died, his youngest brother, Ernest, became King of Hanover. This separation of the two kingdoms pleased the British, because the possession of land in Germany had often forced them to take more part than they wished in European wars, and had thus put them to great expense.

From early childhood Victoria was educated for the great position she was to occupy, and taught to be conscientious, kind, and affable to all. She was a happy little girl, although her father died when she was a mere baby, for she was constantly with her mother, the Duchess of Kent, a very good woman.

No one was allowed to tell Victoria that she might some day be queen, and she was brought up very plainly. We are told that she had a small allowance, and that she had to keep strict account of every penny she spent. Every one was forbidden to give or lend her any money, so that when she wanted to buy something, she had to wait and save up, if her allowance was already gone.

One day when she was out with her governess, she saw a doll which pleased her much, and she felt badly because she could not buy it at once. The shopkeeper, however, put it aside for her; and as soon as Victoria had saved up enough money, she hastened to the place to secure the coveted treasure. But as she stepped out of the shop, a poor woman begged her for something to eat. Victoria, whose money was all gone, hesitated a moment; then, turning around, she begged the merchant to take back the doll and give her her money, which she immediately bestowed upon the starving woman.

When Victoria was about twelve years old, her mother thought it was time that she should be told that she was heir to the crown. So her teacher made her trace a genealogical table of the kings of England, such as you will find at the end of this book. The little girl finally came to her uncles, and then, looking up, said that she could not see who should come after her uncle William, unless it were she.

Her mother gently told her she was right, and after a few moments' deep silence and thought, little Victoria slipped her hand into her mother's, and solemnly said: "I will be good." This resolution, made by so small a girl, has been faithfully kept. She has been a good daughter, a good pupil, a good wife, a good mother, a good queen, and, what is best of all, a thoroughly good woman.

At five o'clock in the morning, on a beautiful June day in 1837, Victoria was roused from her slumbers to receive the visit of the ministers of state. After a very hasty toilet, she went into the room where they were, and these grave men humbly bent the knee before her, calling her their queen. Although only eighteen years old, Victoria received their homage gently and with great dignity, and made them a little speech, in which she expressed her sorrow for her uncle's death, and her earnest desire to rule her people wisely.

Ever since that day, although Queen Victoria has stood alone, the observed of all observers, she has proved so good and earnest that she has won the respect of all the civilized world.

CIX. THE QUEEN'S MARRIAGE.

WHEN Victoria became queen, every one felt a tender interest in the young girl who was thus called upon to stand at the head of a great nation. Her coronation, which took place on June 28, 1838, was one of the grandest sights London has ever seen. She was crowned at Westminster Abbey, in the midst of the peers of the realm, who came up to do homage to her. Each one in turn bent the knee before her, and, removing his coronet, touched the queen's crown, saying, "I do become your liegeman of life and limb and of earthly worship; and faith and love will I bear unto you to live and die against all manner of folk. So help me God."

Even there, at the coronation, the young queen showed how kind-hearted she was; for when a very aged peer stumbled and fell, she stretched out her hand to help him rise, and came down a few steps so that he need not exert himself too much to reach her.

Now you may think it is great fun to be a queen, but

it is really hard work. From the very first, Queen Victoria spent many hours every day going over state papers with her ministers, who carefully explained everything to her. This was far more tedious for a young girl than any lesson could be; for many things were difficult to understand, and all the papers were very dry.

The queen's first minister and her good friend was Lord Mel'bourne, who took a fatherly interest in her, and who once said of her: "She never ceases to be a queen, and is always the most charming, cheerful, obliging, and unaffected queen in the world."

It was while this minister was helping her to govern that a long-planned marriage was arranged between Victoria (the "little Mayflower," as her German relatives called her) and Prince Albert of Saxe-Co'burg-Gotha (go'ta). Victoria being a queen, and Albert only a prince, she was told that it would not be proper for him to propose to her. She therefore had to propose to him; and she once said that it was the hardest thing she ever had to do.

Next, she had to appear alone before Parliament, to tell the House of Lords (which now numbers about 575 members) and the House of Commons (670 members) what she intended to do, and to receive their good wishes. This too was a great trial for so young a girl, but she never had cause to regret it, for her marriage was very happy.

Queen Victoria and the Prince Consort (for so he was later called) were a most devoted couple, and they lived a quiet, beautiful, happy, and exemplary life. Not only was the Prince Consort a good man, but he was wise and well educated, and so modest and unselfish that all he ever asked was to help the queen and her people.

During the following years many changes took place in the royal family, where nine children played in turn in the royal nursery. Changes were going on elsewhere too; for since Victoria had come to the throne, among countless other improvements, there had been established the first penny post, the telegraph, and the Atlantic cable.

To show the people how many new inventions had been made, and what wonderful things the world contains, the Prince Consort planned the first " world's fair," or " peace festival." It was held in the Crystal Palace, near London, and was such a success that it has been followed by many others in different parts of the world. These fairs have been a great help in educating people everywhere, by giving them new and useful ideas.

You will probably often hear it said that Queen Victoria is only a figurehead, and has nothing to do with the government, which is carried on by Parliament and her Cabinet. This, however, is not true; for while Great Britain is a constitutional monarchy, that is to say, a kingdom ruled by the laws of the land, and the queen could not do anything against the law, she can do much with it. Although Victoria is not a genius, she is so well educated and painstaking that it is she who has often suggested many of the improvements which have taken place.

In the government she has had many prime ministers besides Lord Melbourne; for you must know that her ministers resign their office just as soon as the greater part of Parliament does not approve of what they propose to do. Then the queen asks the principal man in the opposition party to be her minister and to select men for a new Cabinet. These members stay in office just as long as the prime minister has the good will of the House of Commons; but when he goes, they go too.

The queen's ministers have been these noted men: Melbourne, Peel, Russell, Derby, Ab-er-deen', Palm'er-ston,

Gladstone.

Glad'stone (the Grand Old Man), Dis-rae'li (Lord Beac'-ons-field), Salisbury, and Rose'ber-y. These ministers have little by little brought about many reforms, among which is a law allowing Jews to be members of both houses of Parliament. Another says that the Irish people need no longer pay taxes for the support of the Church of England, which so few of them attend.

CX. SOME WARS IN VICTORIA'S REIGN.

IF you were to hear all the great and important things which have happened during this, the longest and most glorious reign in English history, it would take a very long time and a much bigger volume than this is now to tell you about them. There have been so many great artists, writers, scientists, statesmen, inventors, and discoverers that the last half of the nineteenth century is often called the Victorian Age.

Since Victoria has been on the throne of Great Britain, there have been many disturbances. When she began her reign, the people who had been suffering from hunger wanted some of the laws changed. The reformers got up a charter, which they said had been signed by five million people, and, marching into London, they rolled it into Parliament in a tub.

The demands of the Chartists, as the charter-signers were called, frightened the people, and many took upon themselves the office of policeman to keep the mob in order. The changes the Chartists had asked for, although not granted then, were gradually brought about by a few great statesmen, such as the ministers already named, and Wilberforce, Brougham (broo'am), Cobden, and Bright.

Changes were made in corn, navigation, and trade laws; for Great Britain now has free trade; that is, goods are brought into the country without the payment of duty.

Queen Victoria has always taken a lively interest in all state matters, and has in many cases felt sorry for the numerous wars fought during her reign. Among these are several wars in Af-ghan-is-tan', fought either against the natives or against the Russians, who quarrelled with the British about the frontier.

Then there have been a number of wars with the Chinese. The first of these wars is, I am sorry to say, not to the credit of the British; for they forced the Chinese to let them have the island of Hong Kong, so as to sell all the opium they wanted to the natives, for whom it is even worse than rum. In another war, an English general, who is generally known as "Chinese Gordon," put down a Chinese rebellion, and in reward received from the emperor a mandarin's yellow gown and some gay peacock feathers, these being among the Chinese, like the Order of the Garter among the English, a mark of especial honour.

In India the British waged two wars against the Sikhs (seeks), defeated them, and took possession of their territory, the Punjab (poon-jahb'). Next they fought against the Burmese, and took possession of Lower Burma. In 1857 broke out the terrible "Indian Mutiny," or the revolt of the sepoys. These sepoys were native soldiers who had been trained to fight by British officers. When new rifles were introduced, and they had to use greased cartridges, the sepoys fancied that the British wanted to make them do what their religion forbade; that is to say, touch grease taken from their sacred animal, the cow, or from the hog, an animal the least contact with which, they fancied, made them unfit to enter heaven.

The officers tried to pacify the men by telling them that they could either grease the cartridges themselves with anything they pleased, or use other guns; but it was too late. The revolt spread from Mee'rut to Delhi (del'lee),

Cawn-pore', and Luck'now. Everywhere the British were killed without mercy, and at Cawnpore men, women, and children were cruelly butchered and cast into a well, after they had heroically defended themselves for many a day.

Memorial Well, Cawnpore.

A brave general named Hav'e-lock fought like a tiger to reach Cawnpore in time to save his countrymen; but he got there too late. In spite of the awful heat, he next hurried on to Lucknow, where he found the English still alive. But there were so many women and children that he could not fight his way out with them. He therefore joined them in their heroic resistance, which was kept up until a brave Scotchman named Campbell came marching to the rescue, just as one of the women had dreamed.

When the English heard the Scotch bagpipes in the distance, playing "The Campbells are Coming," they almost died of joy. Lucknow was relieved; but Havelock, worn

"Relief of Lucknow—Jessie's Dream."

out by his heroic exertions, soon breathed his last. The mutiny was put down, and India was taken away from the East India Company and placed under the rule of the queen.

Since then there have been a few other revolts, which have quickly been put down. But railways, telegraphs, schools, and colleges are making rapid changes in India, where there are more than two hundred million people, speaking many different languages, practising many religions, but all subject to Victoria, who was crowned Empress of India in 1877.

Great Britain also fought one war in Europe, against Russia—a war of which you will hear a great deal. It is called the "Cri-me'an War," and it was during this contest that, owing to a mistaken order, the Light Brigade made the gallant charge at Bal-a-kla'va (1854). Their prompt obedience, their courage, and the death of nearly the whole

Robert Cibb, Artist.
"The Thin Red Line"—93d Highlanders at Balaklava.

company, have made them for ever famous. If you want to hear what dangers they braved, you had better read Tennyson's poem, "The Charge of the Light Brigade," and then you will see why every one admires them.

While the British soldiers were making their names famous in the Crimean War, an Englishwoman, Florence Nightingale, nursed the sick and the dying with such devotion that the men kissed her shadow on the wall as she passed by. Thanks to her exertions, and to those of the kind nurses whom she directed, many lives were saved, and since then hospitals for wounded soldiers have been much improved.

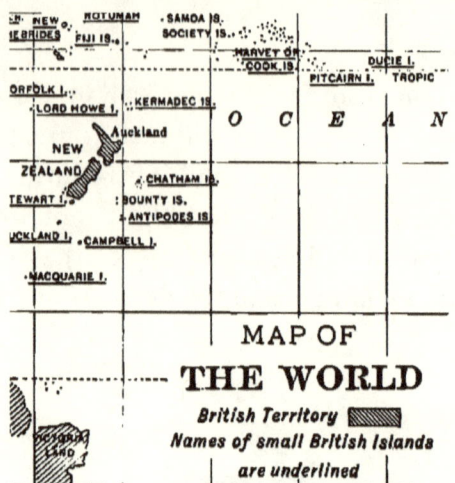

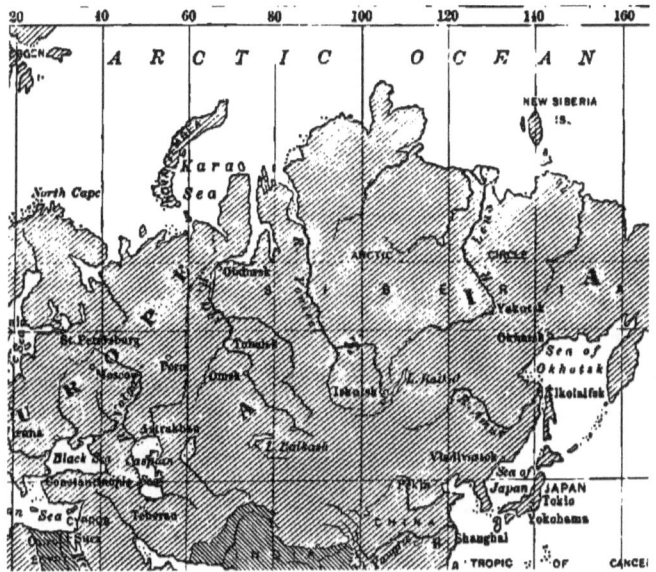

CXI. THE JUBILEE.

GREAT BRITAIN'S wars in Africa have been numerous, for she has fought, north, south, east, and west, against many of the small tribes; and a large part of that continent is now under her rule. In one of these wars the French prince imperial, son of Napoleon III., was killed by the Zu'lus; in another brave "Chinese Gordon" fell at Khar-tum'; and on his way to a third, the Prince of Bat'ten-berg, Victoria's son-in-law, lost his life from fever.

During the Civil War in America, in 1861, England and the United States pretty nearly came to blows; but a kindly message, suggested by the dying Prince Consort, and a prompt and graceful apology on the part of the United States, averted this catastrophe. Later on, when other disputes occurred between the two nations, they were settled by arbitration, which is always the best method for civilized people to adopt as a means of settling disputes.

By all the wars which you have just read about, and by sundry others which we need not mention here, Great Britain has spread her territory farther and farther, and grown stronger and stronger. She has also planted many colonies without having to fight great battles, the most prosperous of these being in Australia, where gold was discovered in 1851. About one quarter of all the people on the globe now belong to Great Britain, for Victoria is said to rule over nearly four hundred million subjects.

The queen married in 1840, and had nine children. A careful mother, she watched over her children herself, praising them when they did right, correcting them when they did wrong, and always giving them clearly to understand that their exalted position demanded that they should set a good example to others.

One day the queen went out with the princess royal, her eldest daughter, to review some troops. Perhaps she was going to bestow "Victoria crosses," which are the medals given to soldiers or sailors for some of the brave deeds such as we love to hear about. The queen's carriage was escorted, as usual, by the magnificent Horse Guards, who stood a short distance off as if they were statues. But although they were so motionless, each man's eyes were fixed upon the royal carriage, and all were ready, at a mere sign, to spring forward to render any service.

Either to show her importance, or to attract the attention of the handsome guardsmen, or from a spirit of mischief, the princess royal, after dangling her handkerchief for a few moments over the side of the carriage, dropped it as if by accident. As it fluttered to the ground the guardsmen rushed forward to pick it up. But the queen, who had noticed her daughter's manœuvres, and who knew she had let her handkerchief fall intentionally, motioned the guards back to their post.

Then, turning to the princess royal, she bade her get out of the carriage and pick up her handkerchief herself, since she had dropped it only to give trouble. In the sight of guardsmen, troops, and the assembled crowd, "Vicky," as her parents affectionately called her, was obliged to wait upon herself. And you may be sure that this wholesome lesson, and the queen's explanation that it was vulgar to try to attract attention, made a deep impression on the princess, who later became Empress of Germany.

After the marriage of this daughter, and after a happy married life of more than twenty years, the Prince Consort, who had always worked very hard for his wife's subjects, fell suddenly and dangerously ill. In spite of the utmost care and skill, he sank rapidly, and died in the queen's arms, whispering loving words to her.

Prince Albert was such a good and noble man that he was mourned by the whole people. They erected a beautiful public monument for him in London, the Albert Memorial, while his sorrowing wife and children put up a private tomb for him at Frogmore.

Victoria's children have all married, and nearly all of them now have large families. . Her eldest son, the Prince of Wales, is named Albert Edward. The queen, who is by this time a great-grandmother, is related to nearly all the crowned heads in Europe, and while one of her grandsons is Emperor of Germany, one of her granddaughters is Czarina of Russia.

Victoria has led a very quiet and retired life ever since the death of the Prince Consort. She lives part of the time in London or Windsor, where she has beautiful palaces. The rest of her time is spent in her seaside home at Os'borne in the Isle of Wight, in her mountain home at Bal-mor'al in the Scottish Highlands, or in travelling.

Victoria is always busy and is always striving faithfully to do her best for her people. When state affairs do not need her attention, she reads, writes, sews, and studies. When she was younger she used to practise on the piano, sing, and draw. And in spite of the fact that she already knew several languages, we are told that, although nearly sixty years old when she became Empress of India, she began to study Hin-doo-sta'nee, so that she could talk in their own language to her Indian servants and visitors.

In 1887 Queen Victoria celebrated her "jubilee," or the fiftieth anniversary of her reign. In 1897 another imposing pageant took place to commemorate the longest and

Albert Edward, Prince of Wales.

most prosperous reign of the best sovereign that England has ever seen. There was a magnificent procession, and the queen heard the Te Deum sung in the big square before St. Paul's Cathedral; for there was no church big enough to contain the many important people who came to do her honour. There were princes and troops from every country, and in the huge crowd were many American children, who, remembering how good the queen has always been, joined the British in crying:

"God bless Queen Victoria!"

GENEALOGICAL TABLE AND INDEX.

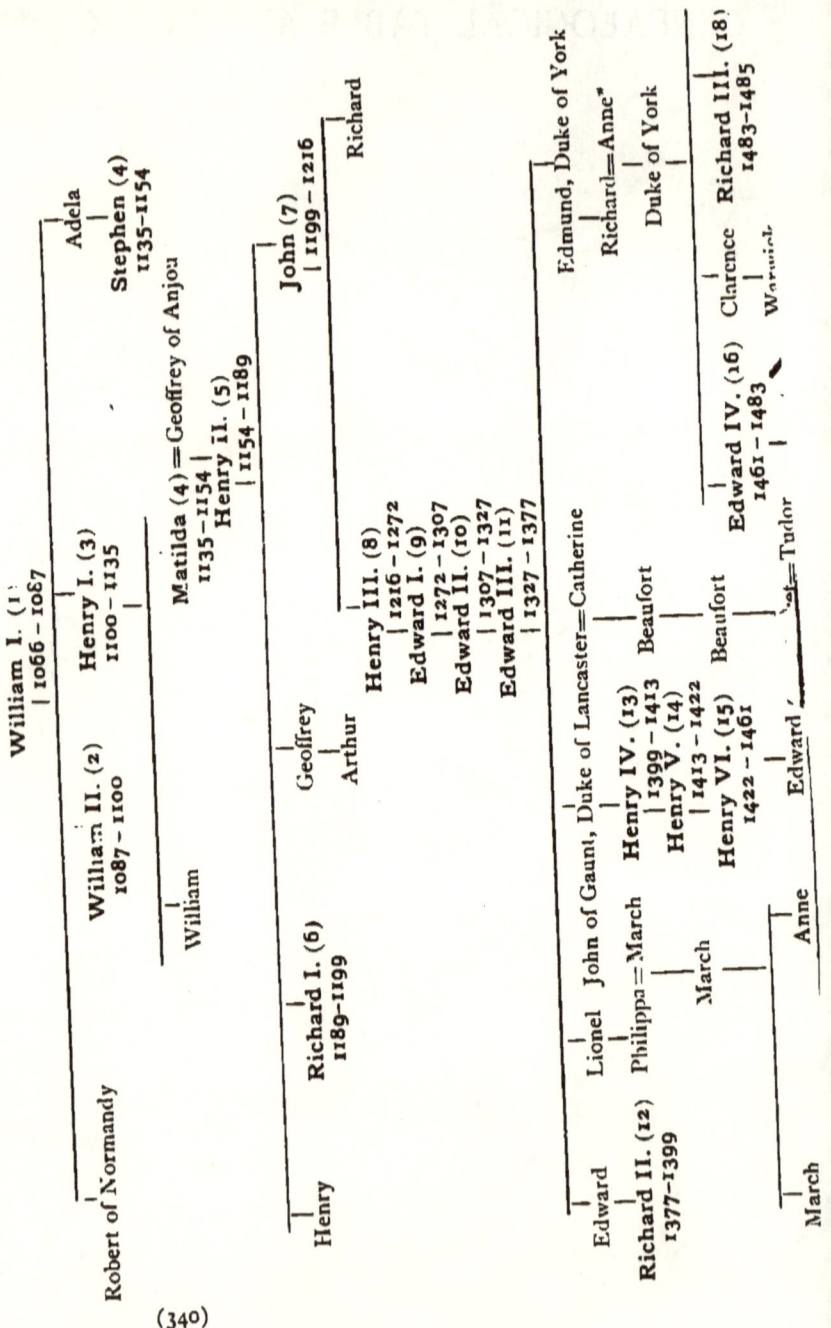

```
                                    Henry VII. (19)=Elizabeth
                                     1485-1509  |         |            ------
                                                                       1483-1483
                                           |                              |
                                           |                         Mary=Suffolk
                                     Henry VIII. (20)                     |
                                      1509-1547                      Frances=Grey
                                           |                              |
                                           |                        Lady Jane Grey
        _____
        |                    |                    |
    Mary I. (22)        Elizabeth (23)       Edward VI. (21)
    1553-1558           1558-1603            1547-1553

                                                            Elizabeth
                                                                |
                                                          Sophia=Hanover
                                                                |
                                                          George I. (30)
                                                           1714-1727
                                                                |
                                                          George II. (31)
                                                           1727-1760
                                                                |
                                                          Frederick
                                                                |
                                                          George III. (32)
                                                           1760-1820
```

James IV.=Margaret=Angus	
James V. Margaret	
Mary Stuart=Darnley	
James I. (24)	
1603-1625	

                    Commonwealth, 1649-1660

                                    Hyde=James II. (27)=Marie
                                         1685-1688
                                              |
                                         Pretender
                                              |
                                      Young Pretender

Charles I. (25)
 1625-1649
      |
      | Anne (29)*
      | 1702-1714
Charles II. (26)   Mary
  1660-1685 |
      | William III. (28)=Mary II. (28)
Monmouth   1689-1702   1689-1694

George IV. (33)   William IV. (34)   Edward
 1820-1830   1830-1837 |
                                         Victoria (35)
                                          1837-

                                          Ernest

Victoria Albert Edward Alice Alfred Helena Louise Arthur Leopold Beatrice

(341)

* This Anne is the same as the one shown at the left as the descendant of Lionel and the Marches.

THE SOVEREIGNS OF ENGLAND.

First, William the Norman,
  Then William his son;
Henry, Stephen, and Henry,
  Then Richard and John.
Next, Henry the third,
  Edwards, one, two, and three,
And again, after Richard,
  Three Henrys we see.
Two Edwards, third Richard,
  If rightly I guess;
Two Henrys, sixth Edward,
  Queen Mary, Queen Bess;
Then Jamie the Scotchman,
  Then Charles whom they slew,
Yet received, after Cromwell,
  Another Charles, too.
Next Jamie the second
  Ascended the throne;
Then good William and Mary
  Together came on;
Then Anne, Georges four,
  And fourth William all passed,
And Victoria came —
  May she long be the last!

INDEX.

Key to pronunciation.—VOWELS: ā in lāte, ă in făt, â in câre, ä in fär, ȧ in lȧst, ạ in fạll, ḁ in wḁs, au in author; ē in mē, ĕ in mĕt, ẹ in vẹil, c̄ in tēr̄m; ī in fīne, ĭ in tĭn, ï in police; ō in nōte, ŏ in nŏt, o in son, ô in fôr, ọ in wọlf, ọ in dọ, oo in loop; ū in tūne, ŭ in nŭt, ɥ in rɥde, ụ in fụll, ü = French u; ȳ in mȳ, ў in hўmn. CONSONANTS: ç in çent, e in ean; ġ in ġem, ḡ in ḡet, G or K = German ch; ñ = ny in barnyard, ŋ = ng, N = ng but is silent; ṣ = z. *Italic letters are silent.*

	PAGE		PAGE
Ab'bess, head of nunnery	58	Aŋ'gli-a, kingdom formed by Angles	34
Ab'bot, head of monastery	57	Aŋ'gli-can Church. See *Church of England.*	
Ȧb-er-deen', prime minister	326	Aŋ'glo-Sȧx'ons	31–76
Ȧ-bọu-kïr', battle of	311	conversion of	39
A-cā'di-a, relinquished by French	295	Heptarchy	36
Ac-co-lāde', bestowing the	161	laws and language of	33, 34, 36–38, 78
A'cre (ā'ker). Napoleon at	311	names of days of week	33
Richard I. attacks	107–109	An'lȧf, Danish leader	53, 54
Act of Set'tle-ment	287	Anne, wife of Richard II.	170, 172
Ad'ams, John, ambassador to England	308	Anne of Clēveṣ, marries Henry VIII.	
Ad'di-son, English writer	295		218, 219
Ad'e-laide, wife of William IV.	321	Anne, Queen, daughter of James II.	282
Ad-ri-ăt'ic Sea, Richard I. on	111	age of literature	295
Æl'la (ăl'a), captured by Northmen	45	death of	296
head of Heptarchy	44	marries Prince George of Denmark	291
Ȧf-ghan-is-tȧn', wars in	328	An'selm, Archbishop of Canterbury	88
Af'ri-ca, wars in	334	An-to-nī'nus, wall of	26
Agincourt (ä-zhăN-koor'), battle of	181	Ȧr'a-bic numbers, introduced	52
Āix-lä-Ch̥ä-pelle', peace of	299, 300	Ar-ġȳle', Duke of	284
Al'bert Ed'ward, Prince of Wales	336	Ar'mour, description of	89, 90
Albert of Sȧxe-Cō'burg-Gō'thȧ, death of	336	Ar-suf', Richard victorious at	110
marries Victoria	324, 325	Ar'thur, King, defeats Saxons	34, 35
Al'bi-on, England called	13	tales of	35, 36
Alençon (ä-lŏN-sŏN'), Duke of	236, 244	Arthur, nephew of John	117, 118
Al'fred, King, conquers Danes	49, 50	Arthur, son of Henry VII.	205
death of	52	As'ca-lon, fortifications rebuilt	110
education of	46, 47	As'eham, Elizabeth's tutor	234
in the herdsman's hut	48, 49	As-san'dun, battle of	64
invents first lantern	51	As-sas'sins, tribe of	109
Alfred, son of Ethelred	68	Ath'el-stan the Glorious, Saxon king,	
Ȧl'vu, Duke of	244	reign of	53, 54
Amiens (ä-mI-ăN'), treaty of	312	At-lan'tic cable, laid	325
An'ġe-vine kings. See *Plantagenets.*		At'ti-la, invasion of	28
Aŋ'gles, settle in Britain	33, 34	Aus-trā'li-a, British colonies in	334
Aŋ'gle-sey, Druids settle in	18	Aus'tri-a, Duke of	108–110
Suetonius attacks Druids in	24	Austrian Suc-ces'sion, War of	299

	PAGE
Aus'tri-ans, Napoleon conquers	311, 314
Av'a-lon, home of fairies	35
Bab'ing-ton, conspiracy of	243
Ba'con, Lord Francis	259
Bacon, Roger, discoveries of	128
Băl-a-klä'vă, Light Brigade at	331
Bā'li-ol, Edward, Scottish king	152
Baliol, John, claims Scottish throne	137
Ball, John, leads mob	168
Bal'lad of Chěv'y Chase	171
Bal-mör'al, Queen Victoria's residence	336
Bạl'tic Sea	31
Bank of England, established	291
Ban'nock-burn	145
Bare'bone, Praise-God	272
Bar'net, Yorkist victory at	194
Bār'ons, draw up Magna Charta	122
join Prince Edward	127
power of	80
ravages of	97
revolt of	147, 148
Bat'ten-bĕrG, Prince of	334
Battle of Nations	315
Battle of the Spurs	206
Battle of the Stand'ard	94
Ba-vā'ri-a, in War of Austrian Succession	299
Ba-yĕux' tapestry	76
Beach'y Head, battle of	289
Beac'ons-field, Lord, prime minister	326
Beaū'fort, Cardinal	187
Beck'et, Thomas à, Archbishop of Canterbury	100
chancellor	99
murdered	102
quarrel with Henry II	101
shrine of St. Thomas	103
Bed'ford, Duke of, death of	186
regent of France	183, 184
Ben-gạl', war in	303–305
Be-ren-gā'ri-a, wife of Richard I.	107
Berke'ley Castle, Edward II. murdered in	149
Ber'tha, wife of Ethelbert	38
Bĕr'wick, taken	146
Bible, divided into verses and chapters	120
King James's	254
translated into English	170
Bir'nam woods	73
Black death, ravages of	159
Black Hole of Calcutta	304
Black Prince, death of	163
in Guienne	162
wins battle of Crécy	154, 155
Blake, Admiral	271, 272
Blĕn'heIm, battle of	292

	PAGE
Blenheim Castle	293
Blon-del', finds Richard I.	112
Bloody As-sī'zes	285
Blü'cher (-Ger), Prussian general	317
Bo-ad-i-cē'a	24, 25
Bo-he'mi-a, King of, at Crécy	155
Bọl'eỹn, Anne, Henry VIII. marries	215
sent to Tower and executed	217, 218
Bŏl'ing-broke. See *Henry IV.*	
Bom-bay', English property	278, 303
Bordeaux (bor-dō'), Black Prince at	162
Bŏs'co-bel, Charles II. at	270
Bŏs'worth, battle of	201
Bŏth'well, Earl of	240, 241
Bou-logne', acquired by English	221
French army at	312
Bourges (boorzh), King of	184
Bou-vĭnes', English defeat at	120
Boyne, battle of the	289
Brĕnne-ville', battle of	89
Bretigny (brē-tēn-yi'), treaty of	163
Bret'wal-da	36
Bright, English statesman	327
Bris'tol, besieged	149
Matilda besieged at	94
Bri-tan'ni-a, Latin name for England	22
Brit'ons, adopt Christianity	26
conquered by Romans	22, 23, 25
driven from England	32, 33, 35
religious customs of	18, 19
settle in England	17
Brit'tan-y, Britons settle in	35
opposed to John	117, 118
Brittany, Duke of, joins Henry IV.	173
Bronze Age, defined	12
Brougham, English statesman	327
Bruce, David, defeat of	157
Bruce, Robert, and the spider	143, 144
claims Scottish throne	137
crowned	140
death of	152
escapes	139
King of Scotland	146
signs treaty with Edward III.	151
victorious	144, 145
Brụ'nan-burgh, battle of	54
Buck'ing-ham, Gloucester's friend	198
executed	200
Buckingham, Duke of (Steenie)	259
adviser of Charles I.	261
murdered	261
Bur'gun-dy, Duchess of, helps Warbeck	204
Burgundy, Duke of	180
Bur'leigh, chief minister of Queen Elizabeth	233, 235
death of	250

	PAGE
Bur'ma, conquered	328
By'ron, Lord, death of	320
Ca-bäl', the	281
Cab'i-net, the	326
Cab'ot, discovers Newfoundland	205
Cade, Jack, rebel	188, 189
Câ'diz, Francis Drake at	245
French and Spanish fleets at	313
Spanish fleet at	244
Caed'mon, story of	41
Caer-lē'on, King Arthur's palace at	36
Çaē'şar, Jūl'ius, in Britain	21, 22
Cä-lā́is', capture of	156, 157
Henry VIII. meets Francis at	210
sole English possession in France	186
Spanish Armada at	245
taken by French	232
Cal-cut'ta, captured	303, 304
Cal'der, Sir Robert	313
Cal-e-do'ni-a, Scotland called	27
Cal'en-dar, change in	305
Camp'bell, relieves Lucknow	330
Campbells, murder MacDonalds	288
Cam'per-down, battle of	310
Cäm'po-for'mi-o, treaty of	311
Can'ning, English minister	319
Can'non, first used	155
Ca-no'va, sculptor	301
Can'ter-bur-y Cathedral	39, 40, 164
Ca-nūte', Danish king	64
and the waves	65, 66
death of	67
King of England	65
Ca-rac'ta-cus, leader of Britons	23
Car'diff Castle, Robert imprisoned in	89
Car-lisle', Edward I. at	140
Car-nar'von, Castle of	132
Câr'o-line, wife of George IV.	319
Carr, James I.'s favourite	256, 258
Cä-så-bi-än'cä, story of	311
Cas-si-tĕr'i-dĕş, Tin Islands	20
Cas-si-vel-lau'nus, leader of Britons	22
Cas-tile', throne of, secured by Lancaster	171
Cäth'er-ine, wife of Henry V.	183
Catherine of Ar'a-gon, divorced	215, 237
marries Henry VIII.	206
marries Prince Arthur	205
Catherine of Brä-gän'za, wife of Charles II.	278
Cath'ŏ-lic Emancipation Act	320
Catholics, Roman, favoured by Charles II.	281, 282
favoured by James II.	285
in Ireland	288

	PAGE
Catholics, Roman, in Parliament	320
in Scotland	224
opposed to Wyclif	171
plots of	242, 252, 253, 254, 255
refuse oath of supremacy	216
set sail for America	263
trouble with Charles I.	261
under Elizabeth	237, 244
under Mary	228, 230
Cav-a-liĕrş' and Roundheads, 264, 265, 270	
Cawn-pōre', revolt in	329
Cax'ton, introduces printing	196
Celts, in England	14–18
Châlons (shä-lŏN'), Little Battle of	129
Chä-lūs', Lord of, besieged	116
Châr'ing Cross, erected	136
Charles I. of England, character, 260, 261	
consents to Petition of Right	261
executed	268
rules without Parliament	262
tried as traitor	266, 267
wages war with Parliament	265
Charles II., appeals to Parliament	267
character	282
crowned	276
death of	282
flight of	270, 271
in Scotland	269
marriage of	278
policy of	277
sells Dunkirk to French	280
Charles V. of Spain and Holland	207
alliance with Henry VIII.	210
Charles VII. of France	184–186
Charles Edward, Prince	299, 300
Char'lotte, wife of George III.	306
Chart'ists, demands of	327
Chau'cer, English author	164
Ches'ter, Roman camp at	25
Chi-nêşe', wars with	328
Chiv'al-ry, age of	159–161, 194
Church of England, in Charles I.'s reign	263
Irish not taxed for	326
James I. favours	252
James II. promises to support	284
restored	277
the national church	233
under William and Mary	288
Churches, built	39, 40, 69
destroyed by Danes	45
founded in Ireland	31
Church'ill, Lady	293
Churls, duties of	36
Civ'il War, in America	334
in England	94, 124, 125, 265
Clăr'ence, George, Duke of	191, 193–195

	PAGE
Clăr'en-don, Earl of	277
exiled	281
Clau'di-us, releases Caractacus	23
sends legions to Britain	22
Clăv'er-hŏuse, commander	277
Clive, Robert	304
Cob'den, English statesman	327
Cob'ham, Lord, burned	180
Col'o-nies, American, proclaim Independence	308
taxation in	307
Colonies, British	307, 332-334
Co-lum'bus, discovers America	205
Com'merce, encouraged	203, 257
Com'mon-wealth, the	260, 271-275
Compiègne (cŏn-pyăñ'), Joan of Arc at	185
Cŏm'ўn, killed	140
Con-sti-tu'tions of Clarendon	99
Becket opposes	101
Con'vents	58
Co-pen-hā'gen, bombarded	315
Côrfe Castle, Edward murdered at	61
Corn laws	319, 327
Corn'wall, Britons in	32
tin mines in	20
Corn-wal'lis, surrenders	308
Cor-o-na'tion stone of Scotland	138
Cŏr'yat, traveller	257, 258
Cŏv'e-nant, the Scottish	263, 269, 277
Cŏv'en-trў, Leofric, Lord of	71
Cran'mer, Archbishop of Canterbury	215
arranges Book of Common Prayer	223
burned at stake	231
character	220
Crécy (crā-sē'), battle of	153-155
Cri-mē'an War	331
Cròm'well, Oliver, and Charles I.	266
death of	275
Protector of Commonwealth	272-274
Puritan leader	264, 265
victory of Dunbar	269
Cromwell, Richard, son of Oliver, 275, 276	
Cromwell, Thomas, and Henry VIII.	218, 219
Crṵ-sāde', first	86
Prince Edward joins last	128
Richard joins third	105, 107
Cul-lo'den, battle of	300
Cum'ber-land, Duke of	301
Cum'bri-a, conquered by Edmund	55
Cur'few bell	81
Cў'prus, Richard captures	107
Dāne'gĕld, Danes' money	64
payment of, stopped	69

	PAGE
Dāne'lagh	45
Danes restricted to	50
Dānes, at war with Saxons,	44, 45, 47, 54
conquered at Ethandun	50
defeated at Stamford Bridge	75
defeated by Edward	55
invade England	64, 74
ravages of	42, 44
Dān'ish kings	64, 67, 68
Danish ships, seized	315
Darn'ley, Lord	238, 240
Dau'phin	184
Da'vid of Scotland, invades England	93
David, successor of Robert Bruce	152
taken prisoner	157
David, Welsh leader	131, 132
Days of week, named	33
Dee, river	60
De-fend'er of the Faith	211
De-foe', Daniel, English author	282
Del'hy̆, revolt in	328
Der'by, prime minister	326
De-spen'sers, father and son, favourites of Edward II.	147-149
D'Este (dās'tĕ), Marie, James II. marries	284
Det'ting-en, battle of	299
Dis-rāe'li, prime minister	326
Dŏmeṣ'day Book	81
Doŭg'las, fights Saracens	146, 147
skirmish warfare of	150, 151
Douglas, defeats Percy Hotspur	171
Douglas, George, assists Mary of Scots	242
Drāke, Sir Francis	245
Drṵ'ids, in Anglesey	18
killed by Suetonius	24
religion of	14-17
Dry'den, poet	282
Dud'ley, lawyer	205, 206
Northumberland's father	207
Dudley, son of Northumberland	226
husband of Lady Jane Grey	229
Du'el-ling, end of, in British army	317
Dun-bar', Scotch defeats at	138, 269
Dunbar Castle, Mary of Scots at	240
Dun'can, King of Scotland, murdered, 73	
Dun'kirk, acquired by Cromwell	274
sold to French	280
Spanish army at	244
Dun'stan, banished	59
influence of	56-58
in power	60
placed among saints	62
Duquesne (dṵ-kān'), Fort, captured	303
Dutch. See *Holland*.	

347

	PAGE
East India Company, formed	257
loses India	330
trading posts of	303
Ed'gar, laws of	60
Edge'hill, battle of	265
Edinburgh (ed'in-bur-ro), captured	300
English army at	224
E'dith, wife of Edward the Confessor	69
Ed'mund, King, conquers Cumbria	55
Edmund Iron'sides, war with Danes	64
Ed'red, defeats Danes	55, 56
under Dunstan's influence	57, 58
Ed'ward the Confessor	69, 70, 73
Edward the Elder, King of Saxons	53
Edward the Martyr	61, 62
Edward I., coronation of	129
death of	140
escapes	127
marches into Wales	132
persecutes Jews	130
reforms of	130
taken prisoner	126
trouble with France	134–136
wins Little Battle of Châlons	129
Edward II., first Prince of Wales,	132, 140
murder of	149
Parliament at York	142
revolt of barons	147, 148
war with Bruce	145
Edward III., crowned	149
death of	165
fights Scots	150, 151
Hundred Years' War	153
seven years' truce with France	159
Edward IV., death of	196
escapes	193
marries Elizabeth Woodville	193
proclaimed king	191
returns to London	195
Edward V., birth of	194
imprisoned and murdered	197, 198
Edward VI., son of Henry VIII.	218
crowned	222
death of	226
education of	223
peasants' revolt	224
plan for his marriage	224
plan for the succession	225, 226
Ed'wy, Saxon king	58
E'gypt, British take possession of	312
Napoleon's victories in	311
El'ba, Napoleon sent to	315
El'can-or, wife of Henry II.	96
imprisoned	104
released	107
Eleanor, wife of Edward I.	128, 136

	PAGE
E-lec'tions, reform in	321
El-fri'da, Edgar marries	61
reigns in England	62
El-gi'va, wife of King Edwy	58–60
E-liz'a-beth, Queen, daughter of Henry VIII.	217, 218
character	234
church policy of	233
crowned	233
death of	252
encourages literature	247, 249
excommunicated	237
Invincible Armada	244–246
plans for her marriage	236
reforms of	235
successor to throne	222, 225
troubles with Ireland	250
troubles with Mary Stuart	242, 243
Elizabeth, wife of Henry VII.	202
Elizabeth Wood'ville, wife of Edward IV.	193
E-liz'a-beth-an Age	247, 249
Em'ma, wife of Ethelred	64
marries Canute	65
Emp'son, lawyer	205, 206
England (ing'glund), origin of name	34
separation from Hanover	321
separation of French provinces	118
union with Ireland	310
union with Scotland	295
Wales annexed	134
England, Church of. See *Church of England*.	
English (ing'glish) language	34, 164
English Reign of Terror	285
Er'nest, King of Hanover	321
Es'sex, kingdom of Saxons	34
Essex, Earl of, Elizabeth's adviser,	250, 251
Eth-an-dyn', Danes conquered at	50
Eth'el-bert, Anglo-Saxon king	38
Eth'el-red the Unready, Anglo-Saxon king	62
pays Danegeld	64
Eth'el-wulf, King, journeys to Rome	46
Eû-gêne', Prince	291, 292
Eves'ham, battle of	127
Ex-com-mu-ni-ca'tion, defined	103
Ex'e-ter, Roman camp at	25
Fair'fax, Puritan leader	264
Fair Ros'a-mond, story of	96, 97
Fal'kirk, Scots defeated at	138
Fâv'er-sham, James II. escapes to	285
Fawkes, Guy, Gunpowder Plot of,	255, 256
Fer'di-nand and Isabella of Spain	205

	PAGE
Feu'dal-ism, decline of	155, 201
introduced	80, 81
Field of the Cloth of Gold	210
Fire, great	279
Fish'er, Bishop of Roch'es-ter	216, 217
Flan'ders, Count of, John's ally	120
Flanders, Philip of Spain in	232
Flint Castle, Richard II. in	173
Flod'den Field, battle of	207
Flor'i-da, boundary in dispute	298
ceded to England	307
Fŏth'er-iŋ-gay Castle, Mary in	243
Fox, Charles	312
France, acquires Calais	232
attacked by John	120
Britons settle in	35
English possessions in, lost	118
helps Greeks against Turks	320
Hundred Years' War	153–159, 162, 163, 180–186
loses colonial possessions	305, 307
makes compact with Spain	298, 299
Napoleon	311, 312
Northmen in	63
recognizes independence of United States	309
Reign of Terror	309
Seven Years' War	301
treaty of Bretigny	163
War of Spanish Succession	290
wars with England	115, 134–136, 153, 180, 221, 223, 311
Fran'cis I., King of France	207
meets Henry VII.	210
Francis II., marries Queen of Scotland	225
"Frank'ing" letters	275
Freă, goddess of beauty	34
Fred'er-ick V., Elector	259
Free trade	327
French and Indian War	301
Fröb'ish-er, commander	245
Frog'more, tomb for Prince Albert at	336
Gäels, driven to Scotland and Wales	18
settle in England	13, 14
Gard'iner, Bishop, adviser of Queen Mary	228, 230
death of	231
imprisoned	224
Gas-coigne', Judge	177, 179
Gaul, invaded by Attila	28
Gāv'es-ton, Piers	141–143
Geoffrey of Anjou (äN-zhoo'), marries Matilda	92

	PAGE
Geoffrey, son of Henry II.	105, 106
George I., death of	298
proclaimed king	296
visits Hanover	297
George II., crowned	298
death of	305
George III. character of	306
crowned	305
death of	319
George IV., regent	315
character of	319
George, husband of Anne	291, 295
Geŏr'gi-a, boundary of, in dispute	298
Ger'man-y, Charles V., Emperor of	207
Victoria, Empress of	335
William, Emperor of	336
in War of Spanish Succession	291
Gi-bral'tar, captured	294
Gil'bert à Becket	99
Gil'das, writes Latin history	41
Glad'stone, prime minister	326
Glăs'ton-bur-y, Arthur buried at	85
Glen-coe', MacDonalds murdered at	288
Glen'dow-er, Owen, leads rebellion	175
Glŏuces'ter, Humphrey, Duke of,	183, 184, 187
Gloucester, Richard, Duke of. See Richard III.	
Gloucester, Robert, Earl of	94, 95
Gloucester, Thomas, Duke of	167
death of	172
regent	171
Go-dī'va, Lady, story of	71, 72
God'win, officer of Canute	67
death of	70
influence of	68, 69
Gor'don, Chinese	328
death of	334
Grand Alliance	291
Great Brit'ain, countries composing	11
Ireland united to	310
kingdom of	295
Great Char'ter. See *Magna Charta*.	
Greek war	320
Greenwich (grĕn'ij) Hospital founded,	291
Greg'o-ry, Pope	38–40
Grey, Lady Jane	226
executed	229
reigns ten days	227, 228
Grey, Lord, executed	197
Gui-enne', Black Prince in	162
English province	118, 153
French monarch occupies	135
Guine-gäte', French defeat at	206
Gun'pow-der, discovered	128
Gunpowder Plot	254–256
Gŭth'rŭm, Danish general	50

	PAGE
Hā'be-as Cor'pus Act	281, 285
Hā'dri-an, wall of	26
Hal, Prince. See *Henry V*.	
Hamp'den, pays ship money	262
Puritan leader	264
Hamp'ton Court, Charles I. at	266
Wolsey at	208
Han'o-ver, Elector of, marries Sophia	296
separated from England	321
Han-o-vē'ri-an kings,	296, 298, 305, 319, 320
Har-di-ca-nute', King	68
Har-fleur', surrender of	180
Hăr'old, death of	75
made king	74
Harold the Harefoot	68
Hās'tings, battle of	75, 76
Hastings, Lord, beheaded	197
Hastings, pirate chief	50
Hat'field House, Elizabeth captive at	233
Hāv'e-lock, in Indian Mutiny	329, 330
Haw'ar-den Castle, captured	132
Hawke, Admiral, destroys French fleet	303
Hawk'ins, commander	245
Hedge'ly Moor, battle of	191
Hĕm'ans, Mrs., poet	311
Hen'gist, leader of Jutes	32
Hen-ri-et'ta Maria, wife of Charles I.	259, 261
Hen'ry I. (Beauclerc, bō-klärk'), King of England	88
death of	92
master of Normandy	89
Henry II. (Short'man-tle), and Thomas à Becket	100, 101
conquers Ireland	103
crowned	96
death of	105
institutes trial by jury	97
public penance of	104
war with Stephen	95
Henry III., crowned	124
death of	129
inglorious reign of	128
Henry IV., crowned	173
death of	178
exiled	173
war with Welsh and Scotch	175
Henry V., battle of Agincourt	181
battle of Shrewsbury	175
conquests in France	182
death of	183
invades France	180
succeeds Henry IV.	179
Henry VI.	183
captured	190

	PAGE
Henry VI., death of	195
deposed	191
marries Margaret of Anjou	187
recrowned	194
Henry VII., character of	205, 206
crowned	201
death of	206
discoveries	205
Earl of Richmond	200
marries Elizabeth	202
the pretenders	203, 204
Henry VIII., alliance with Charles V.	207, 210
character	206
death of	222
Defender of the Faith	211
encourages learning and commerce	220, 221
head of church	216, 218, 219
marries Anne Boleyn	215
marries Anne of Cleves	219
marries Catherine Howard	219
marries Catherine of Aragon	206
marries Catherine Parr	219
marries Jane Seymour	218
proceedings for divorce	212-215
Henry, son of James I.	258
Henry, son of Charles I.	267, 268
Hep'tarch-y	36
Hĕr'e-ford, Earl of	135
Hex'ham, battle of	191
Hi-bēr'ni-a, Ireland called	29
High'land-ers, defeated	287
join Prince Charles Edward	300, 301
Hil'da, abbess	41
Hol'bein, painter	221
Hol'land (Dutch), Charles V., ruler of	207
wars with England	271, 281, 310
wars with France	291, 299
Ho'ly-rood Palace	240
Hom'il-don Hill, victory at	175
Hŏng Kŏng, British take	328
Hor'sa, leader of Jutes	32
Hot'spur, Percy, war with Scots	171, 175
House of Com'mons, origin of,	127, 128, 136
House of Lords	136
How'ard, Admiral	245
Howard, Catherine, marries Henry VIII.	219
Howe, Lord, defeats French	309
Hū'gue-nots, Charles I. aids	261
in England	288
Hun'dred Years' War	153-159, 162, 163, 180-186
Huns, invasions of	28

	PAGE
In-de-pend'ents, in James I.'s reign	254
quarrel with Parliament	266
In'di-a, French and English in	303
French driven out of	305
Indian Mutiny	328–330
placed under queen's rule	330
In-vin'ci-ble Ar-mä'da	244–246
Ire'land (Irish), conquered by Henry II.	103, 104
conquered by Ireton	271
conversion of	30, 31
in Elizabeth's reign	250
rebellion in	289
Roman Catholic Church in	288
united to Great Britain	310
war with Cromwell	269
wars with	173, 263
Ire'ton, subdues Ireland	269, 271
Iş-a-bel'la, Edward II. marries	141
rules during Edward III.'s minority,	150
signs treaty with France	148
Isabella, wife of Richard II.	172, 173
Jăc'ob-ites, adherents of James	287
become loyal subjects	306
in Ireland	289
in Scotland	300
Tories side with	297
Ja-mäi'ca, acquired by Cromwell	274
James I. of Scotland, captivity of,	176, 184
James IV. of Scotland, death of	207
James V. of Scotland, and Henry VIII.	220
James VI. of Scotland (I. of England), character	253
death of	260
divine right of kings	256, 261
favours Church of England	252
Gunpowder Plot	254–256
religious conference	254
James II. of England, crowned	283
death of	290
favours Catholics	285
flees	285
in Ireland	289
rebellion under Monmouth	284
successor to throne	278, 281, 282
James the Pretender	290, 297, 300
Jef'freys, Judge	284, 285
Je-hō'vah	246
Jen'kins's Ear, War of	298, 299
Je-ru'sa-lem, taken by Saracens	105
taken by Turks	86
Jews, in Parliament	326
massacre of	106
persecution of	130

	PAGE
Jews, return to England	275
torture of	120
Jo-an' of Arc, at Orleans	184
burned at stake	186
sold to English	185, 186
victories of	185
John of England, called Lackland	111
crowned	117
death of	124
does homage to pope	119
favours foreigners	125
kills Prince Arthur	118
makes alliances	120
pardoned by Richard	115
John I., King of France	162
Jon'son, Ben, author	259
Jop'pa, Richard I. victorious at	111
Joyce, Captain, seizes Charles I.	266
Judg'ments of God, defined	81
Ju-di'cial duels	81
Jūtes, Teutonic tribe	32–34
Jŭx'on, Charles I.'s chaplain	268
Ken'il-worth Castle, Edward II. at	149
Elizabeth at	249
Kent, Duchess of	321
Kent, Jutes take possession of	34
Khar-tŭm', Gordon killed at	334
King George's War	299
King William's War	290
King's evil	69
Kirk, massacre of	284
Knights, education of	160, 161
new order of, founded	159, 160
Knights of the Round Table	36
Knox, Protestant preacher	237, 238
La Hōgue, battle of	289
Lanc'as-ter, Duke of, power of	167
secures throne of Castile	171
Lancaster, Earl of	143
beheaded	148
revolt of barons under	147
Lancaster, house of	174, 179, 183, 189
Lane, assists Charles II.	271
Lan'franc, Archbishop of Canterbury	82, 84, 85
Lang'ton, Stephen, Archbishop of Canterbury	119
La Ro-chĕlle', Huguenots besieged at	261
Lăt'i-mer, preacher	223
burned at stake	230, 231
Laud, minister to Charles I.	262, 263

	PAGE
Leices'ter Abbey, Richard III. buried at,	201
Wolsey's death at	214
Leicester, Earl of	236
and Mary, Queen of Scots	238
receives Elizabeth at Kenilworth	249
Leipzig (lip'tsiG), battle of	315
Leith	271
Le-ŏf'rĭc, imposes tax	71
Le'o-pōld of Austria	108, 110, 112
Lew'es, battle of	126
Lex'ing-ton, battle of	308
Limoges (lē-mŏzh'), revolt of	163
Lin'coln, French defeat at	125
Stephen defeated at	94
Lin-lith'gōw, captured	144
Lit'er-a-ture, under Elizabeth	247, 249
under Queen Anne	295
Llew-ĕl'lyn (loo-), Welsh leader	131, 132
Loch-lē'ven (lŏK-) Castle, Mary of Scots at	241
Log'a-rĭthms, table of, invented	259
Lol'lards, persecution of	175, 180, 211
teachings of	170
Lom'bards, money-lenders	130
Lŏn'dŏn, mob in	168, 188
plague and fire in	279
rebuilt	280
refuses admission to Margaret	190
Lŏn'dŏn-dĕr-ry, siege of	289
Long Battle, Athelstan wins	54
Long Parliament	272
Lou'is XII. of France	207
Louis XIV. of France	290
alliance against	291
loses American colonies	295
taxation of	309
Louis XV. of France	309
Louis XVI. of France, beheaded	309
Louis XVIII. of France	315, 319
Lŏv'el, Lord, death of	203, 204
Luck'now, revolt in	329
relieved	330
Lū'ther, Martin, preaching of	211
Lut'ter-worth, Wyclif at	170
Mac-beth', story of	73
MacDon'ald, Flora, aids Prince Charlie,	300
MacDonalds, at Glencoe	288
Mad Parliament	126
Ma-drăs', English settlement at	303
Măg'na Chăr'tă, drawn up by barons	122
ratified by Edward I.	135
ratified by Pembroke	124
Maid of Or'le-ans. See *Joan of Arc*.	
Măl'cŏlm I., receives Cumbria	55

	PAGE
Malplaquet (mäl-plä-kä'), battle of	293
Mantes (mŏNt), captured	83
March, Earl of	174, 179
Mar'ga-ret, Queen, defeats Yorkists	190
defeated and captured	194
escapes to France	193
flees to Scotland	191
invades England	191
ransomed by her father	195
Marl'bŏr-ough, Duke of, character	293
commander of the Dutch and English forces	291, 292
victories of	293, 294
welcomes George I.	296
Mar'ston Moor, battle of	265
Mä'ry, Queen, daughter of Henry VIII.	223
death of	232
marries Philip of Spain	228
persecutes Protestants	230, 231
war with France	232
Mary, Queen, daughter of James II.	282
crowned	286
death of	290
marriage to William of Orange	282
Mary Stuart, Queen of Scotland	220
condemned to death	243
escape of	241
imprisoned at Dunbar	240
imprisoned by Elizabeth	242
takes title of Queen of England	237
Mash'am, Mrs., friend of Queen Anne,	293
Mā'sons' Guild, builds cathedrals	128
Ma-til'da, wife of William I.	76, 83
Matilda, wife of Henry I.	88
Matilda, daughter of Henry I.	92
claims throne	93
marries Geoffrey Plantagenet	92
war with Stephen	94, 95
May'flow-er, Separatists sail in	254
Med-i-ter-rā'ne-an Sea	19
Mee'rŭt, revolt in	328
Mel'bourne, Lord	324, 325, 326
Mel'rose Abbey, Bruce buried at	147
Mĕn'aī Strait, English killed at	132
Mĕr'ci-a (-shi-a), kingdom formed by Angles	34
Mĕr'lin, prophecy of	131
Merry England	277
Mil'ton, John, poet	276, 282
Min'den, battle of	303
Mis-so-lŏn'ghĭ, Byron's death at	320
Mŏn'as-ter-ies	31, 40, 57, 69
Monk, General, dismisses Parliament.	276
subdues Scotland	271
Mon'mouth, Duke of	278
tries to secure the throne	284

	PAGE
Mont'fort, Simon de	126, 127
Mont-Saint-Mi-chel', Prince Henry at	85
More, Sir Thomas, chancellor	216
death of	217
his "Utopia"	217
Mor'ti-mer, escapes to France	148
hanged at Tyburn	152
rules during Edward III.'s minority	150
Mur'ray, imprisons Mary Stuart	241
Na'pi-er, John, scientist	259
Na-pō'le-on Bō'na-parte	310
attacks Austria and Russia	314
attempts to cross Channel	312–314
death of, at St. Helena	317
Emperor of French	312
First Consul	311
returns from Elba	317
sent to Elba	315
Nāse'by, battle of	265
Nav-i-ga'tion Act	271
Na'vy, English, founders of	50, 183
increased	60, 235, 320
Nel'son, Admiral	311–313
Neth'er-lands. See *Holland*.	
Nev'ille's Cross, victory of	157
New Am'ster-dam, given to James II.	283
New'cas-tle, coal brought from	179
New England, first colony in	254
New Forest	82
New'found-land, discovered by Cabot	205
relinquished by French	295
News'pa-pers, circulation of first	275
Ni-ăg'a-ra, Fort, captured by British	303
Night'in-gale, Florence, in Crimean War	331
Nile, battle of the	311
Non-con-form'ists, in James I.'s reign	254
Nor'folk, conspiracy of	243
Nor'man-dy, given to Robert	83
Henry I. acquires	89, 91
Northmen settle in	63
seized by William Rufus	87
taken by Philip of France	118
Nor'man kings	76, 84, 88, 93
Nor'mans, become friends with Saxons	164
castles and customs of	78–81
invade England	75, 76
quarrel with Englishmen	134
North A-mer'i-ca, English in	297, 303, 307
North-amp'ton, Lancastrian defeat at	190
treaty of	151
North'men. See *Danes*.	
Nor-thum'ber-land, and Lady Jane Grey	227, 228
executed	228
policy of	225, 226

	PAGE
Nor-thum'bri-a, kingdom of	34
Nor'way, conquered by Canute	65
Norway, Maid of	137
Nor-we'gi-ans, attack England	87
Not'ting-ham, Countess of	251
Nottingham Castle, Mortimer at	151
Nottingham Hill, Charles I. at	265
Nun'ner-ies	58
Oath of supremacy	216
O'Con'nell, Daniel	320
Order of the Garter, formed	159
Or'le-ans, Duke of	180
Orleans, siege of	184
Og'borne in Isle of Wight	336
Ot'ter-burn, battle of	171
Ou'den-ar-dē, battle of	293
Out'laws, infest forests	115
Ox'ford, Wyclif at	170
Oxford Castle, Matilda at	95
Pal'es-tine, Prince Edward in	128
Richard I. in	108–110
Pal'mer-ston, prime minister	326
Par'is, peace of	307
Par'lia-ment, and Henry III.	125
Barebone's	272
Catholics in	320
divided into Houses	136
elects Henry IV. king	174, 175
first real	127
Irish members in	310
Long	272
Mad	126
Rump	266
Scotch members in	295
secures reforms	164
Short	263
struggle with Charles I.	261–267
struggle with James I.	256
under York and Lancaster	195, 196
Parr, Catherine, marries Henry VIII.	219
Peas'ants' Revolt	167–169, 224
Peel, English minister	319, 326
Peep'ing Tom of Coventry	72
Pem'broke, Earl of, regent	124, 125
Pen'der-ell, befriends Charles II.	270
Pen-in'su-lar War	315
Per'cys	171, 175, 180
Per'rers, Alice, and Edward III.	165
Pe'ter the Hermit	86
Peter's pence	45, 46
Pe-ti'tion of Right	261, 286
Phil'ip of France, complains about Richard	110

Philip of France, ordered to invade England	119
takes Normandy	118
Philip II. of Spain, claims English throne	244
courts Elizabeth	236
disliked by English	230
marries Mary	229
victorious at St. Quentin	232
Phi-lip'pa of Hainault (hā-nō')	151
intercedes for burghers of Calais	157
vow of	161
Phœ-nī'cians (-shuns)	19–21
Picts and Scots, driven out of Britain	32
raids of	25–28, 31
Pin'kie, Scotch defeat at	224
Pitt, William, English minister	303, 307
death of	308
Pitt, William, the Younger	308
Pitts'burg, so called in honour of Pitt	303
Plague, ravages of	279
Plan-tăg'e-net kings,	96, 106, 117, 121, 129, [140, 149, 166, 173, 179, 183, 191, 198, 201
Plăs'sey, battle of	304
Plȳm'outh Rock, Pilgrims at	254
Poitiers (pwä-tī-â'), English victory at	102
Pole, Cardinal	230
Poll tax	167, 170
Pontefract (pom'fret) Castle, Richard II.'s death at	173
Pope, the, and Henry VIII.	212, 215
Pope, poet	295
Pôr'tū gal, war against Napoleon	315
Post'age, reduced	321, 325
Post'al service, improved	275
Potatoes, introduced into Ireland	258
Pres by-te'ri an Church in Scotland	288
Press, freedom of	290
Pres-ton-pans', battle of	300
Pre-tend'er, proclaimed James III.	297
in Rome	300
Pri'mate	100
Prince of Wales, first	132, 134
Print'ing, introduced	196, 211
Prŏt'es-tants, crown to go to	287
during Charles II.'s reign	282
during Edward VI.'s reign	221, 224
during Elizabeth's reign	234
during James II.'s reign	285
first	170
Huguenots	261
in Netherlands, revolt of	244
in Scotland	237
persecution of	228, 230, 231
Prussia (prŭsh'a)	299, 317
Pun-jäb', taken by the British	328
Pū'ri-tan party	266, 269
Puritans	234
called Roundheads	264
during Charles II.'s reign	278, 279
during James I.'s reign	254
set sail for America	263
Pȳm, Puritan leader	264
Pyr'a-mids, battle of the	311
Quăk'ers settle in New World	281
Que-bec', captured by British	303
Queen Anne's War	291
Rag'nar Lod'brog, invades England,	44, 45
Rail'road, first English	320
Ra'leigh, Sir Walter, executed	258
imprisoned	253
seaman	245
story of	246, 247
Ramillies (rä-mē-yē'), battle of	292, 293
Road'ing, abbey at	89
Read'ing-glasses, discovered	128
Ref-or-ma'tion, Wyclif	170
Martin Luther	211
Reign of Terror	309
Res-to-ra'tion, the	277
Rev-o-lu'tion, of 1688	287
American	308
Rich'ard I., Cœur de Lī-ŏn', crowned	106
death of	116
in third crusade	107–110
recrowned	113
return of	111, 112
war with France	115
Richard II. of England, abdicates	173
crowned	166
his promises to peasants	168
Richard III., Duke of Gloucester	191
conspires against Clarence	195
crowned	198
death of	201
murders young princes	194, 198
plots with Warwick and Clarence	193
proclaimed Protector	197
Richard, Prince, murdered	198
Rich'mond, Earl of. See Henry VII.	
Rid'ley, burned at stake	230, 231
Rig'ing Castle, Isabella at	153
Riv'ers, Earl, executed	197
Rizzio (rit'se-o), Mary's secretary,	238, 239
Rob'ert I. of Scotland. See Bruce.	
Robert, son of William I.	82, 86
Rob'in Hood, outlaw chief	115
Rob'sart, Amy, wife of Leicester	236
Rôçhe-fôrt', Napoleon at	317
Rol'lo, Rolf Gäng'er	63

	PAGE
Ro′man Cath′o-lics. See *Catholics*.	
Ro′mans, buildings destroyed	33
conquer Britain	22, 25
leave Britain	26, 27, 29
seek Tin Islands	20, 21
Rooke, Sir George, conquers Gibraltar	294
Rōṣe′ber-y, prime minister	326
Roses, War of	189-195, 201
Rouen (roo-ŏn′), besieged and taken	182
Joan of Arc burned at	186
Richard I. buried at	116
Round′heads	264-266
Ro-we′na, Hengist's daughter	33
Roy′al Oak	270
Rump Parliament	266
Run′ny-mēde, John at	122
Ru′pert, Prince	264
Rus′sell, prime minister	326
Russia (rŭsh′a), attacked by Napoleon	314
Crimean War	331
Czarina of	336
helps Greeks against Turks	320
Rye House Plot	282
Ryṣ′wick, treaty of	290
St. Al′bans, battle of	190
St. Au′gus-tīne, converts Anglo-Saxons	39, 41
St. Brice's day, massacre of	64, 69
St. Germain (sȧn zher-mȧn′), James II. at	286
St. He-le′na, Napoleon at	317
St. Pat′rick, story of	29-31
St. Paul's Church	279, 280
St. Pe′ter's Church	45
St. Pierre (sȧn pē-ār′), at Calais	157
St. Quentin (sȧn kŏn-tȧn′), battle of	232
St. Thom′as of Canterbury	103, 104
St. Vin′cent, battle of	310
Sal′a-din, Saracen chief	108, 111
Sal-a-man′ca, battle of	315
Ṣa̱lis′bur-y, Countess of	159
Salisbury, prime minister	326
Săr′a-cens, in Holy Land	86, 110, 111
war with Spain	146
Sat′urn, Roman god	34
Sa-voy′ Palace, French king at	163
Sax′on kings	34-74
Saxons, at war with Danes	44, 45, 47
become friends with Normans	164
defeated by Arthur	35
education and morality of	51, 52
settle in Britain	32-34
Schom′berg, General, killed	289
Seŏne, coronation at	137

	PAGE
Scot′land (Scots), annexed to England	138
conquered by General Monk	271
Presbyterian Church in	288
rebellion in	284, 297
sides with Elizabeth	237
united with England	295
war with England	150, 152, 171, 175, 207, 220, 224
wins independence	144-146, 151
Scots and Picts	25-28, 31, 32
Scri-bā′ri-um, monastery library	58
Scrōpe, Archbishop of York, rebels	176
Sedge′moor, battle of	284
Seine, river	186
Sen′lac, battle	75, 76
Sep′a-ra-tists, sail for New World	254
Serfs, or slaves	36
Sev-en-oaks′, battle of	188
Seven Years' War	301, 303, 306
Se-vē′rus, wall of	26, 29
Sȳ′moṳr, Jane, marries Henry VIII.	218
Shāke′spēare, William	249
Shĕr-iff-mūir′, battle of	297
Sher′wood Forest, Robin Hood in	115
Ship money	262
Shore′ham, Charles II. at	271
Shrews′bur-y, battle of	175
Siç′i-ly, Prince Edward in	129
Sid′ney, Sir Philip, death of	247
Sikhs, English defeat	328
Sim′nel, Lam′bert, pretender	203
Slāv′er-y, abolished in colonies	321
Slave trading, introduced	222
Smith′field, Richard II. at	169
Snōw′don, Mount, Glendower on	175
Welsh on	132
Sol′way Moss, Scotch defeat at	220
Som′er-set, Duke of, closes monasteries	223
executed	225
invades Scotland	224
named Protector	222
Somerset, Margaret's adviser	189, 190
Sŏmme River, Edward III. at	153
So-phī′a, heir to the throne	287, 296
South Sea Bubble	297, 298
Sŏuth′wark, camp at	188
Spain, cedes Florida to England	307
Charles V., ruler of	207
declares war against Napoleon	315
makes compact with France	298, 299
Thirty Years' War	259
tin mines in	19
war with England	245, 313
"Spec-ta′tor," early English magazine	295
Spen′ser's "Fā′e-rie Queene"	247
Spit′al-fields, silk factory at	268

	PAGE
Stam'ford Bridge, battle of	75
Stamp Act	307
Star Chamber	205, 252
end of	264
Steele, English author	295
Ste'phen, King, civil war	94, 95
crowned	93
death of	96
Stir'ling, surrender of	144, 145
Stirling Bridge, English defeat at	138
Stoke, Irish defeated at	203
Stone Age, defined	12
Stone'henge, temple of Druids	17
Straf'ford, Earl of	262–264
Straw, Jack, leads mob	168, 169
Stũ'art, Lady Arabella	253
Stuart kings	241, 260, 276, 283
Sue-tō'ni-us (swē-), Roman general	24, 25
Suf'folk, Margaret's adviser	188
Suffolk, Duchess of	222
Sur'rey, Lord, victory over Scots	207
Sus'sex, Saxon kingdom	34
Sweyn, Danish king	64
Swift, English writer	295
Swit'zer-land, missionaries in	31
Syr'i-a, Napoleon in	311
Ta-la-ve'ra, battle of	315
Tan-giēr', becomes English possession	278
"Tat'ler," first English magazine	295
Tel'e-graph, first	325
Tel'e-scopes, first	128
Ten'ny-son's "Charge of the Light Brigade"	331
"Idylls of the King"	36
"Lady Godiva's Ride"	70–72
Teu-ton'ic race, Angles	33
Danes, or Northmen	42, 44
Jutes	32
Saxons	32, 33
visit shores of Britain	31
Tewkes'bur-y, battle of	194
Thames (tĕmz)	257
Thāneg, duties of	36
Thăn'et, given to Jutes	32
Thirty Years' War	259
Thōr, god of thunder	33
Ti-con-der-ō'ga, captured by British	303
Tinchebrai (tănsh-brā'), battle of	69
Tin Islands	20
Tiū, god of war	33
To-bac'co, introduced into England	253
Tō'ries and Whigs, quarrels of	282, 295
side with Jacobites	297
Tou-lon', recovered by French	310

	PAGE
Tower of London, built	79
Tow'ton, battle of	191
Traf-al-gar', battle of	313
Trafalgar Square	314
Treaty, of Aix-la-Chapelle	299, 300
of Amiens	312
of Bretigny	163
of Campoformio	311
of Northampton	151
of Paris	307
of Ryswick	290
of Troyes	182, 184
of Utrecht	295
of Wallingford	95, 96
of Wedmore	50
Trial by jury, instituted	97
Trials by ordeal	37, 38
Trip'o-li, pirates at, subdued	274
Troyes (trwä), treaty of	182, 184
Tū'dor architecture	206
Tudor kings	202, 206, 222, 228, 233
Tū'nis, pirates at, subdued	274
Ty'burn, place of execution	152, 204
Ty'ler, Wat, leads mob	167–169
Ty-rōne', Earl of, rebels	250
Tyr'rel, Sir Walter	87
United King'dom	11
United States, Civil War	334
recognition of	308
taxation in	307
U'trĕcht, treaty of	295
Van-dyke', Dutch artist	260
Van Tromp, Dutch admiral	271
Ven'er-a-ble Bēde	42
Vic-tō'ri-a, Queen, character of	322
childhood of	321, 322
children	335, 336
coronation of	323
Empress of India	330
improvements during reign of	334
jubilee of	337
marriage of	324
occupations of	336
reforms during reign of	327
Vic-tō'ri-an Age	327
Vi ĕn'na, assembly at	317
Vienne, Jean de (zhŏN dŭ vē-ĕn')	156
Vik'ings. See *Danes.*	
Vir-gin'i-a, granted to Raleigh	247
Vi-tō'ri-a, battle of	315
Vor'ti-gĕrn, death of	34
gives Thanet to Jutes	32
solicits aid from Germans	31, 32

	PAGE
Wăke'field, Yorkist defeat at	190
Wâleş (Welsh), annexed	131, 132
Britons take possession of	32
exterminate wolves	60
language of	35
rebellion	175
Wallace (wŏl'is), William, war with,	138, 139
Wal'ling-ford, treaty of	95, 96
Wal'pole, prime minister	296, 298
Wal'sing-ham, minister to Elizabeth	235
War, of Austrian Succession	299
of Spanish Succession	290-295
of the Roses	189-195, 201
of 1812	315
War'beck, Per'kin, pretender	204
War'wick Castle, Gaveston at	143
Warwick, Richard, Earl of, at Northampton	190
enters London	190, 191
killed	194
revenge of	193
the kingmaker	194
Warwick, Edward, Earl of, beheaded	204
Wạsh'ing-ton, George, American general	308
Wa-ter-loo', Napoleon at	317
Wạt'ling Street	50
Wed'more, treaty of	50
Wel'ling-ton, victories of	315, 317
Wes'sex, Saxon kingdom	34
West'min-ster Abbey, kings buried at	62, 141, 183, 206, 259, 275, 277, 314
Whigs and Tories	282
quarrels of	295-297
White'hall, palace of	208
White Ship, the	91
Whit'ting-ton, Lord Mayor of London	178, 179
Wil'ber-force, abolishes slavery	321
Wil'liam I., builds Tower of London	79
claims throne	74
crowned	76, 78
curfew bell	81
death of	83, 84
Domesday Book	81
feudalism introduced	80, 81
New Forest	82
war with Robert	83
wins battle of Senlac	75

	PAGE
William II., Ru'fus, attacks Prince Henry	85
crowned	84
killed in New Forest	87
seizes Normandy	87
William III. of Or'ange, and Mary	285
campaign in Ireland	289
character of	287
crown offered to	286
death of	296
founds hospital and Bank of England	291
freedom of worship	288
King William's War	290
William IV., reign of	320, 321
William, Prince, death of	91
Win'ches-ter, Alfred buried at	53
Win'dşor Palace, built	165
Earl of March imprisoned at	174
residence of Victoria	336
Win'ter, seaman	245
Wit'e-na-ġe-mōt	37, 47, 55, 61, 64
Wō'den, Teutonic god	32, 33, 36
Wọl'şey, Archbishop of York	208
Chancellor of State	208
fall and death of	214
in Henry VIII.'s divorce case	212-214
Wood'stock, estate given to Marlborough	293
Fair Rosamond at	96
Wọrces'ter, battle of	270
World's fair, first	325
Wren, Sir Christopher, architect	280
Wy'att, executed	229
Wyc'lif, English reformer	164
death of	170, 171
translates Bible into English	170
York, Charles I. at	264
Parliament at	142
Roman camps at	25
York, Duke of, claims throne	188
killed	190
power of	167
Protector	189
York, house of	149, 191, 198
Young Pretender	300
Zu'lus, war with	334
Zut'phen, battle of	247

www.ingramcontent.com/pod-product-compliance
Lightning Source LLC
Chambersburg PA
CBHW030251240426
43673CB00040B/945